Divided Power

*Volume III of the Fulbright Institute
Series on International Affairs*

Divided Power

The Presidency, Congress, and the Formation of American Foreign Policy

EDITED BY DONALD R. KELLEY

The University of Arkansas Press
Fayetteville
2005

Copyright © 2005 by The University of Arkansas Press

All rights reserved
Manufactured in the United States of America

ISBN: 978-1-55728-798-4 (cloth)
ISBN: 978-1-55728-804-2 (paper)
eISBN: 978-1-61075-129-2

25   24   23   22   21   5   4   3   2

Text design by Ellen Beeler

∞   The paper used in this publication meets the minimum requirements of the American National Standard for Permanence of Paper for Printed Library Materials Z39.48-1984.

Series page photo of J. William Fulbright courtesy of Lyndon Baines Johnson Library and Museum. Photo by Yoichi R. Okamoto, serial number A950-32A.

Library of Congress Cataloging-in-Publication Data

Divided power : the Presidency, Congress, and the formation of American foreign policy / edited by Donald R. Kelley.
    p. cm.
  Includes bibliographical references and index.
  ISBN 1-55728-798-8 (pbk. : alk. paper)
  1. United States—Foreign relations administration. 2. Separation of powers—United States. 3. Political planning—United States. 4. United States—Politics and government. I. Kelley, Donald R., 1943–
  JZ1480.D59 2005
  327.73—dc22

2005009287

To Leigh Davis

Contents

1 Answering the "Invitation to Struggle"   1
DONALD R. KELLEY

2 The President, Executive, and Congress: The Same Old Story?   19
BERT A. ROCKMAN

3 Authorizing War: Congressional Resolutions and Presidential Leadership, 1955–2002   39
GARY R. HESS

4 Intraparty Factionalism on Key Foreign Policy Issues: Congress versus Clinton, 1995–2000   65
TERRY L. DEIBEL

5 Explaining Congressional-Executive Rivalry in International Affairs: The Changing Role of Parties, Committees, and the Issue Agenda   111
BRYAN W. MARSHALL

6 Which Dancer Leads? Foreign Trade Policy Making and Divided Government   133
RALPH G. CARTER

7 Long-Term Trends in Congressional Foreign Policy Behavior: Explaining Variations in Contention in the U.S. Senate in the Past and in the Future   149
MARIE T. HENEHAN

8 Seeing Things in Perspective   167
          DONALD R. KELLEY

Contributors   181

Notes   185

Index   209

1 Answering the "Invitation to Struggle"

DONALD R. KELLEY

Introduction: The Fulbright Legacy

To the world, the name J. William Fulbright is synonymous with the academic exchange program that he was instrumental in creating after World War II. A small-town Arkansas boy whose life had been profoundly changed by his years at Oxford on a Rhodes scholarship, he sought to bring similar experiences to American and foreign scholars at a time when the world was realigning itself in ways that defined the next half century of Cold War. In the midst of that growing polarization, the Fulbright exchange program, and the thousands of scholars who crisscrossed the world on its behalf, contributed to an informed dialogue about the nature of the world and the ways in which its myriad differences could be accepted, even celebrated, in a world of Iron Curtains, Berlin Walls, and proliferating and ever more sophisticated weapons.

To a student of American politics, that same name evokes a slightly different, although equally reflective connotation. It is associated with one of the quintessential questions of American democracy: the relationship between the executive and legislative branches of government, in this context concerning their respective roles in the formation of foreign policy. As in any system of divided government, those roles are imprecisely defined and subject to conflicting interpretation. During Senator Fulbright's tenure in office, balancing the powers and responsibilities of the executive and legislative branches was framed by the imperatives of the Cold War. On the one hand, the nation needed strong leadership at a time when it believed it faced implacable foes in the Soviet Union and the international communist movement; whatever the other vagaries of American political life, there was general consensus that the Cold War meant that the very survival of the nation and our way of life were at stake. Conventional wisdom of the day generally vested such strong leadership into the hands of the president, whose symbolic status as leader of the nation (and to many, the "free world") as well as his special roles as commander-in-chief and chief diplomat empowered him to take the lead in dealing with the outside world. But on the other hand, that same conventional wisdom also reminded us that the legislative branch remained an important partner in determining the broad outlines of America's relations with the rest of the world. Even though the call for a loosely defined bipartisanship echoed throughout both the House and the Senate and at both ends of Pennsylvania Avenue, political reality was never far below the surface. While there was little open disagreement over the threat posed by the Soviet Union, there was growing discord over the implications of the spread of communism elsewhere, over who had "lost" China, or over how best to oppose the spread of this pernicious doctrine to Africa, Latin America, and Southeast Asia.

Throughout his political life, J. William Fulbright was at the center of these debates, often in ways that belie simplistic description and explanation. In one of his most quoted comments on the value of a liberal arts education, he spoke of the need to view "things in perspective." That injunction also informed his view of America's place in the world. On the one hand, he clearly supported the bipartisan anti-communist consensus that had emerged at the beginning of the Cold War. Whatever else might be said about it, the Soviet Union was a threatening rival seemingly bent on redrawing the map of the world and challenging the values that Fulbright held dear, and the spread of communism throughout the world was seen as a threat to American interests. On the other hand, Fulbright was reluctant to demonize the communist foe or to dichotomize the world into monolithic camps. Seeing things in perspective meant, in this context, the creation of a nuanced perception of the ideological and nationalist factors that animated the international communist movement; communism came in many different incarnations, as did individual communist leaders who mixed their own sense of national history and identity with whatever they eclectically borrowed from Marx, Lenin, or Stalin. For Fulbright the question became to sort out the wheat from the chaff, to distinguish the essential and immediate threats from the peripheral issues to which the label of communism had been applied, fairly or unfairly. Making that assessment became increasingly difficult throughout the senator's tenure in office. In the Soviet Union, the implacable Joseph Stalin was replaced by the reform-minded, if erratic Nikita Khrushchev and then by the business-like, if uninspiring Leonid Brezhnev. Even more confounding was the growing role of communist insurgents at the core of anti-colonial national liberation movements which sought to advance an agenda of national independence and economic and social reform. While America proffered its own vision of a democratic, noncommunist future for the third world, there were no clear guidelines that separated unacceptably dangerous communist revolutions from more benign transformations that did not exactly conform to American preferences.

Perhaps inevitably, the growing debate over the *ends* of American foreign policy—how to comprehend and oppose the spread of communism while avoiding dangerous overcommitment of American resources to ill-conceived or unwinable struggles—soon also became a debate over the *means* through which it was formulated. Here again, Fulbright was a man of many parts, his perceptions of the respective duties of the executive and legislative branches informed by his desire for competent leadership exercised within the context of an informed debate. He certainly supported strong presidential initiatives in moments of crisis, backing Truman's actions in Korea, Eisenhower in Lebanon, and urging even stronger action on Kennedy during the Cuban missile crisis. In a move he later regretted, Fulbright played an important personal role in securing the passage of the Gulf of Tonkin resolution in 1964, which President Johnson took as unquestioning legislative endorsement to escalate the American role in Vietnam. There is little in these actions to suggest that Fulbright was inherently opposed to the exercise of strong presidential power, especially at times when quick, decisive action was required. That said, there is no doubt that Fulbright is most vividly remembered for his growing opposition to the Vietnam War and for his efforts to reassert the role of Congress in foreign policy formation. As chair of the Senate Foreign Relations Committee, he conducted insightful hearings into the conduct of the war, emerging as one of the most vocal and respected critics of the imperial presidency. No less significantly, his actions contributed greatly both to the changing legal framework and the public mood of reluctance that followed the war's end.

When he reluctantly left office, defeated in his 1974 bid for reelection, Senator Fulbright could doubtless reflect that his injunction to see "things in perspective" had left a mixed legacy. As befits the nature of the Cold War itself, some things were clear; there *was* an enemy to be opposed, and *somebody* had to rally the nation to the task. But other things were less precisely defined; *where did we draw the line between real enemy and unrelated conflicts, and who should rally the nation to such a task?*

Framing the Question I: Institutions and Nested Games

Our intellectual task would be far easier if we could limit our examination of the role of the president and Congress in foreign policy formation to a particular set of legal issues and institutional relationships. Such simplicity does not exist. Some things are constant, such as the constitutionally mandated division of powers that Edwin Corwin describes as an inexorable "invitation to struggle" over the inseparable questions of *what* the nation's foreign policy will be and *who* will have the upper hand in making it.[1] But the modalities of this struggle are subject to redefinition over time and space. The only certainty is the *possibility* of disagreement, coupled with the seemingly durable acceptance by all parties that the parameters of the conflicts and the mechanisms of their resolution will be defined by the conventional legal wisdom and political realities of the day.

But if the likelihood of struggle and the general outlines of the playing fields are known with some certainty, what remains unknown or ambiguous, and how do we deal with it? If it is our task to pose an exceedingly general question—what is the relationship between the executive and legislative branches in the formation of foreign policy?—what other factors or variables must be introduced into the equation? If our limited certainties tell us *what* probably will happen—there is a high probability of struggle over these issues—and *where* the struggle will occur—within the accepted institutional, legal, and political realities of the day—where do we go from here?

The answer to that question, at least in general terms, lies in our recognition that the formation of American foreign policy is best described as a classic "nested game." The term was coined by George Tsebelis to describe a complex multi-actor and multilevel decision-making nexus in which policy outcomes are determined by the interaction of multiple structural and incentive factors.[2] In simpler terms, each actor plays games in *multiple arenas*, all of which are connected both by the involvement of that and other actors whose interactions persist over time and by the interplay of motivations and priorities attached to various policy outcomes. To complicate matters, any actor's behavior in one arena has implications for his or her involvement in all other arenas. At least in the short run, the actors operate within reasonably clear roles, although there is always some latitude, and the roles evolve over time. Moreover, the roles are essentially institutionally or situationally defined; presidents are supposed to act like presidents, legislators like legislators, lobbyists like lobbyists, and so on. But in the broader perspective, every actor plays many roles, each defined by the multiple and overlapping arenas which the actor perceives as relevant to his or her own identity and interests. Put in these terms, this means that no actor has the luxury or clarity of a single point of view. Every issue, every decision has implications that ripple out over all other actors in all other arenas. While each player can attempt to decide which "arena" is most important at that moment in time, no one can ever completely unpack a decision and reduce it to a single frame of reference. Every decision is "nested" in time and space, affected by political and institutional precedent and shaping events that follow, and affected by and affecting what occurs in all connected arenas.

As Tsebelis points out, there is an additional complicating factor: there are really two kinds of nested games. The first is about the *substance* of policy and is played out by actors, each of whom operates within multiple and frequently overlapping arenas. The internal logic of each arena will define the question and, hopefully from the player's perspective, suggest the optimum policy choice from that point of view alone. But since actors operate in multiple and frequently conflicting arenas, they will receive conflicting signals and incentives. The decision is reached, at least from each player's perspective, when he or she chooses the relative priority of the arenas.

The second game is about what Tsebelis terms *institutional design.* This game is about the rules of the game itself, that is, how decisions are made and how the various arenas interact with one another. This game is best thought of as exemplified by the traditional Russian *matryoshka,* the nested wooden doll in which each doll contains a smaller version of itself. In this sense, each larger doll determines the context within which all smaller dolls can exist, or more precisely from our point of view, each larger arena defines the formal and informal rules of the game for the smaller ones within it. What is at stake is *how* the decision will be made, and this question simultaneously affects both the substance of the policy outcome itself and the relative power and authority of those institutions and players who participate in a particular arena. Sometimes the decision maker resolves the conflict among contending arenas by deciding which is more important: the substance of the decision itself, or the issue of how and by whom the decision is made. If the former choice prevails, each actor will try to balance personal and institutional priorities of each arena in ways that maximize desirable policy outcomes; "given my many priorities and loyalties," he or she will reason, "the best obtainable policy is," and the sentence will be completed by a solution that presents the best *compromise* of priorities, not a single optimal choice. If the latter choice prevails, emphasis will fall on questions of rule and boundary maintenance, that is, the relative authority of each arena, the rules that govern internally how they make decisions, and boundary maintenance among them.

And now it gets really complicated. What if both kinds of nested games are in play at the same time? What if for some players the most important question is the *substance* of policy, or in the complicated world of nested games, about the best combination of policy outcomes dictated by that individual's prioritization of the many different arenas in which he or she plays? But for others, *procedural* questions about how the decision is made are more important than substance, placing them in a game of *institutional design*. If each game has its own complex internal logic, what about the interplay of the two? The answer, again in theory, is derived from the final consensus among all players in all arenas about which game is more important, that is, whether the present encounter should be considered primarily a substantive or procedural game.

This brings us to a more sophisticated understanding of why the particular "invitation to struggle" that characterizes American foreign policy seems dauntingly complex. The two differing kinds of nested games overlap not only in terms of space—institutional space, in this sense—but also in terms of sequencing and temporal overlap. There are really two games in play, one dealing with the creation of a general consensus shared by a preponderance of the most powerful players about whether the current game is about policy (the "normal" nested game) or the rules of the game (the "institutional design" nested game), and the second about structuring the outcomes of the game that everyone (hopefully) has agreed to play. In the clearest scenario, the two would occur in temporal sequence; first we decide what kind of game it is, and then we play it. But in reality, the two stages occur in rapidly alternating sequence or virtually simultaneously. They overlap, or conflicting interpretations coexist for prolonged periods of time, each rooted in a particular institutional constituency. As intended by the drafters of the Constitution, a final answer is never given, because there can be no final answer—only new iterations of the same basic questions redefined in time a place by the shifting nature of conventional constitutional and political wisdom, by the questions faced by policy makers in both branches, and by the personalities, quirks, and foibles of the actors themselves.

Framing the Question II: Context and Conventional Wisdom

If the "invitation to struggle" is endemic to the constitutional and institutional realities that frame the making of American foreign policy, it stands to reason that this struggle also takes place within a broader political, cultural, and intellectual context. These contextual realities define a sort of "conventional wisdom" that plays an important role in how the invitation to struggle is answered. To be sure, such conventional wisdom does not dictate a monolithic view either of the substance of policy or how decisions should be reached. Rather it establishes an intellectual, perceptual, and moral framework—a limited consensus, at best—that sets forward the rules of the playing field and articulates areas of agreement and disagreement. That which is constant—the ambiguity inherent in the Constitution itself and the proclivity to struggle over its interpretation—is joined by constantly shifting conventional wisdom of the day. At any moment there probably exists a widespread consensus on how the game is to be played and what outcomes may be reasonably expected; without such agreement the game would be difficult to comprehend and the outcomes hard to predict. But conventional wisdom is a moving target, subject to change over time. And more intriguing, if we imposed the nested games model described above, conflicting conventional wisdoms will emerge. Each arena may have its own slightly different version, or its own slant to generally accepted precepts, governing the perceptions of rewards and strategies from that perspective, and these "wisdoms" may change at different times or at different speeds.

An understanding of the interplay of the executive and legislative branches in the making of American foreign policy also therefore requires that we carefully examine the nature of these conventional wisdoms. Like all complex realities, these "wisdoms" are usually reduced to stereotypes vested with strong symbolic meaning. They are both *descriptive,* defining the world around us, and *prescriptive,* telling us the appropriate goals to seek and how to reach them. "Isolationism," one of the major elements of American conventional wisdom of the nineteenth century, was more than just a statement of policy; it evoked a mindset that defined America and its place in the world, and was thus vested with emotional and prescriptive as well as cognitive and referent meaning. What follows is an attempt to sketch out the most significant conventional wisdoms of the late twentieth and early twenty-first centuries, at least as they define the parameters of the "invitation to struggle" envisioned by Corwin.

THE VIETNAM WAR AND THE POST-VIETNAM SYNDROME

Perhaps more than any other military engagement, the Vietnam War left its mark on how America thinks about the formulation and assessment of foreign policy. To be sure, other wars exacted greater tolls in terms of human life or ended in ways that even more significantly defined America's role in the world. Because it ended in defeat and so bitterly divided the nation, the war legitimated what was at first called the "post-Vietnam syndrome," a mixture of legal changes and cultural norms that redefined how the United States would enter into armed conflicts and debate its commitments and conduct even while American forces were still in the field. Even more significant, the war changed the way in which leaders would think about the personal and political costs of such commitments, and how political activists would engage those leaders and mobilize supporters and critics of their policies. A new generation of political and military leaders would soon emerge who were concerned about the details of engagement and disengagement and who were better aware of the political significance of their actions. And even when the United States shed its visible reluctance to act like the superpower that it always was—a reengagement that came, in typical American fashion, with Reagan's rediscovery of the "evil empire" of the Soviet Union—it remained committed, at least in rhetoric, to the need for clear "mission statements" and "exit strategies."

GLOBALIZATION, REAL AND IMAGINED . . .

Over the last quarter century, the phenomena of *globalization* have come to join the pantheon of conventional wisdoms. The plural form is purposeful, if a bit awkward; it is meant to suggest that we have accepted a number of overlapping "globalizations," which, when taken *in toto,* have redefined the way in which we think about the context of U.S. foreign policy. Most easily visible is the creation of a global economy, which has been variously celebrated as the key to growing interdependence and prosperity or condemned for its deleterious impact on sustainable development, the environment, and standards of living in less developed, cheap-labor nations to which production has been "outsourced." No less significant, however, is the growing recognition of what may be termed "cultural globalization." It includes both the ubiquitous presence of essentially Western and usually

American commercial and entertainment forms—the McDonalds and Wal-Marts, as well as the global distribution of American films and television, although in some venues such as music there has long been a multidirectional flow—and the more subtle dissemination of attitudes, values, and for want of a better term, aspirations for freedom, a better life, and hope for the future. What Samuel Huntington has termed the "third wave of democratization" that has swept the world with increasing force over the last two decades has been animated as much by a revolution of rising expectations as by the inherent failures of authoritarian regimes.[3]

These overlapping facets of globalization have developed both real and mythic roots. In many ways, globalization is an objective reality that cannot be ignored; trading networks link the world in ways not thought possible fifty years ago, and satellite communications and computer networks have created a real-time capability to view the best and worst of human affairs. The instruction booklet that begins "some assembly required" now always comes in five or six languages, and the note at the bottom of the label that says "made in" usually names a nation distant from the consumer. Even the opponents of globalization must acknowledge its ubiquitous presence and relentless momentum, arguing for the most part that it should be tempered by a framework of social and moral considerations as well as shaped by its economic and technical imperatives.

Globalization also embodies a mythic dimension, evoking deeply rooted cultural shibboleths that link it to the humanistic tradition of Western culture and to the ideas of progress and perfection as the most laudable of human goals. In a world of global trade and culture, we are easily seduced to think in terms of the creation of the "global village" in which we all reside. We all are, or so the mythology would tell us, essentially the same, seeking the same private and frequently public goals, and beset by the same enemies and demons that keep us from such self-fulfillment. Moreover, we are "perfectible," at least in the sense that rational individual and collective action can move us further down the road labeled "progress." Even the critics who bemoan the destruction of cultural distinctiveness implied by the mythic creation of the global persona limit their practical recommendations to the creations of mechanisms that would sustain some diversity in the face of broader integration.

. . . AND EXCEPTIONALISM, REAL AND IMAGINED

Certainly there can be no doubt that the debate over globalization has shaped the contemporary conventional wisdom within which American foreign policy is formulated. But there is an equally strong and deeply rooted aspect of

American conventional wisdom labeled *exceptionalism* that stands in sharp contrast. In its simplest form, it argues that America is "special," unlike any other nation. To be sure, many nations laud their special contributions—French wine, a Polish polonaise, German technology—and some export their culture as if it were a marketable commodity. For America, the notion of exceptionalism was borne of history and geography; its original settlers "escaped" from an oppressive Europe, seeking their own version of religious and eventually political freedom, and the formidable expanse of the Atlantic Ocean and the vast open lands to the west guaranteed them time and space for experimentation. That sense of escape and isolation easily morphed into a feeling of cultural and political superiority that endowed the nation with a special mission—to set itself apart from the "corrupt" societies of Europe (the *old* world) and to improve, if not perfect, the economic, social, and political forms embodied in this unique experiment (in contrast, the *new* world). Those missions gave America license to engage and disengage from world affairs at times and places of its own choosing and permission to create its own yardsticks and values by which to define friend and foe, choose goals and means, and assess success and failure.

Such exceptionalism found its nineteenth-century manifestation in the doctrine of isolationism, to which the nation returned briefly after World War I. The end of the next global war permitted no return to simpler times; after World War II America was now a superpower, and, like it or not, it was drawn into a protracted and indecisive conflict, the oxymoronic "cold war" in which decisive victories escaped all contending forces. In a bi- and then multipolar world, America could at best be the first among equals, the most powerful nation in a coalition of forces that opposed the spread of communism. In that sense, it was no longer "exceptional," that is, able to make the rules of the game and choose the time and place of its involvement. While America retained the sense of moral superiority implied by exceptionalism, it nonetheless found itself a part of a team, a first among allies aspiring to be equals.

The end of the Cold War revitalized the sense of American exceptionalism. While globalization had woven a more complex world than that of 1945, the new realities of the post–Cold War world fit nicely with the previous American mindset. We had "won" the Cold War, at least in the sense that the other side had self-destructed under the weight of cumulative economic and social problems, and the "victory" affirmed our superiority, especially since we had been the "leader" of the free world. The spread of democracy throughout the former communist world and elsewhere proved the innate superiority of the West, as did the rapid shift to market economies. The onus of American failure in Vietnam was erased, although much of the operational caution remained. More important, the United States was left as the world's only superpower, possessing—if not before September 11, knowing how or why to use it—the preponderance of military and economic power. And not surprising, Americans took exaggerated credit for making it all happen, and for shoring up the new democracies of Eastern Europe and the former Soviet Union. Once again, it was easy to think that events had proven us to be on the side of history with a unique and singular role to play in shaping the post–Cold War world.

FROM COLD WAR TO . . .

One of the most important elements of the conventional wisdom that shaped the formation of American foreign policy over the last half century was the Cold War, or perhaps more correctly, Cold Wars, since the over forty years of this global confrontation proceeded through many a number of bipolar and multipolar stages. Its mutations aside, it did provide an important definitional clarity that named (and demonized) the enemy—the communist movement in all of its established and potential incarnations—and identified (and sanctified) its opposition—the "free world," led, of course, by the United States. As with most of the other "conventional wisdoms," it acquired a mythic quality that informed and colored the way America looked at the world and the ways in which its leaders sorted out the tasks before them. In one way or another, most of the elements of American foreign policy came to be viewed through that prism. That tendency of thought produced two consequences. First, the propensity to view all things through the Cold War prism led us not to recognize the beginning of economic, political, and social trends that eventually would shape the post–Cold War world. Among these were the emerging global economy and regional trading blocs and the complex interdependencies and rivalries associated with them; the nascent and then firmly institutionalized political integration of new entities such as the European Union, and the cautious experimentation of other regional or bilateral associations; the emergence of China and Japan as regional and eventually global powers, and the rising importance of other nations such as Brazil and Mexico; the growing salience of a global, albeit Western-dominated, culture, which paradoxically confirmed (and in part created) common values and expectations while speeding a revolution of rising economic, social, and political expectations; the emergence of cultural and religious "fracture points" that led analysts like Samuel Huntington to describe the post–Cold War world in terms of a "clash of cultures" rather than in terms of geopolitical or ideological divisions;[4] and the growing loss of a sense of "history," at least in Francis Fukuyama's formulation that history required epic struggle.[5]

Second, the end of the Cold War, even if regarded as a victory for the capitalist and democratic West, wiped the intellectual slate clean and left us with few immediately apparent points of reference. The "enemy" was gone, and the new nation-states that emerged in its place professed fealty to our notions of democracy and market economies. Given the American propensity to define itself with reference to the "other," this was a disorienting hiatus. While some debated if a new enemy would soon emerge (China led the list for some, Muslim fundamentalism for others) or how to spend the "peace dividend" that would result from decreased military budgets, others pondered the commitments that might be necessary for the United States to engage the world in humanitarian and nation-building efforts. The institutionalized dichotomization of executive and legislative roles in foreign policy formation shed no light on this new debate, nor did the conventional distinctions between Republicans and Democrats or conservatives and liberals. None of the internal or external reference points of past divisions served as a guide to the meandering debate over the nature of the post–Cold War world, and while most commentators bandied the term "new world order" as if they knew what it meant, there was little consensus about the nature of that outside world or America's place in it.

For George Bush, the first of the post–Cold War presidents, the dilemma was resolved by substitution: the Iraqi invasion of Kuwait provided both the enemy and the cause. The former—Saddam Hussein—could easily be demonized, and the latter—the liberation of a victim of aggression, with a strong whiff of crude oil in the air for the realists—could be sold to both houses of Congress, the American public in general, and to the ad hoc coalition that Bush skillfully assembled. Limited in time and place, the conflict appeared to reach closure when Iraqi forces were driven out of Kuwait and when Baghdad seemingly accepted weapons controls and inspections. Gulf War I proved that America's values and capabilities were still intact, and that the rest of the world would respond to its leadership. If this were a new world order, it was one that the United States could understand and control.

To its credit, the Clinton administration, which came to office hoping to marginalize foreign policy issues in the interest of domestic reforms, further explored the implications of a new world order by opting for "assertive multilateralism" and committing itself to humanitarian intervention and nation-building, especially in former communist states. Perhaps inevitably, it soon found itself facing the dilemmas that inherently flowed from a rhetorically pleasing but vexingly vague definition of the scope and purpose of American power. Preoccupied with its own domestic political problems and caught up in the growing commitments brought on by "mission creep" and the lowest-common-denominator nature of coalition driven foreign policy, Clinton and his advisors grew increasingly conventional and pragmatic. No less important in this transformation was the increasingly partisan and ideological nature of the executive-legislative relationship. For six of Clinton's eight years, he faced a Democrat-controlled House and Senate, a reality further complicated by the fact that the parties themselves were increasingly internally divided on foreign policy issues. Out of a combination of understandable frustration and political wisdom, the administration soon learned the value of bargaining and consultation with legislative leaders on both sides of the aisle and seldom asked for more than it was already sure it could get.

In the broader perspective, the first decade of the post–Cold War era still contained some reassuringly familiar elements. Gone, of course, was the single, all-defining enemy of world communism. But in its place had emerged positive goals that were at least consistent with the rhetoric, if not some of the realities, of the Cold War itself. Democracy was to be encouraged; even though there now was a more complex assortment of them as a consequence of the "third wave" of democratization. Alliances, both formal and informal, were to remain an important part of the *modus operandi* of American foreign policy; NATO was to be expanded and revamped to suit the new world order and to deal with the instabilities produced by the disintegration of former communist states such as Yugoslavia, and the sort of ad hoc alliances cobbled together for Gulf War I were touted as productive supplements to formal alliance structures. There was fairly widespread agreement about newfound issues whose recognition had been delayed by the Cold War, although there was less agreement about how to respond. The striking difference—the piece missing from the puzzle—was the "other," the nation or the philosophy (or both together) that could be set in contrast, sometimes uniting the nation in a bipartisan response but always clarifying the issues and providing the prism through which the formulation of America's response to the post–Cold War world would be viewed.

That piece of the puzzle seemed to emerge on September 11, 2001.

September 11, 2001 . . .

It is tempting to argue that the terrorist attacks on September 11, 2001, filled in all the gaps, but it would be at best a partial truth. The destruction of the World Trade Center, the attack on the Pentagon, and the aborted attack on the Capitol building that ended in a farm field in western Pennsylvania brought both the *reality and the specter* of international terrorism home to Americans. But the two were not the same. The reality was unmistakable; in ways not true since television brought the Vietnam conflict home to America, violence entered our living rooms in palpable and inescapable ways. But these events also manifested a less tangible, although nonetheless compelling, facade. They assumed a spectral dimension, entering into the mythology of our era. As the dictionary informs us, a specter is less than completely tangible, a "ghost" or an "apparition" that looms over detailed reality and portends ill fate on those in its shadow. Just as Karl Marx had warned Europe in the *Communist Manifesto* that the "specter" of communism was haunting Europe without spelling out a more precise road map for revolution, the specter of international terrorism now was manifest on American shores, and in some ways, the specter was more frightening than the reality itself. To be sure, its precursors had been there in the bombing of American embassies abroad and in an earlier attack on the World Trade Center itself. But the events of September 11 crossed a threshold—a threshold that could never be defined until *after* it has been breached—that altered *but did not clearly redefine* the nature of the threat or the modalities of the American response.

To that ambiguity, Americans responded with typical American style. The point is meant to be more than just a circular argument. Rather it is to suggest that the response to September 11 evoked a set of established responses rooted deeply in the American culture and the nature of its political system. It was, in a sense, as if the nation once again went into search mode, scanning its history, its previous experiences in such critical moments of redefinition, and the institutionalized processes through which it engaged the discovery, definition, and response to newly perceived realities. As it had done before, it created a new conventional wisdom that would frame the American response. To be sure, that process is still underway, and there remains much serious debate about the nature of the primary threat and the substance and style of the American response. At the time of this writing, the same president, George W. Bush, remains in office, and there has been only one congressional election that did not engage anti-terrorism issues in meaningful debate. Moreover, the nation is still deeply involved with the inconclusive consequences of military campaigns in Afghanistan and Iraq putatively launched as a consequence of the new war on terrorism.

But if the response to the post–September 11 world remains a work in progress, the mindset with which American leaders will confront the problem was far clearer—and typical of the way in which a nation's culture and political institutions have interacted in the past. Once again, the "invitation to struggle" over the direction of American foreign policy would be framed by a new conventional wisdom consistent with the past. As before, America's *perceived* vulnerability would be the starting point for casting that new worldview. It was now perceived that America faced a new level of threat, now manifested not because of the advanced technology or military strength of the enemy but because of the nation's openness to penetration and the ubiquitous nature of both targets for and weapons of terrorist action. The enemy could be, and probably was, already among us, or could penetrate our defenses with little difficulty. As in the Cold War, the homeland once again was vulnerable, not to intercontinental ballistic missiles or bombers but to the insidious attack of terrorists. And as in the Cold War, the American response sought to deal with the problem by taking action both at home and abroad.

Just who were these new enemies, and how should we think about the nature of the threat they posed? As before, the enemy became the mirror image of our perception of ourselves; if "they" were the advocates of terrorism, global instability, and non-democratic states, "we" were the proponents and defenders of peace, globalization, and democracy. Terrorist organizations such as al-Qaeda and "rogue states" such as Afghanistan, Iraq, and North Korea were proffered as the threat to both global and domestic stability, their leaders demonized and their aspirations and grievances denied legitimacy.

The post-September mindset also carried its own, admittedly simplified, theoretical raison d'être. Just as a few key arguments such as George Kennan's "Mr. X" article or Walt Rostow's *Stages of Economic Growth* initially shaped American thinking about the Cold War, there quickly emerged some new "truths" that defined the post–September 11 reality. One was the unquestioned assumption of American hegemony and its special responsibility for maintaining the new international order. The end of the Cold War had left America as the world's dominant military and economic power, and that carried profound implications for its role in dealing with terrorism and rogue states. While there was plenty of room for debate over how long that hegemony would last and how to use it in the short term, there was little disagreement that with such power came special responsibility.

A new operational code emerged, containing both an analysis of the primary sources of instability in the post–September 11 world and a set of sticks and carrots through which Americans would engage the world. At the core of the diagnosis were the notions of "fragile" or "failed" states. Such states were the major source of instability in the world because they had already failed, or were at imminent risk of failing, the basic test of governance in at least two ways. Within their own borders, they were unable to provide effective government, to meet the material needs of their people, to create a sense of community, and, most important, to win the support of their people through democratic elections. They tended to generate, or to provide sanctuary for, extremist movements and terrorist and revolutionary groups. Beyond their borders, such fragile states easily morphed into the "rogue stages" of the international system, often in conflict with their neighbors and seemingly always in search of any means, including weapons of mass destruction, with which to act out their self-proclaimed role of bad boys.

In its most assertive form, American policy would confront rogue states through whatever means necessary to end their support of international terrorism (thus protecting American interests and the American homeland) and the threat they posed to their neighbors (thus stabilizing volatile regions such as the Middle East). While the Cold War doctrine of containment was never relevant, at least in the geographical sense, there was the same sense of a muscular American willingness to resort to military action and to deny the enemy safe haven. The "stick" of American foreign policy was based on its military prowess and its willingness, unilaterally if necessary, to apply it. But there also was a carrot—a positive enticement—in the American arsenal. Consistent with the assumption that the global spread of democracy would eventually become a stabilizing force in the international arena, American policy averred that the creation of capable democratic states would undercut terrorism. To the extent possible—actively, in the case of the rogue states that had been the targets of intervention and now would (hopefully) be rebuilt as viable democracies through extensive American guidance and aid, and more indirectly through diplomatic and economic pressure in other cases—American policy would encourage progress toward democratization, especially in the Middle East.

On the home front, there were striking similarities between the Cold War and the post–September 11 response in terms of the conceptualization of the nature of an internal threat. Just as the early years of the Cold War produced a mindset that justified the search for traitors and enemies and to the creation of what might be termed a "national security state," America's newfound vulnerability to penetration by terrorists led to the creation of the Department of Homeland Security, which was broadly tasked with the defense of the nation against terrorist action. To the nation's credit, the level of national paranoia never rose to that of the "red scares" of the 1930s or McCarthyism of the 1950s, and great care was exercised not to place the Arab American community per se under a cloud of suspicion. That said, surveillance of any individual or group suspected of sympathy with terrorist elements dramatically increased, and the nation's borders were more carefully watched.

Also reminiscent of the Cold War was the qualified bipartisanism of support for efforts to confront the post–September 11 threat. While there was no protracted discussion over the need to respond forcefully to the new challenge, and little open disagreement with the initial commitment of American forces in Afghanistan and Iraq, there quickly emerged a heated debate over a number of issues, including the American ability single-handedly to create viable democracies in both nations, whether the greater threat came from rogue nations or from less well organized terrorist networks, and whether the United States should proceed unilaterally in the face of such threats. The growing partisanship fueled these debates, as did the approaching 2004 presidential election.

Conclusion: Invitations, Wisdoms, and the Tasks before Our Contributors . . .

What, then, is the task set before us? If we follow Senator Fulbright's injunction to see "things in perspective," it is to examine the relationship between that which is seemingly constant—the institutionalized, if ambivalent and constantly reinterpreted, division of powers and responsibilities mandated by the Constitution—and the changing "conventional wisdoms" that define the intellectual and contextual nature of the playing field at any particular moment in time.

All of that cannot be accomplished in one volume, no matter how talented and ambitious the contributors. What our authors bring to the task is a diversity of perspectives. Some approach the question from a historical vantage point, stressing the shifting balance between continuity and change. Bert Rockman notes the recurring themes—the "same old story," he calls them—that permeate and define the parameters of the relationship. Gary Hess, the sole historian in the study, traces the relationship from 1955 to the present day in terms of the always controversial issue of war powers and executive leadership. Terry Deibel and Marie Henehan, respectively, focus on the impact of internal party factionalism and the changing nature of the Senate as factors that shape the alignment of political forces that affect the struggle. Henehan attaches particular importance to the changing nature of the international system in defining the executive-legislative relationship, arguing that such exogenous factors have often been overlooked in more conventional analysis that focuses on the interplay of purely domestic political forces. Bryan Marshall focuses on the changing role of parties, committees, and the issue agenda. Ralph Carter points out how new issues such as foreign trade shift the policy agenda and reshape the battle over foreign policy.

Taken *in toto,* our contributors offer a series of snapshots of reality. Yet such a montage is instructive. Each snapshot illuminates a particular moment of reality in the complex relationship between the executive and legislative branches, and each illustrates the complex interplay between the ever-changing "conventional wisdoms" that situationally define time and place and the less malleable aspects of institutional and constitutional reality that frame the struggle over American foreign policy.

2 The President, Executive, and Congress

The Same Old Story?

BERT A. ROCKMAN

With the insight of a scholar who has studied the modern presidency, Bert Rockman poses a fundamental question: can you have a rational debate over foreign policy given the pressures generated both by the institutional features of divided power in the American system and the political realities that must confront any politician, even Senator Fulbright, as he picks his way through the thicket of policy choices and domestic political realities? Rockman notes that Fulbright was critical of two features of Congress's impact on foreign policy: first, it has a tendency to micromanage policy choices and to interfere in the implementation of programs, and second, it fails to engage the executive branch in a high-level, meaningful debate over foreign policy, frequently demurring on important questions or choosing political expediency over hard choice. Unfortunately, the prospects for clear debate have been diminished by the complex and daunting realities of the post–Cold War world, including the uncertain impact of the events of September 11; the globalization of the economy and its implications for American producers and consumers; the increasing partisanship, frequently bordering on polarization, of American politics and the potential for occasional periods of divided government; and the rising decibel level of America's domestic "culture war," and its tendency to affect the way in which Americans interact with the world.

Introduction

Within the American political class, at any point in time, there are a few individuals with both intellectual credentials and a commitment to serious thinking about policy that give them considerable *gravitas* when they speak or, on occasion, write. The late senator J. William Fulbright was clearly one of these few extraordinary politicians. Their ranks thicken and thin over time, and although Senator Richard Lugar (R-Indiana) may, by reputation, intellect, and thoughtfulness in regard to foreign policy issues, come closest to Fulbright in today's Senate, he is unable to command the attention that Fulbright gained during his chairship of the Senate Foreign Relations Committee in the 1960s and early 1970s.

Fulbright was the author of several books.[1] Perhaps none had the impact of his *Arrogance of Power* published in 1966 in the midst of the Vietnam War and in close propinquity to the Senate Foreign Relations Committee's and Fulbright's relentless interrogation of Johnson administration decision makers about the conduct of U.S. policy in Southeast Asia. *The Arrogance of Power* was both a critique of American policy in Southeast Asia and, more generally, of the Cold War frame that drove policy in that region. But it also critiqued American political institutions with respect to the oversight and making of foreign policy, and particularly with respect to the quality of legislative deliberation in foreign policy making. Fulbright was dismayed by the reflexive, rather than reflective, quality of American foreign policy in the Cold War era and by the quality of debate, or lack thereof, regarding American foreign policy options, particularly in the Congress. It is possible and indeed quite probable, that were he alive today, his concerns would be deepened significantly despite the passing of the Cold War.

This chapter aims first to analyze the main themes of Fulbright's concerns, especially with regard to the quality of the foreign policy debate and the roles and responsibilities of the legislative and executive branches, then secondly to account for changes in the international and foreign policy-making environments and their possible implications since the time (1966) that *The Arrogance of Power* appeared and during which Fulbright's own visibility may have been at its zenith. Third, the chapter then sets forth a research agenda that might help us grapple with the extent to which the quality of foreign policy debate has plummeted, remained about the same, or even improved. Finally, the chapter concludes with a discussion of how much, if anything, has really changed in the foreign policy-making environment between Congress and the president since the mid-1960s.

The Old Story

When Senator J. William Fulbright's book, *The Arrogance of Power*, appeared in 1966, the United States was struggling with a still-escalating and costly involvement in Vietnam. Fulbright's Senate Foreign Relations Committee conducted an interrogation of top-level Johnson administration officials as to how the United States came to escalate the war, the bases of the congressional resolution (the Tonkin Gulf resolution) that resulted in the war's escalation, and, ultimately, the Johnson administration's plans for bringing the conflict—or at least American involvement in it—to an end. The committee hearings were spearheaded by Fulbright himself as its chair. He had obviously come to regret his role in pushing the Tonkin Gulf resolution through the Senate in 1964—a resolution that he thought was confined to a much narrower mandate than the Johnson administration chose to give it. At the forefront of Fulbright's concerns was the lack of debate about the broader issues of a large-scale American intervention in the war in Vietnam, the absence of what he regarded as true Senate consultation prior to any escalation, and, in general, the balance of institutional forces in the conduct of American foreign policy. Fulbright was deeply concerned about the institutional balance and the proper roles of the executive and the Congress, especially the Senate. But he was equally concerned about the lack of serious ideas and analysis in American foreign policy. His concern was that the Cold War provided a climate for simple-minded and pseudomoralistic thinking.

Consequently, Fulbright pushed a two-front engagement. One front required an invigorated set of ideas to move U.S. foreign policy toward a more subtle and nuanced foreign policy, tempered by a comprehension of complexity and less driven by reflexive responses to perceived communist transgressions. The other front required a different institutional balance, one that he believed was warranted by the Constitution, and which would conceivably subject the executive to more critical policy scrutiny. In order to achieve that institutional balance, of course, Congress would be required to live up to what Fulbright understood to be its genuine constitutional responsibilities.

New Foreign Policy Thinking

Senator Fulbright was a public intellectual, but also a practicing politician. The latter role requires deft maneuvering and the frequent taking of positions designed to reduce personal political vulnerability rather than to reflect an academician's conception of logical consistency. Fulbright's long career produced sufficient grist for nearly any mill. But persistent patterns also could be discovered in Fulbright's thinking about international affairs. In many respects, his thinking could be characterized as Burkean. Be skeptical of grand schemes and broad-scale abstractions and of American-centric perspectives on global issues. Respect the past. Respect geopolitical realities. Understand culture and history and respect their stubbornness to conform to an American perspective on the world.

Elements of both idealism (the cultural exchange ideas behind the Fulbright fellowships) and political realism pervaded Fulbright's thinking. Realism dictates an understanding based upon history and the interests of various actors. Subtlety, nuance, and diplomacy are essential to carrying out policies founded on geopolitical and cultural realities. Although realism ultimately must be predicated on the necessity of force, military responses are more often than not likely to be self-defeating unless there is an appreciation for conditions in the field. Simple military responses to an adversary's initiatives can prove to be dangerous.

Thus, a realistic assessment of the Soviet invasion of Afghanistan on the eve of 1980, for example, might well have led to a policy of laissez faire. The Soviet invasion was compelled by many things, but above all by concern that the radical communist leader who had come to power in Afghanistan by overthrowing the Soviet's previously installed puppet leader was stirring fierce opposition from tribal traditionalists in the hinterland beyond Kabul. The Soviets feared radical Islamic movements on its doorstep adjacent to its own Muslim populations in central Asia. It would have been well enough merely to articulate discontent with the Soviet position. But during the Reagan administration, loose and wildly inaccurate talk about "freedom fighters," armed by that administration with an impressive array of weaponry, sowed the seeds for much greater destruction in Afghanistan. It propelled the creation of murderous warlordism, the coming to power of the oppressive Taliban regime, and ultimately providing the base for the al-Qaeda terrorist strikes in the American homeland itself. No one at the time, for sure, could see all or even any of that coming. But realism, as understood by Fulbright, required an understanding of facts on the ground and the likely consequences of altering them. He was dismissive—and rightly so—of those inclined to see foreign policy as part of a Manichean struggle undisturbed by complexity. In the caricatured labels used to displace careful description, Fulbright was a dove. In the word association that appends to that descriptor, Fulbright was labeled by the hardliners as "soft," which in those days meant "on communism." In reality, Fulbright was a hard thinker with little patience for weak-minded formulations that saw single answers behind every problem and a single adversary stirring up every problem. But simple answers and simple formulations make for better political slogans and have more staying power in the minds of policy makers and citizens alike.

Is it plausible or even possible, therefore, to have rational foreign policy discussions in our public life and to have considered outcomes as the basis of foreign policy? Fulbright understood that for this to come about, there was both a need to rid ourselves of platitudinous moralizing in our habits of thought (by letting thought not be based on habit) and to bring forth an institutional balance to provide more and better informed debate within Congress and a more even balance of power between Congress and the executive branch. Fulbright was of two minds about executive discretion. While the executive retains significant control of information and a capability to initiate covert and even overt military operations, and at times had abused those advantages, Fulbright also feared that Congress was too parochial in its interests to hold the executive accountable. Learning little from the Gulf of Tonkin resolution of thirty-eight years before, Congress passed an equally broad grant of military authority to the executive in 2002 for the use of force in Iraq, and potentially other places. The authority ultimately was exercised with dubious results in both instances, and only when the results became unsatisfactory did Congress and opposition politicians become emboldened to oppose it. This was all a little late, but an old story. Could, and above all would, Congress become more responsible? Can, and will, it become less inclined to micromanage for constituency and pork-barrel benefits and more engaged with broader policy questions on which it might partner with, not merely submit to, the executive?

INSTITUTIONAL ISSUES

Two basic concerns about the role of Congress are reflected in Fulbright's thinking. One is that Congress, especially the House of Representatives, too often micromanages foreign policy. It tends to be hyperactive and intrusive on small matters and interferes with the executive in the operations of foreign policy rather than influencing its direction or strategic purpose. Fulbright considered direction and strategic purpose to be legitimate grounds for congressional involvement, but operational intrusion to be far less so.

Congress, as Fulbright saw it, too often intervened for parochial, narrow-minded reasons in order either to satisfy particular constituencies at home or the preconceptions of particular well-placed members such as committee or subcommittee chairs.

The second institutional concern was that Congress failed to engage the executive in constructive debate about the course of U.S. foreign policy. This is really the flip side of congressional parochialism. Congress was apt to intervene too much in small matters and to be passive on large ones. Above all, it was insufficiently willing to debate the fundamental premises of policies wedded to conventional wisdom. In sum, Fulbright's concerns were that Congress was remiss in carrying out its shared responsibilities to formulate and critique foreign policy. Thus, Congress ought properly to intervene less but in more serious and consequential ways with respect to policy direction. Congress's institutional failure in this regard was a failure to tackle seriously the ideas and premises behind U.S. foreign policy.

CONGRESSIONAL PAROCHIALISM

The tension between thinking in long-term interest and acting on behalf of short-term interest is basic to representative institutions and their elected officials. As a general matter, politicians tend to discount the longer-term future for the exigencies of the present or the electoral pressures of the near future. These tendencies may well be exacerbated by certain features of representative institutions, especially when their members are the products of a district-based winner-take-all logic. Under these conditions, politicians are particularly susceptible to critical constituencies and interests within their districts or states. It is likely that those voices will be heard and advocated by the politicians, especially if they are connected to the politicians' parties. Certainly, these pressures are felt relentlessly in areas such as trade, international agreements involving regulation, and frequently in such areas as defense procurement.

Fulbright, however, seemed to have in mind a different form of parochialism, one stemming from deep-seated popular prejudices carried forward, rather than contested or deflected, by the public's representatives. Too few legislators presumably were Burkean trustees of the public's interest. While the public is interested in being safe from external threat, it seems little willing to bear nondefense costs for enhancing American policy aims, such as foreign assistance, which the public generally perceives as constituting a far larger percentage of the federal budget than is actually the case. The parochial perspectives of publics, Fulbright concluded, were too often reinforced by equally parochial politicians. During the 1960s, the particular thorn in Fulbright's side was the chair of the House Appropriations subcommittee that appropriated funds for most nondefense foreign aid programs —Representative Otto Passman of Louisiana.

Is parochialism—defined either by isolationism or unilateralism—however, simply an alternative set of ideas about the appropriate conduct of U.S. foreign policy? While Passman's particular niggardliness on foreign aid appropriations and his desire to attach strings to virtually any aid package might well have been small-minded and counterproductive to then-current U.S. foreign policy aims, it also could be argued that a fortress America policy might have made the United States more secure or at least required it to bear less of the cost of collective security arrangements. An isolationist policy—as distinct from unilateralist interventionism—conceivably might have resulted in fewer U.S. military engagements with commensurately lower losses of blood and treasure. One cannot say for certain what differences the involvement of American power has made in the world or precisely how American involvement has affected American security. Much can be conjectured, but little can be settled. While Representative Passman was hardly a theorist of international relations, it is possible to imagine constructing a reasonably strong intellectual framework for a policy of isolationism of the sort that Passman advocated. Indeed, Fulbright himself was being skewered after the Senate Foreign Relations Committee hearings as an advocate for a more isolationist (less interventionist) foreign policy posture, certainly with regard to military deployments.

At least by Fulbright's more Platonic standards of the national interest, Congress too often fixates on the localistic benefits and important local constituencies of its individual members and focuses too little on the broader national picture. In this regard, Congress reflects the political incentives structured into its form of geographic representation with a relatively high level of candidate-centered visibility and accountability.

A second institutional concern of Fulbright's was that Congress failed to engage the executive in constructive debate about the course of U.S. foreign policy. As noted, Congress was apt to intervene too frequently on operational matters, yet be too passive on policy guidance. Above all, Congress was insufficiently willing to debate the fundamental premises of policies wedded to the prevailing foreign policy paradigm. Fulbright's concern was that Congress was remiss in carrying out its shared responsibilities to formulate and critique foreign policy. Congress needed to intervene less but in more serious and consequential ways with respect to policy direction.

Fulbright was especially concerned about what he regarded as the constitutionally special role of the Senate in foreign policy and the insulation it was intended to provide in the Constitution from momentary passions. The Senate's unique role gave it opportunities to engage the larger questions of foreign policy and, in the broadest sense, to educate the public. But the Senate was failing to take full advantage of these opportunities, and as it had become over time a more representative body it was more likely to mimic public prejudices and to follow uncritically the policy assumptions of the executive. Fulbright, in essence, wished not only to renew American foreign policy, he also wished to reinvigorate the Senate's role as a partner in foreign policy making.

The Foreign Policy Debate

Has the quality of debate declined or risen in the nearly forty years since Senator Fulbright articulated his misgivings? This is not impossible to measure, but there are few ready-made measures to discern what has transpired. Above all, quality is an elusive concept—all too frequently merely in the eye of the beholder. As the beholder here, I am tempted to provide a Potter Stewart–like answer to the question of quality, to wit, "I know it when I see it."[2] As for quality, we probably know it when we read or hear about it. But I will try to suggest later in this chapter some indicators that we might look for in assessing the quality of debate.

Looking at relatively recent events, for example, one might compare the quality of debate in the Congress regarding the resolutions to use military force in the first Gulf War under President George H. W. Bush and that of 2002 under President George W. Bush. Or, one might compare the debate in Westminster in 2003 regarding the Blair government's policy in Britain to align itself with the United States and the debate that took place in Congress a few months earlier.

In regard to the 2002 Iraq resolution, debate in Congress was relatively perfunctory with only a few members of the Senate decrying the wide latitude asked for by the administration and granted to it. Only a few senators, most notably Robert Byrd (D-West Virginia), Chuck Hagel (R-Nebraska), and Ted Kennedy (D-Massachusetts), expressed strong reservations about the beat of the war drums and the evidence being mustered to go to war on the part of the presidential administration. The Democrats' party leadership in the Senate and all of its soon-to-be seekers of the presidential nomination fell into line and voted for the resolution. Nothing could have dramatized more the vacuity of discussion in Washington than the Republican House majority's substitution of "freedom" for "French" as a modifier for fried potatoes. There was, of course, no real discussion as to whether the French had it right or the Germans, Russians, and Chinese as well. The war resolution debate was not ultimately about the use of force, but about the timing of it before United Nations arms inspectors could complete their task. The second Bush administration threw caution to the winds, and most senators and members of the House did likewise, displacing policy caution for political caution.

By contrast, the debate surrounding the first Gulf War found more agreement on ends (getting the Iraqis out of Kuwait) but disagreement as to means, and the vote in each chamber for the use of force resolution was closer. Debate, especially in the Senate, was remarkably free of rancor and engaged with the question of what forms of coercion could achieve results.

Context is, of course, vital. In 1990, American forces had not been engaged in a major way since the Vietnam War that influenced thinking about major military undertakings outside of homeland defense for some time. No one could be sure about the costs, but fears of another debacle with high casualties were in the air. In that context, there was probably more burden on the administration to make its case, and the fact that it sought and gained extensive international cooperation was helpful to making its case.

By the time 2002 came around, events had changed matters considerably. First, all national security issues were being conducted with the backdrop of the cataclysmic events of 9/11 and the rally around President George W. Bush as the incumbent. Second, the Vietnam syndrome of a costly drawn-out slog had since been replaced by the Gulf War I syndrome —a quick overwhelming military victory with few casualties. The former provided motivation for preemptive war against potential threats; the latter provided confidence in military capabilities.

Politically, Democrats found themselves on the wrong end of the first Gulf War debate, mainly voting against immediate military force when the use of that force was judged to be successful. Furthermore, for some time Democrats were disadvantaged in the public's mind on national security issues as the party less able to defend the country's national security. While national security issues faded in relative importance after Gulf War I, they resonated far more powerfully after the destruction of the World Trade Center and the attack on the Pentagon on September 11, 2001. Republicans gained further advantage especially after the rout of the Taliban in Afghanistan before the end of 2001. Under these circumstances, Democrats were in more mood for cover than for debate, especially if they had national political aspirations. Thus, the 2002 war resolution debate was limited to a few iconic politicians expressing their reservations through the media, especially Senator Byrd and Senator Hagel (who later wound up voting for the resolution).

Obviously, the message here is that political context counts. A president was riding high in 2002. The country had come under attack. Military means appeared to have a recent history of success. Democrats were chastened both by their prior behavior (as a party) and by public perceptions that they were less able to defend the country during a time when salience on that matter had risen dramatically.

The quality of debate—or even the existence of one—depends considerably on the quality of the actors but even more on the extent to which debate is perceived as an option. When the existence of debate is itself debatable, there is not much likelihood that a vigorous consideration of policy or policy assumptions will take place. The Democrats fled the scene in 2002 giving the president a green light on the Iraq resolution because they were unwilling to be tainted with opposing a president made popular by the threat of terrorism and by his administration's vigorous posture toward any conceivable threat. There was more advantage for them to be seen debating prescription drug coverage than an impending war. Afraid of their own shadows or perhaps with nothing to say, little was said and thus George W. Bush was given his due—perhaps far more than his due. Mostly the few who did engage the issues of the Iraq resolution were politically safe or too old or unlikely to have further political ambition. When debate is most needed, ironically, it is least likely to be generated.

A Changing Environment for Making Foreign Policy

Much has changed in the environment of foreign policy making as well as in the foreign policy environment. With respect to the latter, obviously the Cold War is long gone and so is the Cold War world of "their" surrogates and "ours" in conflicts both overt and covert in less developed and politically unstable countries across the globe. Likely conflict between nation-states in the old, traditional sense has been greatly reduced. The world is now less structured. Terrorist networks, traditional warlords, and weak states unable or unwilling to exert authority are now the chief threats to American security interests. Threat itself has become globalized in that terrorism can strike nearly anywhere.

The global economy is, of course, another dramatic change from the mid-sixties to the present. What precisely are American interests now, and how, if at all, can they be advanced and reconciled with improvements in international living standards? And how much of the global economy's effects can be influenced by public policy. Often, the answers are that what may be good for the workers in less developed countries is good for consumers of the developed countries but not for the workers in these countries whose jobs have been outsourced.

Clearly, the international environment has changed and the world is less predictable and more disorderly than in the Cold War days. The new conditions, which also include an expansion of international regulatory regimes, are a good bit more complicated than the Cold War issues and the occasional regional hot wars or civil wars often fought by surrogates of the cold war principals. The new issues are even more demanding of serious thought and policy debate. Terrorism, as one of these critical issues, has yet to produce that serious analysis in overt political debate within our institutions. The drastic change in the foreign policy environment has been accompanied by equally substantial changes in the foreign policy-making milieu.

One factor that may have an influence on foreign policy in the new era has been the polarization between the parties. It would be an exaggeration, however, to suggest that there ever was for any sustained period of time a bipartisan foreign policy consensus. There were moments when that did occur, and perhaps notably for a time in the 1950s when the Eisenhower administration and the Democrats' leaders in Congress were largely in accord during the Cold War era. The growth in party polarization has meant more acrimony and more controversy in foreign policy issues, traceable to the protracted political fallout over Vietnam. During the Reagan administration, for example, there was at least as much or more party division over foreign policy issues than over domestic ones. Does this partisan division create knee-jerk reflexes or can it serve to sharpen and accentuate the distinctive premises behind policy? These premises were perhaps obscured by the relatively bland Cold War consensus of the 1950s and 1960s prior to the escalating costs of the Vietnam War. It is not clear precisely what has happened, if anything has, other than that foreign policy postures now more predictably cleave along party lines, once party positions have formed, typically *ex poste*. Deep division, unfortunately, may not lead to much deep thinking. And on matters of national security, Democrats typically want to see how events play out before articulating a position that might accentuate their party's vulnerabilities (and their own). When it is safe to be critical of the use of force, they will be. Before then, they are more likely to hedge their bets—a lesson learned from the debate leading to the resolution on Gulf War I.

Issues of global regulation and multilateralism versus unilateralism also divide the parties more deeply than they have since the period before U.S. entry into World War II. Trade is an unusual exception. While trade agreements bring forth a good bit of division between the parties on Capitol Hill, the executive is generally favorably disposed toward them regardless of the president's party.

Divided government has also been a more frequent phenomenon since the mid-1960s. Although divided government had relatively little impact on foreign policy during the Eightieth Congress and the Eisenhower-Johnson-Rayburn years, the effects of divided government began to grow stronger through the 1980s during the Reagan years and continued beyond. Divided government became the norm. But even that has been superseded by *closely divided* government, whether or not the legislative and executive branches are controlled fully or partially by different parties. The division has produced an increased level of acrimony and dissensus, at least judged by what may have been the abnormal two-decade period after the end of World War II. It is not clear if the greater degree of acrimony is in part attributable to the division of government or to the closeness of its division.

To the extent that policy divisions followed along party lines, divided government made foreign policy making more acrimonious. In this way, foreign policy matters came to reflect domestic issue cleavages. Presidential appointments especially grew more contentious than in the past, and much of this contentiousness was based on domestic political issues and sometimes on perceived personal slights. Opposition to the confirmation of James Hormel as ambassador to Luxemburg during the Clinton administration was solely based apparently on the fact that he was openly gay. The reign of Jesse Helms, the cantankerous senator from North Carolina as chair of the Senate Foreign Relations Committee from the Ninety-fourth to the Ninety-seventh Congresses (1995–2003), was responsible for sinking a number of prospective appointments, including that of a former Republican Justice Department official and Senate nominee, William Weld, and for delaying a far greater number as a bargaining tactic. But the trend was there when Democrats controlled the Senate as well and stiffed some of the nominees of the Reagan (in its last two years) and Bush I administrations, including the Bush I nominee for defense secretary, John Tower. To some degree, the shooting down of prospective appointments reflected the higher level of contentiousness and orneriness in American politics and the mapping of domestic political cleavages onto foreign policy and foreign policy personnel choices.

The domestic "culture wars" especially have found their way into foreign policy decisions since the era of President Ronald Reagan. Among these decisions are those involving financial support for family planning and population control. These choices, however, often have emanated from the executive branch in the form of executive orders and often were reversed through the same device when an administration of the opposing political persuasion came to power. These hot-button issues are a function of the expanded agenda of cultural politics in the United States, and the cultural politics cleavage now being largely coincident with the positions of the two main political parties. They also reflect the expanded activities of international organizations and nongovernmental organizations involved in international activities such as population planning. More activities in international, as in domestic, matters also produce more controversy, and that may be the main story here. Four decades ago, many of the cultural conflicts had been kept beneath the surface, and there also was less visible NGO activity on the international scene regarding issues that evoke cultural controversy. Domestic policy controversies have been overlaid on international policies as a consequence of a cultural cleavage in the United States that has become overtly partisan and very intense. The results often place U.S. policies at odds with those of other economically developed democracies.

In addition, a principal line of cleavage on foreign policy stretching back to much of the preceding century has been resurrected—the isolationist/internationalist strain. Since the post 9/11 war on terror began, however, the isolationist strain has taken on an aggressively unilateralist tinge. The major issues here involve going it alone or concerting action (meaning negotiating with other actors to build support) with international or multinational organizations as well as adhering to or joining in international agreements. The political divisions by party are now the key to these perspectives more than the regional divisions of an earlier era.

Partisan politics and sound bites tend to distill the necessary debate about the conditions and circumstances of unilateral and multilateral action into moralistic bromides and cheap shots to appeal to partisan audiences. But no debate is more urgently needed than the conditions for the unilateral and multilateral exercise of power, and the conditions for the use of military power and how it should be utilized (the Colin Powell doctrine of massive force versus the Donald Rumsfeld doctrine of mobile force). Senator Fulbright, I suspect, would have been rightly suspicious of the George W. Bush administration's rush to war in Iraq, but he might have been equally skeptical of the invitation by the opposition candidate that a multilateral force should be created to enjoy the privilege of being shot at in a war disapproved of by the constituent governments of this (so far) hypothetical multilateral force. Unless serious debate occurs before force is committed, ex post constraints on options will be substantial. That is the reason to have serious debate before making a commitment rather than after.

Yet if Senator Fulbright were disconcerted about the lack of debate surrounding the Cold War consensus that helped produce the Vietnam debacle, he might be equally disconcerted by the dissensus that has gripped American foreign policy making since the Carter administration, and which has grown more rigid and partisan with time. Moreover, the constancy of parochial behavior, now fervently part of the domestic cultural wars, affects our foreign policy capabilities even though cultural micromanagement is as likely to be wielded now from the presidential administration as from Congress. Fulbright likely would have found this state of affairs disheartening.

Of course, this is the substance not merely the process of foreign policy, and, as noted earlier, one person's definition of parochial is someone else's definition of a broader worldview. When Otto Passman sought to torpedo foreign aid and multilateral approaches, he was expressing a larger worldview of isolationist unilateralism. When Jesse Helms, through somewhat different venues and means, more or less followed in the Passman tradition, if more venomously, he too was expressing the same isolationist and unilateralist worldview. A sophisticated foreign affairs audience may deem this worldview to be stupid or silly or provincial, but it obviously is not so to those holding it.

Precisely what issues should we be debating then? Is it all just a matter of what worldview we wish to promote? Should it be the constitutionally appropriate process of governing and the roles of executive and legislative institutions? Or ought the focus to be on the quality of the debate that takes place and, thus, getting to the underlying assumptions, diagnostics, and prognostics of foreign policy choices? In reality, it is all of these things. Obviously, though, it is difficult to separate the quality of debate from positions we think should be arrived at. Despite the difficulty of doing that psychologically, it is vital to do it analytically. Is it plausible, after all, that a Passman-Helms policy perspective could be effectively justified on the basis of analytics? We can not know until we do the hard work to analyze precisely what risks, costs, and benefits that policy perspective entails. Indeed, it is certainly plausible that positions regarded as being outside of the foreign policy mainstream are ones that we need to pay attention to if they are (and can be) effectively argued.

The Quality of Debate

Serious foreign policy debate is essential to making wise and judicious choices and to averting tragic ones. Omniscience is not guaranteed, of course; it is, in fact, very unlikely. Mistakes and reasonable, but often wrong, guesses are more probable. Like most complex choices, decisions are often between less than desirable outcomes and worse ones. We do, however, have a better chance of making reasonable, informed, and wiser decisions if we unfreight ourselves of foolish premises and myths. A powerful myth that derives in part from Wilsonian idealism and also from not having had a full-scale foreign war on American soil is the idea of the United States as a zealous bearer of mankind's best intentions. Military force may, of course, be the instrument of those intentions. Neoconservative utopianism reflects this view that the United States can and will do good on behalf of all mankind by bringing force when necessary (and it often seems to be necessary) to ensure the triumph of its position. The choices, in this utopian (and very nonconservative) mindset are not between bad and worse, but between good and evil. And so it would be evil to fail to correct what is bad in the world. This view has been particularly strong in both the Reagan and especially the Bush II administrations. It is, of course, morally difficult to argue that deterring evil is bad unless it leads to worse things, which history suggests it well can. The utopian myth is part of the freight carried in the U.S. foreign policy debate, and reducing choices to the morally virtuous and the morally bad is a great advantage to the adherents of the utopian myth.

For debate to be meaningful, it is truly helpful if it informs decision making rather than rationalizing or critiquing decisions that already have been made. Is it possible to do that?

Two critical but opposing assumptions govern the likelihood of there being meaningful debate in foreign policy or, for that matter, on matters of public policy generally. The first might be regarded as the *quality of the elite* assumption; the second, the *structural incentives* assumption. The former assumption emphasizes who the elites are from the standpoint of their intellectual characteristics and interests. What are they capable of? What questions will they ask? Can they absorb, and are they open to, complexity? Obviously, these are not easy matters to discern, and it is also clear, as noted at the outset, that only a few members of the congressional elite have both sufficient interest and dedication to foreign policy issues to be, as Fulbright was, a recognized authority in foreign policy. It is hard to say whether the quality of the legislative elite has improved, fallen, or been constant in regard to its foreign policy understanding. That depends upon the time range being measured, but, even more, on the complexity of operationalizing the ability of the members of Congress and the senators. We can safely say, however, that insipid people are not likely to inspire high-quality debate. But the obverse is not necessarily true, that is, smart people may not necessarily engage in high-quality debate because political incentives dictate otherwise.

First, members of Congress have enormous responsibilities, one of which is continuous fund raising. Second, members have to respond—or have a position—on a wide variety of issues. It is hard to know a lot about everything. Third, their position typically has to resonate to critical party and electoral constituencies. Fourth, everyone has to watch for the soundbite blow back, for example, the twenty-second statement that an opposition research team can use in a political advertisement. Fifth, as parties polarize, it becomes harder to take positions that cut against the party grain.

In sum, structural conditions and incentives facilitate or impede opportunities for elites to shine if they are bright enough to do so. It is purely a speculation on my part that in an approximately thirty-year period the structural impediments to high-quality debate have risen while the quality of the legislative elites may have fallen. But that, to be sure, requires specification before supposition can be turned into meaningful evidence.

In the United States, as in most other democracies, there are a variety of forums—think tanks, academic centers, advisory groups, and media—in which policy, including foreign policy, can be debated. In forums most dominated by specialists, these debates can be illuminating. It is even probable that within the inner sanctums of government, policy debates can sometimes produce searching questions, a demand for facts, and challenges to assumptions. Of course, we cannot know this conclusively except through memoirs and views of participants, which are usually also self-serving.

It is also possible that behind closed doors in executive session, there may be more illuminating and frank debates than there are in open hearings or on the floor. But, as with policy debate in the executive branch, we do not have first-hand reports. So we can only know what happens in open committee/subcommittee sessions and on the floor.

Given these significant caveats, can we shed light on the comparative state of policy debate in the Congress? Can the Congress, and especially the Senate, serve as a beacon of informed foreign policy discussion? Under the hyperpoliticized conditions noted, that is probably unlikely. Still, it is helpful to propose here a set of criteria by which we can examine in a comparative way the quality of foreign policy debate in Congress, particularly in the Senate where more of it is likely to take place since there is no set limit on the time of floor debate and because of the Senate's unique responsibilities in foreign policy. What are the indicators of quality we should look for? I suggest several below that I believe can be subject to some form of content analysis.

First, does a speaker note *ramifications* of an action or of inaction? Taking this further, we can ask (a) how *specific* are the ramifications noted? (b) *how much* discussion is there of them? (are they throwaway lines or is there an effort to tackle consequences?) (c) are there particularly efforts to deal with *adverse consequences* that may follow from the speaker's position? Thinking about consequences of policy, especially adverse consequences of a favored position, is an indication of complexity and the ability of a speaker (or the speaker's speech-writing staff) to weigh costs and options.

Second, to what extent does a speaker use *data?* Does a speaker refer to evidence and to the source of the evidence, such as a study by the Congressional Research Service (CRS) or the General Accountability Office (GAO) or other publicly available source? When obtainable and valid, systematic evidence is to be preferred to anecdotal evidence. Information that comes from publicly available sources is also better than evidence gleaned from covert sources. Data are the essential constituents of reasoned discourse and of separating fantasy from reality.

Third, is there *clarity and consistency* of objectives, and is *means-ends* thinking in evidence? Arguments where the frame of reference continually changes are disreputable. During the first Gulf War, the rationale for U.S. policy was high-mindedly described as a defense of international principles of nonaggression against sovereign nations and also, more crassly, as being necessary to protect American jobs (presumably based on the possible impact of Saddam Hussein's control of Kuwaiti oil resources). The latter view was articulated by then secretary of state James Baker at one point. During the second Gulf War, and in violation of the nonaggression principle articulated during the first Gulf War, the rationale shifted from the imminent threat of weapons of mass destruction to the uncontroversial proposition that Saddam Hussein was a villainous character. Relating means to ends, as well, is equally essential. The current war on terror, for example, is filled with brash global trash talk from both the Bush administration and its challengers designed to bolster our spirits. But neither the Bush administration nor its challengers have indicated just how they plan on strangling the terrorists. Nor have they even begun defining precisely just what victory over terrorism really means. Clarity, consistency, and means-ends relationships are essential to avoid falling into platitudes that momentarily lift public spirits and, not coincidentally, also the chances for election of the public speakers.

Fourth, is there *nonanalogic reasoning* or, alternatively, a tendency to resort to shopworn analogies? The Munich analogy misinformed the deepening commitment of the United States in Vietnam. Analogic reasoning is typically overly inclusive, meaning that it parallels a few superficial elements between cases without establishing a logic for the case at hand and drawing evidence from its history. The Munich analogy and the related Domino theory voiced as critical to the U.S. military effort in Vietnam assumed that there was a single aggressive regional power with designs and capabilities to control the region. In the rhetoric of the Johnson administration, particularly, the dominant regional conqueror was presumed to be Maoist China—a logic that assumed a separation of communism from the nationalist conflicts that had arisen in the past between Vietnam and China, and which would arise again in 1979 with a military skirmish between the two. In other words, the Munich analogy and the Domino metaphor were each false, overgeneralized, and inadequately grounded in regional realities.

Fifth, are *attributions of bad intent* on the part of potential adversaries absent or present in debate? Attributions of bad intent imply a moralistic good versus bad mindset (which is occasionally appropriate), but, like politics in any setting, issues often arise over conflicting interests. Misunderstandings of intent can lead to wars or to catastrophic policies that reverberate against one's long-term interests as in the case of the U.S. response to the Soviet invasion of Afghanistan. It is, of course, vital to distinguish between aggressive behavioral propensities and behavior reflecting long-standing concerns or interests. While mischievous behavior may not be tolerable in either case, moralistic suppositions will reduce the room for bargaining and negotiation under conditions where bargaining and negotiation can work, for example, during the Cuban Missile Crisis. Empathy, on the other hand, can help us see the options as adversaries understand them. Understanding the thinking of an adversary is likely to be crucial in preventing the escalation of conflicts and in possibly resolving disputes.

Conclusion

Despite the many reservations I have heretofore expressed about the opportunities for meaningful debate, foreign policy discussions are often conducted with appropriate seriousness, a demand for evidence and consistency of analysis, and a willingness to think past the conventional wisdom of the day. There is no lack of serious debate. Unfortunately, there is too often a lack of serious *public* debate as we move closer to the final stages of public policy making.

Unlike academicians or other experts, the politicians who make, or ratify or veto, the critical foreign policy decisions are not free agents. They are also infrequently intellectuals, although they are equally infrequently lacking in intelligence. But they are strapped for time and also anxious not to have their words come back to haunt them politically. With few exceptions, our national legislators especially have much to lose by investing a great deal of time in complicated foreign policy issues. They usually find it easier to sail with the prevailing winds when they exist or under their party's banner. The U.S. system of government emphasizes legislative specialization among a class of politicians who also have to be generalists to their public constituencies. A few invest the time to go beyond the surface; most do not.

Nor does our system value eloquence on the floor or the direct and sometimes searing questioning of the executive leadership as may be found in the Westminster systems. The Westminster systems also may enforce through direct questioning a higher degree of preparation and serious thinking among the executive leadership than in the American system. Minds unchallenged grow wobbly. The Westminster model does appear to lead to a higher quality of debate, although the course of debate may influence decisions even less in the Westminster systems than in the American case.

Quality of debate, as noted, is an elusive matter. I have suggested some indicators that might tell us whether there are greater or lesser levels of debate in a given setting over a specified time range. In the end, however, it is likely that the story is not fundamentally different from that which Fulbright decried. The executive branch controls the policy agenda significantly in international affairs. And while the instruments of policy making (the agencies and staff units) are typically competent at the very least, they can rarely be better than their leadership. But even high-quality leaders for a variety of political reasons and other constraints often make low-quality policies, while lesser-quality leaders are unlikely to make high-quality policies. Quality of personnel in political leadership positions may be a necessary condition for quality decision making, but not a sufficient one.

A few senators of inordinate wisdom and courage and even some members of the House (with less opportunity and lower visibility, however) will rise to challenge the prevailing wisdom and raise vital questions. In the main, though, our system of divided authority continues to suffer from the same old problems that so worried Fulbright. On the whole, the executive gets to define the agenda, and when the agenda reeks with bellicosity, the congressional lamb usually meekly lies down before the executive lion. Few questions are asked ex ante and even fewer courageous choices are made. Numerous recriminations, however, follow when things do not go according to plan. Hindsight remains perfect; foresight is all too scarce. And foresight will remain scarce in the absence of challenging debate. Fulbright, no doubt, would not be surprised. For all too sadly, Congress abdicates its responsibilities for helping shape the contours of our foreign policy or of providing informed debate. In these respects, the executive-legislative relation in foreign policy remains very much the same old story.

3 Authorizing War

Congressional Resolutions and Presidential Leadership, 1955–2002

GARY R. HESS

Gary Hess reminds us of the central importance of the question of war powers in defining the relationship between the executive and legislative branches. The status of that relationship is a constantly shifting target, defined in part by constitutional interpretation and accompanying legislation such as the War Powers resolution and in part by the attitudes of incumbent chief executives and the political realities of the moment. From a historical perspective, support for a strong and proactive presidency has shifted from "liberal internationalists" to "conservative unilateralists," while advocacy of an active role for the legislature has shifted from conservatives to liberals. Presidential interpretation of the Constitution is also significant. Eisenhower and Johnson initially saw congressional resolutions authorizing the commitment of U.S. forces as constitutionally necessary, although Johnson later changed his mind. In contrast, George H. W. Bush and George W. Bush denied that such resolutions were constitutionally mandated but nonetheless sought congressional approval on the grounds of political expediency.

Introduction

On five occasions since 1955, Congress has passed resolutions granting the president prior authority or approval to wage war. The effect of each resolution was to transfer the ultimate decision for war to the discretion of the president. The first two such resolutions of 1955 and 1957, directed at crises in the Taiwan Straits and Middle East respectively, did not result in presidential implementation of their war-making provisions. The three most recent resolutions, however, provided the constitutional authority for presidential decisions for war against North Vietnam in 1965 and against Iraq in 1991 and 2003.[1]

The resolutions have satisfied neither proponents of executive power nor defenders of congressional war-making prerogatives. The former, which have shifted from "liberal internationalists" of the early Cold War to "conservative unilateralists" in recent decades, consider such resolutions a political convenience, not a constitutional necessity. The latter, whose core political constituency has changed from conservative to liberal, resent the resolutions as a "blank check" that leaves Congress responsible for war without formally declaring it. Although began in the interest of promoting executive-congressional cooperation in war making, the war-authorizing resolution thus has become a part of the political and constitutional "struggle for control"—as Edwin Corwin famously described it—of foreign policy.

The resolutions have similar histories. First, each was initiated by the president at a time of crisis and was justified as essential to U.S. national security. The resolutions were presented to Congress as an instrument of deterrence: the show of national resolve and unity would make war less likely. Second, congressional consideration of the resolutions reflected in varying degrees concern about whether approval would compromise the separation of powers and the constitutional authority of Congress to declare war. This led to the practice of attaching provisions giving Congress power to terminate the resolutions without presidential approval and to unsuccessful motions in two instances to require that the president return to Congress for a formal war authorization if efforts to avoid war failed. Third, in each case, the imperative of national security—heightened by the pressure to stand by the president in a crisis—worked to his advantage. With his control of diplomacy and deployment of forces, the president was able to time his request so as to gain maximum political benefit. In only one case was the vote close. Fourth, approval of the resolutions reflected broad bipartisan support. In only one instance did the president's party control both houses of Congress, so in the other cases, he was dependent upon the support of congressional leadership as well as the rank-and-file of both parties. He benefited from the erosion of partisanship in the "rally around the flag" atmosphere that presidents helped to create. Partisan differences, however, were significant in the votes on the 1991 and 2002 war resolutions. The similarities among the resolutions, however, conceal significant differences. The most striking is the changing attitude of the president toward Congress. President Dwight D. Eisenhower was respectful of Congress's constitutional authority to declare war and was committed to the proposition of executive-legislative collaboration in crises where the use of military force might be employed. Lyndon B. Johnson, influenced by Eisenhower's practice, likewise considered congressional support essential as he responded to the Vietnam crisis. In advancing the Formosa, Middle East, and Gulf of Tonkin resolutions, Eisenhower and Johnson embodied a solicitous approach toward Congress; they saw the resolutions as constitutionally necessary. During the controversy over the Vietnam War, especially after the criticism of former congressional supporters, Johnson shifted ground and denied the necessity of congressional authorization. His defiant stance, contending that the commander-in-chief power enabled him to wage war, marked a change in presidential attitude toward Congress that was reflected in the ways that Presidents George H. W. Bush and George W. Bush approached Congress in 1991 and 2002, respectively. They regarded the resolutions as unnecessary on constitutional grounds, but as a domestic or international political imperative.

The Formosa Resolution

Assuming the presidency in 1953 as war and negotiations dragged on in Korea, Eisenhower was convinced that his predecessor, Harry S. Truman, had made a serious mistake in failing to gain congressional authorization for the war. Eisenhower believed that congressional authorization was essential not only on constitutional grounds, but also to assure domestic support and to project American resolve internationally.[2] At the same time, Eisenhower wanted to preserve executive flexibility in crisis situations. Like other presidents, he was determined not to compromise his power as commander-in-chief, but he did not feel threatened by recognizing the constitutionally mandated congressional role in war making.

The Formosa resolution was an integral part of Eisenhower's policy during the extended crisis that began in September 1954 when the People's Republic of China (PRC) started shelling Chinese Nationalist-held offshore islands. Three weeks earlier, PRC foreign minister Chou En-lai restated the communist commitment to "liberate" Taiwan. The shellings were seen as the first step toward an attack not only on those islands, but also as a possible first step of an invasion of Taiwan and the elimination of the Nationalist government. Quemoy, the target of the shellings, and its sister island Little Quemoy were part of a number of islands that had remained in Nationalist hands when Jiang Jieshi's government took refuge on Taiwan in 1949; to the north of the Quemoys, which lay directly across from the port city of Amoy, were the nineteen islands of the Matsu chain, which controlled access to Foochow. Still farther north were the Tachen islands. The Chinese Nationalists had some 75,000 troops on these islands (50,000 on Quemoy) which were used to harass the mainland. The Seventh Fleet, which Truman had sent into the Formosa Strait on June 27, 1950, in an effort to keep the conflict that had just erupted in Korea from spreading, still protected Taiwan itself, but there was no American shield over the offshore islands.[3]

Over the next several weeks, Eisenhower moved to provide U.S. support of Jiang Jieshi's government, while preserving flexibility in defining the limits of that support. In December, the United States completed a mutual defense agreement with the Nationalist government, but it committed the United States only to the defense of Taiwan and the Pescadores and made no mention of the offshore islands.

The congressional resolution was proposed at the moment Eisenhower had decided "the time had come to draw the line."[4] Eisenhower's objectives were to deter the PRC and to avoid provoking a war. As the PRC continued to build up forces on the mainland and to construct jet airfields across from Taiwan, its planes on January 10 raided the Tachens. Eight days later, the PRC launched an amphibious assault on the island of Ichiang, which lay seven miles north of the Tachens, overwhelming the small Nationalist force stationed there. Eisenhower stated that since that island had no relation to the defense of Taiwan, no action to defend it was necessary. The next day two hundred PRC planes bombed the Tachens. Privately, Eisenhower made plans to abandon the Tachens entirely, and prepared to help the Nationalists evacuate the islands once Jiang had been convinced that it would not weaken his over-all position. Besides abandoning a strategically unimportant foothold, withdrawal from the Tachens also helped to project an image of reasonableness.[5]

It was in this crisis atmosphere that Secretary of State John Foster Dulles and Admiral Arthur H. Radford, chairman of the Joint Chiefs of Staff, met with congressional leaders on the morning of January 20 to advance the president's interest in a resolution. A draft resolution had been prepared by the State Department, but it was not shared with the congressional leaders.

Reflecting the views that Eisenhower had expressed in an earlier meeting with him, Dulles based the case for a resolution on constitutional, strategic, and diplomatic grounds. On the first, the secretary defined the powers of the president narrowly. He dismissed the contention that the president had the inherent authority to protect Formosa, saying that the power Truman had exercised to defend Formosa derived from his war powers, but with the Korean War Armistice that authority had become doubtful. When asked whether the president would need congressional authorization once the treaty with Formosa was ratified by the Senate, Dulles pointed out that the treaty specified that any U.S. action to defend Taiwan would be in accord with constitutional processes. Besides arguing the constitutional necessity of authorization, Dulles contended that the resolution would strengthen the U.S. position and would reduce the risk of war. The American position in the crisis had deteriorated because of its uncertainty, but now the combined strategy of a treaty, a resolution, withdrawal from the Tachens, and reinforcement of Quemoy and Matsu would make clear that the United States would retreat no further. The probing of the PRC would end.

Senator Leverett Saltonstall (R-Massachusetts) posed the important constitutional question: can Congress give the president the power to use troops without making it a declaration of war? Dulles replied that he was not suggesting a war declaration, and Saltonstall suggested that the resolution was simply a general approval to use troops to help defend the United States. To that, Dulles said yes, "and to use the armed forces to secure Formosa and the Pescadores and whatever might be necessary to their defense." At other points in the conversation, Dulles was pressed, especially by Senator Earle C. Clements (D-Kentucky), to state that the resolution constituted a "drawing the line" from which the United States would retreat no further. While that had been implicit in Dulles's earlier comments, the secretary avoided such a commitment, noting that while clarity of purpose was necessary, so too was flexibility. Accepting the administration's response to the crisis, the leaders discussed at some length the timing of the resolution, that is, whether it would be better to approve it or the treaty first. Dulles held that since Eisenhower needed congressional authorization in any event, there was no reason to delay the resolution. There was concern that announcement of the resolution might provoke PRC military action, so it was agreed that the news release on the meeting would state only that it was a briefing on the situation.[6]

Assured of support from the leadership, Eisenhower formally requested the resolution in a message to Congress on January 24. He stated: "The situation has become sufficiently critical to impel me . . . to ask the Congress to participate now, by specific resolution, in measures designed to improve the prospects for peace. These measures would contemplate the use of the armed forces of the United States if necessary to assure the security of Formosa and the Pescadores." The limits of the authority that he was seeking were vague: "I do not suggest that the United States enlarge its defensive obligations beyond Formosa and the Pescadores as provided by the Treaty now awaiting ratification." Since armed attack on "closely related localities" might, however, determine the success of an attack on Formosa and the Pescadores, it was necessary that the authority granted by Congress extend to their defense, but "only in situations which are recognizable as parts of, or definite preliminaries to, an attack against the main positions of Formosa and the Pescadores." While authority for some actions that might be required were inherent in his executive powers, "a suitable Congressional resolution would clearly and publicly establish the authority of the President as Commander-in-Chief to employ the armed forces of this nation promptly and effectively . . . [and] would make clear the unified and serious intentions of our Government, our Congress and our people." It would also "reduce the possibility that the Chinese Communists, misjudging our firm position and national unity, might be disposed to challenge the position of the United States, and precipitate a major crisis which even they would neither anticipate or desire." Finally, Eisenhower stressed the need for preemptive congressional action: "The United States must remove any doubt regarding our readiness to fight . . . To make this plain requires not only Presidential action but also Congressional action. In a situation such as now confronts us, and under modern conditions of warfare, it would not be prudent to await the emergency before coming to Congress. Then it might be too late. Already the warning signals are flying."[7]

Congressional contingency authorization of war was unprecedented.[8] "The resolution Eisenhower wanted was something new in American history," Stephen Ambrose writes, "[n]ever before had Congress given the President a blank check to act as he saw fit in a foreign crisis."[9] Herman Phleger, the legal advisor in the State Department who helped draft the resolution, called it "monumental . . . [for] never before in our history had anything been done like that." Seeing presciently the resolution as precedent, Phleger observed that it solved for future presidents the problem of criticism that Truman had faced because of his failure to obtain congressional assent for war in Korea.[10]

Congress quickly and overwhelmingly gave Eisenhower what he wanted. The day after his message, the House of Representatives, by a vote of 410 to 3, approved the Formosa resolution. The administration lobbied against a Senate amendment to "draw the line" so as to exclude defense of Quemoy and Matsu. With that amendment defeated, the Senate on January 28 approved the resolution by a margin of 83 to 3. The resolution specifically authorized the president "to employ the Armed Forces of the United States as he deems necessary for the specific purpose of securing and protecting Formosa and the Pescadores against armed attack, this authority to include the securing and protection of such related positions and territories of that area now in friendly hands and the taking of such measures as he judges to be required or appropriate in assuring the defense of Formosa and the Pescadores."[11]

The ambiguity of the resolution, which was part of Eisenhower's overall strategy of avoiding a commitment to defense of the offshore islands, has been praised by some scholars, most notably Robert Divine. In *Eisenhower and the Cold War,* Divine writes that by "introduc[ing] a note of deliberate ambiguity into American policy . . . [Eisenhower] kept the Chinese Communists off balance. . . . The beauty of Eisenhower's policy is that to this day no one can be sure whether or not he would have responded militarily to an invasion of the offshore islands, and whether he would have used nuclear weapons."[12] However, critics of Eisenhower have pointed out that the practical effect of the resolution was to commit him to the defense of Quemoy. Indeed, in letters in early February to NATO commander general Alfred Gruenther and British prime minister Winston Churchill, Eisenhower acknowledged the difficulty of distinguishing between an attack on Quemoy that was limited to the island and one that was preliminary to an assault on Taiwan.[13] In *Deterrence in American Foreign Policy,* Alexander L. George and Richard Smoke observe that "by endorsing an extension of the U.S. commitment, even in the conditional terms of the Formosa Resolution, [Eisenhower] had substantially narrowed if not virtually lost his freedom of action to withhold use of American forces to prevent the loss of Quemony, should it become necessary to do so. If such a contingency had arisen it seems inconceivable that Eisenhower would not have invoked the Formosa Resolution. For as Eisenhower himself practically admitted on various occasions, it was difficult to imagine a full-scale Chinese Communist attack on Quemoy which was not part of a campaign against Taiwan as well."[14] Even Divine acknowledges that "in his attempts to placate Chiang and the China bloc in Congress, [Eisenhower] had come dangerously close to committing the United States to defend the offshore islands against any Chinese attack."[15]

If the Formosa resolution narrowed Eisenhower's options, it also placed Congress in a position of supporting whatever level of U.S. military power

Eisenhower might choose to employ. Nuclear weapons were not part of the discussion with congressional leaders, nor were they considered in the brief congressional debate on the resolution. Yet within six weeks, as the crisis worsened, both Eisenhower and Dulles threatened the use of nuclear weapons, touching off much criticism in the United States and abroad. Several members of Congress questioned the strategy, but Congress's capacity to exercise restraint on the executive was limited by the open-ended nature of the Formosa resolution.[16]

Whether Eisenhower's policy is judged as a shrewd use of diplomatic and military power or an ill-conceived strategy that risked a major war over islands of questionable strategic importance, the war-authorizing resolution had been introduced as a technique of deterrence and a means of deference to Congress's war-making powers.

The Eisenhower Doctrine and the Middle East

Two years later, a solicitous Eisenhower turned again to Congress. In the aftermath of the Suez Crisis of the fall of 1956, he feared that the prevalent anti-Westernism in the Middle East would enable the Soviet Union to gain influence, if not control, which would be disastrous to the economies of Europe and to the American global interests. To counter that threat, the United States needed to assert its power independently of the discredited British and French. The Eisenhower administration crafted a Middle Eastern policy that sought to put the Soviet Union "on notice" that the United States would protect Western interests and to bolster the confidence of the pro-Western governments.[17]

On New Year's Day 1957, Eisenhower invited thirty leading senators and congressmen to the White House. In a four-hour meeting, the president, Dulles, and other executive branch officials outlined plans for what became known as the Eisenhower Doctrine, a strategy of containment that combined increased economic and military assistance with the threat of U.S. military intervention. In preliminary remarks, Dulles noted that the U.S. position during the Suez Crisis had enhanced its prestige in the Middle East, but the Soviet government—suffering from increased nationalism in the satellite countries and internal challenges—might "recoup . . . its position by a victory in the Middle East." Eisenhower then spoke of the historical Russian interest in the Middle East and the erosion of British and French power that had created a "vacuum that must be filled by the United States before it is filled by Russia." He sought broad authority to use military power in event of a Soviet attack. Only an unequivocal stand would deter the Soviets: "the United States must put the entire world on notice that we are ready to move instantly if necessary." He assured the congressmen that if circumstances permitted, he would follow constitutional procedures before committing U.S. forces, but that might not be possible since in "modern war [it] might be a matter of hours only." If Congress gave him the authority he sought, "it might never have to be used." While most congressional members were supportive, a few raised political and constitutional issues. Congressman John McCormack, Democrat of Massachusetts, questioned whether Eisenhower needed the authority that he was requesting; did he not already have power to carry out his objectives? Eisenhower stressed that "greater effect could be had from a consensus of executive and legislative opinion." He was concerned about situations where he might be required to consult with Congress before acting and spoke of the desire of Middle Eastern countries for "reassurance now that the United States would stand ready to help." Eisenhower said that if the Soviets started moving troops into the area, he would have time to go to Congress, but he needed to be able to move fast if communists starting instigating coups in Arab states; any U.S. military intervention, however, would be only at the request of the threatened government. What he sought was a resolution "contain[ing] clear indication that the United States would act only where requested, and that the United States was not being truculent." In closing, Eisenhower "reminded the legislators that the Constitution assumed that our two branches of government should get along together."[18] The meeting with congressional leaders, while inevitably leaving a number of "loose ends," left little doubt of support for his program.

In a special message to Congress on January 5, 1957, the president personally presented his doctrine for stabilizing the Middle East. Since countries threatened by the Soviet Union could not count on the United Nations for protection, it was necessary for the United States to provide support. And it was important for Congress and the president to stand together: "I deem it necessary to seek the cooperation of Congress. Only with that cooperation can we give the reassurance needed to deter aggression." Eisenhower reiterated the point: "Basic United States policy should now find expression in joint action by the Congress and the Executive." Specifically, he requested authorization of economic and military assistance programs, an additional $200 million in economic and military assistance beyond present allocations, and the use of force. In Section 2 of the resolution presented by the White House, the president was "authorized to employ the armed forces of the United States as he deems necessary to secure and protect the territorial integrity of any such nation or group of nations requesting such aid against overt armed aggression from any country controlled by international communism."[19]

The Middle East resolution differed from the other war-making resolutions in that it addressed a general threat in an entire region and in that it came in the aftermath of a crisis, rather than in the midst of one. Essentially it sought to rebuild U.S. strength to avert another crisis. These considerations enabled Congress to devote greater attention to the Eisenhower Doctrine commitment than it did to the Formosa resolution. The Eisenhower Doctrine encountered considerable criticism. Much of it focused on aspects other than the war authorization provision; there were concerns, for instance, that increased assistance to Arab states would be detrimental to Israel and that the "go-it-alone" approach undermined the Western alliance. With respect to the threat to U.S. interests, critics observed that the greatest likelihood of Soviet influence was in countries that would not request U.S. assistance and that the greatest challenge to the stability of pro-Western countries came not from "international communism" but from Arab nationalism personified by Egyptian president Gamal Abdal Nasser. Further, in an unanticipated outcome of the announcement of the Eisenhower Doctrine, Arab leaders resented what they saw as the imperial implications of the American policy in general and the prospects of military intervention in particular. Former secretary of state Dean Acheson characterized the Eisenhower Doctrine as "vague, inadequate, and not very helpful."[20]

As a result of these concerns and the lack of a crisis demanding immediate action, congressional consideration of the Middle East resolution was more thorough than in the case of the Formosa resolution. After two weeks of hearings in its Committee of Foreign Affairs, the House of Representatives on January 30 approved the Eisenhower Doctrine with minor modifications by a margin of 355 to 61. One of the amendments applied to the war-making authorization, specifically its termination. Like the Formosa resolution, the draft Middle East resolution expired when the president determined that conditions made it no longer necessary. The House added a provision giving Congress the power also to terminate the resolution through a concurrent resolution, which requires only a majority vote by each house and is not submitted to the president for signature or veto.[21]

More extended debate took place in the joint hearings and executive sessions of the Senate Committees on Foreign Relations and Armed Services. In sessions that continued for nearly four weeks, Dulles defended the Eisenhower Doctrine; most of the testimony focused on the implementation of military assistance programs, and relatively little on the constitutional issues of war authorization.[22]

That part of the debate, however, reflected criticism of Eisenhower's proposals from two different constitutional perspectives. First, a number of senators were concerned about transferring war-making power to the president without explicit congressional action based on the immediate circumstances. Senator Estes Kefauver (D-Tennessee) foresaw the resolution transferring war making "to people who are going to decide it on facts which may or may not be convincing enough to the Senate." Senator Wayne Morse (D-Oregon) proposed an amendment that restricted presidential power:

> Prior to the employment of armed forces the President shall give notice to Congress. If, in the judgment of the President, an emergency arises in which such notice to Congress is not possible, he shall, upon the employment of armed forces, forthwith inform Congress and submit his action for its approval or disapproval.[23]

With the administration opposing the Morse amendment as infringing on the president's power to use armed forces, it failed by a vote of 28 to 64.[24]

Besides concern about the "blank-check" nature of the draft resolution, other senators saw the president requesting authority that he already possessed as commander-in-chief. Dean Acheson testified that the request was "not only unnecessary but undesirable" and said that what the president really needed was a "sense of the Senate" resolution. Senator J. William Fulbright (D-Arkansas) expressed concern about the implication of a "timid" president needing congressional authority; he said:

> Experience tells us that when the highest interests of the country are at stake, an Executive who is timid represents a far greater danger to the preservation of our constitutional system than does one who exceeds the letter of the law in a vigorous use of Executive Power to defend the Government, the Nation, and the Constitution.[25]

The Senate majority leader, Lyndon B. Johnson (D-Texas), likewise feared that the administration's proposal would have "created a precedent for a weaker Presidency." Questioning whether Congress should be authorizing power it did not have, senators were reluctant to be committed to the outcome of actions that the president could take on his authority.

The Senate adopted a revised resolution that combined an essential "sense" of congressional policy with contingent support of presidential use of force. After extended discussion, the Senate Foreign Relations Committee, voting along straight party lines, adopted an amended version of Section

2 of the resolution. With Fulbright playing a prominent role, the reference to congressional authorization was eliminated; instead, Congress affirmed that the United States was "prepared" to employ force if the president determined it was necessary. This change did not limit presidential power; in fact, it may have enhanced it. But the modification weakened somewhat the joint congressional-executive position that Eisenhower cherished. Two other changes were also made in Section 2: (1) the use of force was made subordinate to a declaration of U.S. interest in the preservation of the status quo in the Middle East; (2) the use of force had to be consistent with the treaty obligations and Constitution of the United States. Johnson gained Eisenhower's approval of the amended section.[26]

With these changes, Section 2 of the resolution as adopted by the Senate read:

> The President is authorized to undertake, in the general area of the Middle East, military assistance programs with any nation or group of nations of that area desiring such assistance. Furthermore, the United States regards as vital to the national interest and world peace, the preservation of the independence and integrity of the nations of the Middle East. To this end, if the President determines the necessity thereof, the United States is prepared to use armed forces to assist any such nation or group of such nations requesting assistance against armed aggression from any country controlled by international communism; provided that such employment shall be consistent with the treaty obligations of the United States and the Constitution of the United States . . .[27]

On March 5, the Senate, by a vote of 72 to 19, approved the modified Eisenhower Doctrine. Two days later, the House, by a vote of 350 to 60, approved the Senate version.[28]

Eisenhower praised the congressional action and glossed over the changed language. On March 7 a reporter asked whether with "the original concept suggested in your version of authorizing you to use the Armed Forces [being] stricken out . . . does [your approval] mean that you accept the constitutional interpretation that you have always had, as Commander-in-Chief, the right to send the Armed Forces into such a situation in the national interest without that specific authorization?" Eisenhower's reply skirted the question:

> Well, I don't think . . . that I have to go into the constitutional argument again. I would point out that I haven't spent my life in

the study of constitutional law. I do think the legislative history of this resolution shows that the Senate approves—the Congress approves of what we are trying to do in the area, and that is the important thing.[29]

Eisenhower's interpretation of the congressional action as an affirmation of his objectives was justified. He had again gained the congressional support that he deemed essential, and his own power as commander-in-chief had been enhanced in the process. As Walter LaFeber writes: "The passage of the Eisenhower Doctrine had interesting political overtones. A Democratic Congress formally surrendered some of its power, especially that of controlling the outbreak of war, to a Republican President."[30]

Eisenhower's leadership on the Formosa and Middle East resolutions represented an accommodating approach. There was no threat to use military power on his own as commander-in-chief if Congress did not grant his request. He did not exploit the emotions of a crisis. The package of economic assistance with the use of force in the Eisenhower Doctrine may have had a political calculation to it, but Eisenhower believed that the two elements of U.S. power could not be separated. While the draft Middle East resolution may have been constitutionally flawed, the congressional version provided a remedy that gave Eisenhower the power that he sought.

The Gulf of Tonkin Resolution

The Vietnam War changed the presidential-congressional relationship over the war-making power. It began with a presidential request in the tradition of Eisenhower. In a message to Congress on August 5, 1964, Johnson, who had been Senate majority leader when both of the Eisenhower resolutions were passed, requested approval and support "to take all necessary steps, including the use of force to protect any member or protocol state of the Southeast Collective Defense Treaty requesting assistance in the defense of its freedom." This was the third such presidential request within a decade. Like the Formosa resolution, this resolution occurred in the context of a crisis, in this instance a naval confrontation of American and North Vietnamese vessels in the Gulf of Tonkin. The 1964 resolution drew substantially on the language of the Middle East resolution.

Unlike the earlier resolutions, however, a resolution with respect to Southeast Asia had been planned by the executive branch for several months. Since early 1964 the White House and the State Department had anticipated a congressional resolution that would give the president wide latitude to utilize military force to assure the survival of a beleaguered South Vietnam. After considerable discussion, the State Department drafted a resolution on May 24 that included both an open-ended war authorization and specific fiscal allocations for its implementation; a revised draft of June 11 eliminated the budgetary provision and set forth three different ways of justifying the military authorization. While Johnson and his advisors agreed that the worsening political-military situation in Vietnam necessitated such a resolution, they delayed introducing it because of concern that it would detract attention from the consideration of the Civil Rights Bill. Convincing congressional leaders of the need for the resolution would take much time unless, as Secretary of Defense Robert McNamara remarked on June 10, "the enemy acts suddenly in the area. . . ." In the absence of North Vietnamese provocation, McGeorge Bundy, the president's special advisor for national security affairs, urged that Johnson plan for meetings with congressional leaders to line up support; by stressing the resolution as a deterrent to North Vietnam, Johnson could carry all but the most recalcitrant members of Congress. (Only the chronic critic Wayne Morse was specifically written off.) It also seemed politically expedient to have the resolution passed by the time of the Republican convention in mid-July. Recalling the criticism of Truman's failure to gain congressional support for war in Korea, Johnson told his advisors: "By God, I'm going to be damn sure those guys are with me when we begin this thing!" He added at one point: "They may try to desert me when we get in there." Johnson, however, deferred formal action, but quietly he, Rusk, and the under secretary of state George Ball met with key senators throughout June and July, trying to gain support for the resolution whenever it was introduced as a demonstration of American resolve that would deter North Vietnam. The senators were assured that there were no plans to broaden the U.S. military involvement. In the meantime, the State Department considered what additional limited military actions the United States could undertake without a resolution.[31]

Then came the "sudden enemy action" of which McNamara had spoken. On August 2, three North Vietnamese patrol boats fired on the U.S. destroyer *Maddox* in the Gulf of Tonkin off the coast of North Vietnam. The *Maddox* sustained nominal damage, but it returned fire, and together with aircraft from the carrier *Ticonderoga* sunk one and damaged two of the patrol boats. Johnson responded with a protest to North Vietnam warning of "grave consequences" of further unprovoked attacks; he also enlarged the U.S. presence in the Gulf of Tonkin, dispatching another destroyer, the *C. Turner Joy,* to join the *Maddox.* Then on the evening of August 4, the

Maddox reported an imminent attack and aircraft took off from the *Ticonderoga* to protect the destroyers in the Gulf of Tonkin. The Johnson administration's reports on these incidents mislead the American public. Ignored were the intelligence-gathering function of U.S. naval vessels in the Gulf of Tonkin, recent American-supported South Vietnamese attacks along the North Vietnamese coast (which the North Vietnamese likely associated with the presence of the *Maddox*), and, most significant, the lack of firm evidence that the North Vietnamese had actually engaged in any hostile act on August 4. With disregard for the political consequences should the shallowness of the administration's "case" ever become public, Johnson seized on the opportunity to demonstrate American power and resolve.[32]

The war resolution came off the table. Without insisting on verifying the authenticity of the reports of the second attack, Johnson moved quickly. On the evening of August 4, he met with the National Security Council and then with congressional leaders before making a televised address to the public. At the first meeting, he decided to authorize a retaliatory air strike against North Vietnam and to seek congressional support of a revised resolution. At the beginning of the session with congressional leaders, Johnson said he "wanted to counsel with you" in a confidential manner for "some of our boys are floating around in the water." In this tense and emotional situation, the congressional leaders all lined up behind Johnson's military action and promised support of the resolution. Johnson remained solicitous, saying, "I wanted the advice of each of you and wanted to consult with you. . . . I wanted to get the Congressional concurrence. I think it would be very damaging to ask for it and not get it." The support was there for the asking. As the meeting closed, one Republican congressman told him, "it will pass overwhelmingly as far as I am concerned," and a Republican senator added, "by the time you send it up, there won't be anything to do but support you."[33]

Later, as U.S. aircraft began their attacks on North Vietnamese facilities, Johnson speaking from the Oval Office told the American public that "aggression against the peaceful villagers of South Vietnam had now been joined by open aggression on the high seas against the United States . . . [but the U.S. response] for the present, will be limited and fitting. . . . We still seek no wider war."[34] He did not mention the congressional resolution.

Johnson's message to Congress the next day drew upon the precedent of the Eisenhower resolutions as he requested approval of what was formally known as the Resolution to Promote the Maintenance of International Peace and Security in Southeast Asia, but which mercifully became known as the Gulf of Tonkin resolution.[35]

Linking North Vietnamese attacks in the Gulf of Tonkin with "its deliberate and systematic campaign of aggression . . . against its neighbors," the resolution stated that Congress "approves and supports the determination of the President, as Commander-in-Chief, to take all necessary measures to repel any armed attack against the forces of the United States and to prevent further aggression . . . [and] to take all necessary steps, including the use of force, to protect any member or protocol state of the Southeast Asia Collective Defense Treaty requesting assistance in defense of its freedom."[36]

With the American public and press strongly supporting the president's action, congressional consideration of the resolution was perfunctory. Fulbright lent his prestige to the resolution by agreeing to introduce and manage it in the Senate. After the formal introduction on the morning of August 6, McNamara testified before a joint session of the Senate Foreign Relations Committee and the Armed Services Committee. In the Senate debate, which lasted less than ten hours, Fulbright supported the administration's explanation of the Gulf of Tonkin incident and the implications of the resolution. Questions about the purpose of U.S. vessels in the Gulf of Tonkin and the reasons why North Vietnam would provoke war with the United States were dismissed; Fulbright warned at one point not to have "any illusions about the aggressive designs of North Vietnam and its Chinese Communist sponsor."

The constitutional ramifications of the blank check were understood, but gave most senators little reason for concern. Senator Jacob Javits (R-New York) was candid:

> We who support the joint resolution do so with full knowledge of its seriousness and with the understanding that we are voting a resolution which means life or the loss of it for who knows how many hundreds or thousands? Who knows what destruction and despair this action may bring in the name of freedom?

Senator Daniel Brewster (R-Maine) asked if the resolution would "authorize or recommend or approve the landing of large American armies in Vietnam or in China," to which Fulbright replied that "the resolution . . . would authorize whatever the Commander in Chief feels is necessary." Senator Gaylord Nelson (D-Wisconsin) pressed the same point as Brewster:

> Am I to understand that it is the sense of Congress that we are saying to the executive branch: "If it becomes necessary to prevent further aggression, we agree now, in advance, that we may land as many divisions as deemed necessary, and engage in a direct mili-

tary assault on North Vietnam if it becomes the judgment of the Executive, the Commander in Chief, that is the only way to prevent further aggression"?

Fulbright responded that he could not provide assurances that such action would not be taken, however much he would deplore it. When Nelson pressed a concern that the resolution conveyed "the impression that [Congress] consents to a radical change in our mission or objective in South Vietnam," Fulbright reiterated the administration's contention that the resolution was consistent with existing policy. Senator John Sherman Cooper (R-Kentucky) asked, "Then, looking ahead, if the president decided it was necessary to use such force as could lead to war, we will give that authority by this resolution?" Fulbright replied, "That is the way I would interpret it." When Nelson suggested an amendment that Congress opposed an extension of the war or the dispatch of U.S. forces into combat, Fulbright refused to accept it on the grounds that while it was a statement of policy with which he agreed, its adoption would delay action on the resolution. Throughout the questions on the implications of the authority being granted the president, Fulbright pointed to two congressional remedies should it disapprove of his actions: imposition of the provision for a concurrent resolution terminating the resolution; and impeachment. ("We always have a reserve power, when we see the President has made a mistake. We can always later impeach him, if we like.") Brewster, Nelson, Cooper, and others who shared their doubts, however, fell into line and supported the resolution.

As the administration had anticipated, Morse strenuously opposed the resolution. He foresaw "that history will record that we have made a great mistake in subverting and circumventing the Constitution of the United States. . . . We are in effect giving the president . . . war-making powers in the absence of a declaration of war. I believe that to be a historic mistake." Joining Morse was just one other senator, Ernest Gruening (D-Alaska), who called the resolution "a predated declaration of war" and, moreover, "in a war in which we have no business." The House of Representatives devoted four hours to the resolution. On August 7, it gave unanimous approval (416 to 0), while in the Senate that same day only Morse and Gruening voted no as eighty-eight senators voted in favor. Exploiting the shadowy incident in the Gulf of Tonkin, Johnson had easily gained the authority which he had long wanted but which had seemed politically risky until August 4.[37]

The Gulf of Tonkin resolution became a focal point of the criticism of the war that it had authorized. congressional critics of the war, led by

Fulbright, felt betrayed as evidence surfaced of Johnson's distortion of the events of August 2–4. Many senators and congressmen subsequently claimed that in voting for the resolution, they had wanted to show support for the president in a time of crisis and to send a strong message to North Vietnam. They had not intended to be approving a policy that would eventually take 500,000 American troops to fight what by 1967 had become the most divisive war in American history. Given the clarity of the language of the Gulf of Tonkin resolution and the opportunity to modify it as it was being considered, these rationalizations hold little substance.[38] The issue came into clear focus in August 1967. During hearings of the Senate Foreign Relations Committee, Fulbright charged that the administration had gone to war without a declaration. An exasperated Under Secretary of State Nicholas Katzenbach responded: "Didn't that Resolution authorize the President to use the armed forces of the United States in whatever way was necessary? Didn't it? . . . You explained it, Mr. Chairman."[39]

That same month Johnson boldly asserted presidential prerogatives. Defying his congressional critics, he redefined his position on the Gulf of Tonkin resolution. He told a press conference that his administration never believed that the resolution was necessary to authorize his actions in Vietnam. In sum, the president now claimed that his power as commander-in-chief was sufficient to wage war.[40] Johnson's stance was embraced by his successors.

The Johnson administration's defiant stand helped to spur Fulbright's determination to repeal the Gulf of Tonkin resolution, which was finally achieved in 1971. Yet the repeal of the Gulf of Tonkin resolution was something less than a full-scale reassertion of congressional war-making prerogatives, for the administration of Richard Nixon, which had initially opposed repeal, supported it on the grounds that the president had authority to wage war without it. This led to the curious situation where repeal became attached to a cutoff of funds for the U.S. incursion in Cambodia, and to which the administration engineered an amendment to the effect that it would not "impugn the president's power as commander in chief to protect U.S. forces wherever deployed." An enraged Fulbright voted against the repeal in that form, but he did subsequently introduce a concurrent resolution repealing the Gulf of Tonkin resolution without conditions.[41]

Congressional determination to reassert its constitutional prerogatives led to the passage, over Nixon's veto, of the War Powers resolution in 1973. Despite the effort of the resolution to accommodate presidential ability to dispatch forces in a timely manner when circumstances necessitate with the ultimate authority of Congress to declare war, the resolution has tended to accentuate the differences between the executive and congressional branches. Its record has been mixed. All of his successors except one have followed Nixon's contention that the resolution is unconstitutional, but they have also complied with some of its provisions. Congress also has been reluctant to utilize provisions of the resolution that would enhance its authority. Finally, the resolution has suffered from what some critics s ee as inconsistent and ill-conceived provisions, including one of dubious constitutionality.[42]

Gulf War I

So when after a lapse of twenty-five years, the practice of the war-authorizing resolution was resurrected by President George H. W. Bush in January 1991, the tone of presidential-congressional relations had changed. During the first few weeks after the Iraqi invasion of Kuwait in August 1990, Bush built international support for United Nations–imposed sanctions against Iraq. At home, he enjoyed strong congressional and popular support for his policy, including the dispatch of U.S. forces to Saudi Arabia to defend that country. By mid-September, Bush and his advisors, however, were contemplating the use of force against Iraq, which they recognized would be a controversial step. Bush's diary entry of September 13 underlined his concerns and an effort to draw from the "lessons" of Vietnam: "My gut wonder is, how long will they be with us? How long will the Senate stay supportive, or the House? Once there starts to be erosion, they're going to do what Lyndon Johnson said: they painted their asses white and ran with the antelopes."[43]

Bush drew upon his recollection of Johnson's leadership on the Gulf of Tonkin resolution as a model. He viewed such a resolution as a political move, not a constitutional necessity. He recalls:

> I wanted to find a way to get Congress on board with an unmistakable show of that support for what we were doing, and what we might have to do. Early in September I had asked Boyden Gray to look into how Lyndon Johnson at the time of the Gulf of Tonkin Resolution in 1964 had worked hard to get individual members of Congress, and Congress itself, to go on record in support of what he was doing in Vietnam. He urged joint hearings of the committees on foreign relations and armed services in both Houses, and asked Congress to insist on roll calls so the record would be complete. In the end, he got a unanimous vote out of the House—414 [sic] to 0—and a Senate count of 88 to 2. I realized the Vietnam War was different, but his effort made a big impression on me,

and I began to think about seeking a similar congressional vote of support.[44]

Bush, however, did not seek the congressional resolution until January 1991. To some extent, this resulted from Congress's unsolicited show of support, manifest in the passage of similar resolutions in the House and Senate in early October which supported his objective of reversing aggression and the imposition of sanctions against Iraq; the resolutions also called for continued efforts to reach a diplomatic solution to the crisis.

Most of the Democratic party majority in Congress, including its leadership, were known to be opposed to the use of force, so as Bush planned for shifting the U.S. military mission to one with an offensive capability, he was aware that such a step would undermine his support in Congress. In early November, while Congress was in recess, he authorized a doubling of the U.S. military presence in Saudi Arabia. That was followed by a diplomatic campaign, spearheaded by Secretary of State James Baker, to line up UN Security Council support for the use of force. UN Security Council Resolution 678, passed on November 30, 1990, authorized UN members "to use all necessary means" to restore regional peace and security if Iraq failed to comply with earlier resolutions to withdraw from Kuwait by January 15, 1991.

These steps strained relations with Congress. The Senate majority leader, George Mitchell (D-Maine), issued an ultimatum: if Bush wanted war, he would have to request a congressional declaration; there was no constitutional authority for him to act without it. Fifty-three House Democrats and one senator filed a suit in federal court to prohibit Bush from using force without congressional authorization. Even Republicans, who were supportive of Bush's threat to use force, were disturbed by what seemed to be indifference to congressional prerogatives. Congressional hearings found a number of former civilian and military officials questioning the wisdom of Bush's military plans. So by the time that the UN Security Council gave near unanimous support to Resolution 678, Bush had concluded that a congressional resolution would likely fail. He did little to improve matters when in a meeting with congressional leaders, he said that he would continue to work with them, but that he did not need their approval to liberate Kuwait.

In the end, Bush decided to seek congressional support. On January 8—a week before the UN ultimatum would take effect and on the eve of a meeting in Geneva between Baker and Iraq foreign minister Tariq Aziz that was seen as the last chance for peace—Bush sent a carefully worded message to congressional leaders. He did not concede any aspect of what he considered his constitutional prerogatives. He chided Congress to act in the national interest. It would have been "constructive" for Baker in his meeting with Aziz to have had such support, and Bush added, somewhat disingenuously, that he would have welcomed a resolution earlier. He stated: "There is still opportunity for Congress to act to strengthen the prospects for peace and to safeguard this nation's vital interest . . . [by] adopt[ing] a resolution stating that Congress supports the use of all necessary means to implement U.N. Security Council 678." The ultimate authority, Bush asserted, was his, and he was asking Congress to endorse whatever he decided: "I am determined to do whatever is necessary to protect America's security. I ask Congress to join with me in this task. I can think of no better way than for Congress to express its support for the President at this critical time."[45]

In a press conference the next day, Bush refused to concede that his request reflected a constitutional obligation. When asked whether he needed the resolution and whether he would be unable to act if it failed, the president replied: "I don't think I need it. . . . There are different opinions on either side of this question, but Saddam Hussein should be under no question on this: I feel that I have the authority to fully implement the United Nations resolutions." He added in response to a follow-up question: "I still feel that I have the constitutional authority—many attorneys have so advised me." Later Bush fell back on the argument that "there have been a lot of uses of forces in our history and very few declarations of war. But I have tried. I have done more consultation with Congress than any other President."[46]

However begrudging the request, Bush had gone to Congress. Given the well-known position of many members that Bush was rushing to war and that sanctions had not been given sufficient time, there was a risk of rejection, which (despite Bush's denials) would have weakened the U.S. position internationally. That possibility, however, also worked to Bush's advantage, for many members of Congress, even those with doubts about the wisdom of the president's course, would be reluctant to undermine American leadership. Bush also benefited from the timing of his request; with the UN coalition poised to attack Iraqi positions in Kuwait, the imperative for congressional action was much greater than it would have been had it been present with a similar resolution earlier. Waiting until the last minute worked to his advantage. The most compelling reason, however, for taking the calculated risk of seeking congressional support was Bush's recognition that it was necessary politically. An opinion poll in early January showed that 60 percent of Americans believed that Bush needed congressional authority before taking the country to war. The greater political risk would have been to act without going to Congress.[47]

By the time that congressional debate began on January 10, Bush benefited as well from Iraqi intransigence in the Baker-Aziz meeting, as Bush called it: "a total stiff-arm . . . total rebuff." That helped as well to shift public opinion (by narrow margins) in favor of war as opposed to continuing sanctions. Given the urgency of time, congressional consideration was limited to intense (and extravagantly praised) debate in both houses that took place before packed galleries and a vast television audience. The Republican leadership introduced resolutions in both houses that blended the president's request with an assertion of congressional prerogatives. After restating Iraq's record of defying UN resolutions, the resolution "authorized" the president to use American forces pursuant to UN Security Council Resolution 678. Before taking that step, he was to report to Congress that all peaceful efforts to secure Iraqi compliance had failed. The resolution also stipulated that its provisions derived "specific constitutional authorization" from the War Powers resolution. The Democratic party leadership offered an alternate resolution directing the president to continue diplomacy and economic sanctions and, if that failed, to return to congress for authorization to use force; it failed, however, to gain a majority in either house. So the Republican resolution, designed to attract bipartisan support, was the focus of the three days of debate.

Since the resolution had attempted to finesse the constitutional issues dividing Congress and the presidency, the debate dealt mostly with whether or not war was necessary. There was, however, some strident criticism of Bush for maneuvering Congress into a last-minute decision on war and for denying the constitutional authority of Congress to declare war. Democrats George Mitchell, Patrick Leahy of Vermont, Daniel Patrick Moynihan of New York, Joseph Biden of Delaware, and Edward Kennedy and John Kerry of Massachusetts assailed a resolution which left the decision for war in the hands of the president. Moynihan warned that passage of the resolution would mean "that the primacy of the Congress on this issue under the Constitution will have been denied." Kennedy predicted that passage of the resolution "will haunt us for years to come," and to Biden, it "would be a mistake of historic proportions." Supporters of the resolution rarely answered these charges, other than to observe that the resolution upheld congressional prerogatives; rather they stressed the importance of congressional support as a means of demonstrating national resolve that might in fact lead to Saddam Hussein backing down.

In the end, both houses of Congress approved the war resolution. It was the closest vote on going to war in U.S. history: 250 to 183 in the House, 52 to 47 in the Senate. However contentious the debate and however narrow the margin, the constitutional provisions had been followed to the satisfaction of the vast majority of Americans, so that Bush could claim after the vote: "we have now closed ranks behind a clear signal of our determination and our resolve . . . to Iraq that it cannot scorn the January 15th deadline."[48]

Still Bush refused to concede the constitutional issue. When he signed the resolution on January 14, he followed praise of Congress for supporting his policy with the following stipulation:

> As I made clear to congressional leaders at the outset, my request for congressional support did not, and my signing this resolution does not, constitute any change in the long-standing positions of the executive branch on either the President's constitutional authority to use the Armed Forces to defend vital U.S. interests or the constitutionality of the War Powers Resolution.[49]

Gulf War II

The attitude of the second President Bush proved identical with that of his father. When eleven years after the Persian Gulf War, President George W. Bush confronted a defiant Iraq, he too turned reluctantly to Congress for support. From the time that the Bush administration began to talk openly in early 2002 of the necessity of "regime change" in Iraq and of the possibility that preemptive war might be the means of accomplishing that objective, Bush and others in his administration contended that he had sufficient authority as commander-in-chief to wage war. Like his father before him, the current president sought congressional support for political, not constitutional, reasons. Neither could ignore the pressures from congressional leaders, including many Republicans, demanding that Congress's constitutional role in war making be acknowledged. In addition, public opinion polls in 2002 as in 1991 indicated that Americans by substantial margins believed that congressional authorization was necessary. In other ways, the circumstances differed. These reflected a significant change in the U.S. relationship with the United Nations. While the first Bush had built a solid base of support in the United Nations before seeking congressional backing which he saw as necessary to buttress his position within the United States, the second Bush went to Congress as a means of strengthening the U.S. position in trying to gain UN support for the campaign against Iraq. The lukewarm response to Bush's speech to the UN General Assembly meeting in September 2002 reinforced the necessity for building the congressional base.

In the executive-congressional interaction over the 2002 resolution, the administration held all the high cards. Bush's decision to seek a war resolution in early October had the political advantage of forcing members of Congress to take a stand on the issue prior to the midterm elections. For that reason, Democratic leaders had wanted to postpone the matter until after November, but they could not ignore the White House claim that national security demanded immediate action. To defy Bush on national security was difficult, for ever since the terrorist attack a year earlier, he enjoyed high approval ratings. Members of Congress, especially those who were in tight reelection races, took enormous risks in opposing the administration on an issue of national security. Bush benefited as well from the extent to which the public accepted the administration's contention of a connection between Saddam Hussein's regime and international terrorism. This "link" enabled the White House and its congressional supporters to respond to some Democrats who contended that preemptive war against Saddam Hussein would detract attention from the nation's priority: the war on terror. Indeed, the White House made clear that it would use its resources against congressional opponents of the resolution. This threat underlined the extent to which the Democrats as a party were vulnerable on issues of national security. The fact that most Democrats had voted against the Persian Gulf War resolution, which had led to a triumphant war, put the party in general, and its leadership in particular, on the defensive when it came to another war in the Middle East. The final advantage of the administration was that once it moved forward with the resolution, Democrats were anxious to get it passed so that they could attempt to focus the public's attention on other issues prior to the elections.

The Democratic leadership in 2002 was thus anxious to accommodate the White House. With the exception of Senator Bob Graham of Florida, the several Democrats who had (announced or otherwise) ambitions for their party's presidential nomination in 2004 did not want to risk appearing to be weak on the war issue. One such aspirant, the Democratic leader in the House of Representatives, Richard Gephardt of Missouri, said that his vote against the Persian Gulf War resolution had been a mistake, and that the war on terror had changed everything; he took a prominent role in working with the White House on the 2002 resolution. Although most House Democrats did not follow him, Gephart was representative of a significant shift among Democratic leaders between 1991 and 2002. Unlike the congressional debate eleven years earlier, this time only a handful of senior Democrats—like Edward M. Kennedy of Massachusetts, Robert Byrd of West Virginia, Patrick Leahy of Vermont, and Carl Levin of Michigan—

questioned whether the Bush administration had made a convincing case for war, and only rarely was the issue of preemptive war as a strategy raised.

Underlying the Bush administration's rationale for war was Iraq's threat to U.S. national security through its duplicitous development of chemical and nuclear weapons, the violation of the disarmament provisions of the agreement ending the 1991 war, and its capacity to support terrorist groups in their anti-American campaigns. The resolution authorizing force to achieve regime change in Iraq passed by substantial majorities: 296–113 in the House and 77–23 in the Senate. Partisan differences were again significant, however, and perhaps most notable was the fact that a majority of Democrats in the House of Representatives did not follow their leadership, 81 voting in favor and 126 against the resolution. In the Senate, 28 Democrats voted in favor and 21 against. The resolution, which passed both houses on October 11, authorized the president to use armed forces "as he determines to be necessary and appropriate in order to (1) defend the national security of the United States against the continuing threat posed by Iraq; and (2) enforce all relevant United Nations Security Council Resolutions regarding Iraq." In language similar to the Persian Gulf War resolution, Congress affirmed that its authorization was based on its obligations under the War Powers resolution.[50]

Conclusion

Whatever its imperfections, the war-authorizing resolution seems destined to become a continuing means of compromising differences over war making. The change in the tone and substance of the process over forty-five years speaks to the continuing difficulties of reconciliation. The approach of Eisenhower toward Congress has essentially been repudiated by his successors, who have played the politics of the war-making resolution shrewdly. Congress, in approving presidential requests, has been able to maintain a degree of constitutional principle by referring to the War Powers resolution. In the end, though, the war-authorizing resolution has become an instrument in the growth of presidential power.

4 Intraparty Factionalism on Key Foreign Policy Issues

Congress versus Clinton, 1995–2000

TERRY L. DEIBEL

Terry Deibel points out that the end of the Cold War initially produced a foreign policy that was "more disjointed, arbitrary, and unpredictable," in part because of the lack of a perceived external threat until the terrorist acts of September 11, 2001, and in part because of the increasing partisanship of American politics and the phenomenon of divided government. Further complicating the partisan divisions was the tendency of both parties to divide internally into factions. Among Democrats, these included the "idealists," who sought to apply the party's philosophical agenda abroad, and the "pragmatists," who were less ideologically motivated. For Republicans, the line was drawn between the party's "unilateralists," who argued that intervention abroad should occur for limited strategic, not humanitarian or idealistic reasons, and its "internationalists," who agreed with fellow Republicans on the nature of the threats facing America but argued for multilateral responses. Alignments on particular issues would sometimes cut across party labels. Deibel argues that this particular alignment of forces may now have passed because of the impact of September 11 and the presence of unified government under Republican control.

Introduction

From the time the Republican party won control of both houses of Congress in 1994 until it captured the White House in 2000, the administration of Democrat Bill Clinton battled the Republican Congress for control of American foreign policy.[1] Although the majority party on the Hill never produced a broad document setting forth its views, conservative Republicans' statements and actions on various legislative issues during that six-year period did seem to add up to a more or less coherent approach to statecraft, and one that was quite different from that taken by the prior Republican administration of George H. W. Bush. Similarly, many Democrats in Congress differed from the Clinton administration's foreign policy and expressed those differences in their comments and votes on key issues. Behind the very public executive-legislative and Democrat-Republican struggles over foreign policy, in other words, there were intraparty factions at play, factions that often had a decisive impact on outcomes.

The purpose of this chapter is to define and demonstrate the existence of these foreign policy factions, not only as aggregates within the parties in Congress, but also in the cases of individual senators and representatives, as demonstrated by their votes on a selection of high-visibility foreign policy issues. What follows is, first, a brief description of four intraparty factions, along with the philosophical views and issue stances that defined them. Then I present voting data for fifty-nine senators and seventy-five members of the House on a dozen key issues, followed by descriptions of the legislative-executive play on each and explanations of why the votes tallied indicate membership in a particular faction. The chapter ends with some overall conclusions on the data presented.

Defining Post–Cold War Party Factions

In retrospect, American foreign policy during the 1990s seems to have followed a unique pattern. It was more disjointed, arbitrary, and unpredictable than it had been during the long contest with the Soviet Union or than it seems to be in the current war on terrorism. Although many inside and outside the Clinton administration tried during the decade, no one could come up with a strategic construct that tied the era's statecraft together. One reason for this incoherence, of course, is that statecraft in the nineties was much more affected by internal factors than before or since. The lack of an immediate and visible external threat unconcentrated the foreign policy mind, as it were, allowing America's leaders the luxury of indulging partisan loyalties, special interests, economic concerns, personal ambitions and animosities, and other matters that intrinsically had little to do with the situation beyond our shores.²

Another reason the 1990s were different is that the post–Cold War era, like all postwar periods, witnessed a natural resurgence of congressional influence in foreign policy, redressing the extraordinary powers that presidents tend to accumulate in wartime. It is remarkable that in key areas of American statecraft, from foreign affairs agency reorganization to the overthrow of Saddam Hussein to ballistic missile defense, President Clinton eventually abandoned positions he once strenuously argued for and all but adopted the policies of the Republican opposition in Congress. Clearly, one cannot understand American foreign policy in the 1990s by looking only at the White House.

Although relationships between the executive and legislative branches were dominated by partisanship and personal vindictiveness during Clinton's impeachment and the 2000 presidential campaign, a careful look at their foreign policy struggles during the second half of the 1990s reveals a far more complex and interesting pattern. It was factional as much as partisan, and underneath the personal animosities lay serious intellectual differences about how to deal with the post–Cold War world. In fact, each party was split over foreign policy, split deeper than post-impeachment or campaign bitterness, deeper even than the differing economic interests that bankroll candidates and officeholders. The parties split over foreign policy because their core values on governance, the beliefs that make people *become* Democrats or Republicans, have foreign policy implications that run headlong into the realities of the post–Cold War world.³

Take the Democrats. The Democratic party's basic mission, its reason for being, is to help the disadvantaged in society, to relieve human suffering and uplift the downtrodden.⁴ When it comes to foreign policy, though, such a mission runs into an immediate problem. How does one distinguish between the suffering of Americans and foreigners, or even between the suffering of one foreigner and another? It is impossible to do so on moral grounds, yet the United States does not have the wherewithal to deal with the suffering of all humanity; we cannot lift up all the downtrodden even in our own country. Still, Democrats cannot let go of morality, for it is their sense of morality that enjoins and justifies their party's mission in the first place.

It is on this dilemma that the deepest, most fundamental foreign policy split within the Democratic party takes place. Democratic *idealists* are explicit about wanting to apply the party's *raison d'être* overseas, to relieve foreign suffering even as they try to help those in need at home. Whether it was atrocities in the former Yugoslavia, or a usurpation of democracy in Haiti, or genocide in Central Africa, or a military rampage in East Timor, they were ready during the Clinton years to use American aid and, if necessary, American armed forces to help. Democratic *pragmatists* are more cautious. They do not question the desirability of relieving human suffering overseas, but they are acutely sensitive to the many constraints on governing, and they recognize that overseas interventions can be costly and risky affairs, particularly where idealist goals seem to require the use of military force. Priorities must be set, pragmatists argue, and they thought that the Clinton administration should mainly devote its limited time, policy energy, public support, and financial resources to the domestic program on which the president was elected.

Now Democrats in Congress tend to be idealist; indeed, it can be argued that any party tends to express its more extreme or ideological side on the Hill. Members are not only elected from smaller (and thus plausibly more homogeneous) constituencies than the president, but are also freer to indulge themselves rhetorically since they bear less responsibility under the Constitution for the conduct of foreign policy.[5] Parties in the White House, however, are pushed toward moderation by day-to-day contact with foreign issues and the people who represent them,[6] and presidents tend to be centrists anyway because they are elected by all the people.[7] When a party controls both branches of government, as the Democrats did in 1993–1994, one can expect a tug of war between its moderate and extreme factions.[8]

Pushed by the Democratic majority in Congress and by advisors like Secretary of State Warren Christopher and National Security advisor Tony Lake, the Clinton administration's first two years were marked by idealist statecraft. But the president was not much engaged in foreign affairs, and the administration's early policies lacked the courage of the idealists' convictions. It dithered on Bosnia while the Serbs pursued ethnic cleansing, abandoned nation building in Somalia at the first American casualties, let a deal restoring democracy in Haiti be mugged by thugs on a Haitian dock, and publicly abandoned its effort to promote human rights in China via trade in the face of Beijing's intransigence.[9]

It was not until he lost Congress to the Republicans, essentially destroying his chances of major domestic reform, that Clinton began to focus on foreign policy as an arena in which he could act with less support from the Hill. And it was not until the threat and then the use of force brought peace in Haiti (in September 1994) and Bosnia (in the Dayton Accords of late 1995) that he learned how determination could lead to foreign success—and how foreign success could pay political dividends at home.

In the latter part of its first term, as a result, the Clinton administration began to exemplify Democratic pragmatism. During the late 1990s it acted to relieve human suffering overseas only in places where, like Kosovo, idealist impulses were balanced by hard national interests, while strictly limiting U.S. military involvement in matters of purely humanitarian concern, like Central Africa or East Timor. It abandoned its early goal of assertive multilateralism and avoided idealist treaties banning land mines or establishing an international criminal court. As noted above, it adopted a number of Republican programs it had denounced for years, along with increased defense budgets. "Promising too much can be as cruel as caring too little," the president concluded; "we cannot become involved in every problem we really care about."[10]

What about the Republicans? Their core mission is to ensure equality of opportunity, to get government out of the way of competition.[11] For Republicans, international as well as domestic affairs follow the logic of this mission: they are competitions for wealth and power in which Americans should use every means available to prevail. Fortunately, as the world's sole remaining superpower, the United States usually can outcompete its international rivals—if it is willing to bear the costs and risks of acting alone. Unfortunately, however, such costs and risks are growing as states rapidly become more interdependent and economies more globalized. If Democrats are ill-equipped to deal with the ubiquity of inequality in the world, then, Republicans face the dilemma of how to deal with growing constraints on any nation's unilateral actions.

It is on this dilemma that the deepest, most fundamental foreign policy split within the Republican party takes place.[12] Republican *unilateralists*, who controlled their party in the Congress after the conservative victory in the 1994 elections, came to Washington with a mandate to balance the budget and cut the government down to size. They had little military or foreign experience, and a sense that the end of the Cold War meant the end of serious threats from abroad led them especially to favor cuts in the foreign affairs budget. Most believed that the United States should intervene abroad only in defense of its own security and prosperity and not for humanitarian or idealist reasons. Many were also nationalists, worried about protecting American sovereignty from the effects of globalization and from the very international bodies that the administration felt were essential to deal with its dangers.

When it comes to American statecraft, unilateralists prefer the harder, coercive tools to the softer, cooperative ones. In the late 1990s they demanded and enacted substantial reductions in foreign aid, opposing in particular aid to Russia, aid to Mexico after the 1995 peso crisis, and new financing for the International Monetary Fund. They also cut appropriations for the State Department and were able to eliminate the Arms Control and Disarmament and U.S. Information Agencies, folding their functions (but not their funding) into State. Sometimes they resisted funding the results of U.S. cooperative diplomacy, including the 1994 effort to end North Korea's nuclear programs and the Wye River accords on the Middle East.

Unilateralists are strongly opposed to international organizations, seen as "more government" on the international level and dangerous to American sovereignty. In addition to holding over a billion dollars in U.S. arrearages to the United Nations hostage for several years, they called for crippling cuts in funding for several of the UN's specialized and related agencies. But the activity of international organizations that unilateralists hate most is peacekeeping, which turns the military into a cooperative instrument, furthers idealist causes in which they do not believe, and offends nationalism by raising the possibility that U.S. troops might serve under foreign command. Unilateralists thus oppose paying our share of UN peacekeeping expenses or supporting peacekeeping with in-kind contributions, and they voted against U.S. involvement in both Bosnia and Kosovo.

The unilateralists opposition to cooperative efforts can lead to an "all-or-nothing" approach to statecraft, a tendency to throw the United States' considerable weight around in the world with an "in your face," "take it or leave it" kind of attitude. They preferred to overthrow the government of Iraq rather than negotiate with it, to directly challenge China on Taiwan and Tibet rather than engage it. Unilateralists also have no faith in international law or treaties to protect America, and they worked to defeat both the Chemical Weapons Convention (where they failed) and the Comprehensive Nuclear Test Ban Treaty (where they succeeded). Their alternative to such cooperative and multilateral efforts against the spread of weapons of mass destruction is rapid deployment of ballistic missile defenses—at the cost of another multilateral agreement, the 1972 Anti-Ballistic Missile Treaty with Moscow.[13] The pattern common to most of these cases is the same: a bias against multilateral, conciliatory efforts—where goals may have to be compromised to achieve a successful conclusion—in favor of solo American action on maximum American terms.

The other Republican faction is the *internationalists,* and they have quite a different approach to the party's dilemma of how to apply a Darwinian mission to an increasingly interdependent world. They agree with their unilateralist colleagues on the competitive nature of world politics, the desirability of using American power to the fullest, and the importance of concrete national interests. But unlike unilateralists they believed even before 9/11 that the post–Cold War world contained serious threats to those interests, and that it also contained extraordinary opportunities to shape world politics to America's benefit. Most of all, they argued that the United States can often use cooperative and multilateral tools to lower costs and risks if it is willing to compromise maximum goals to some extent and provide sustained leadership.

Though there were and are Republican internationalists in Congress, the administration of George H. W. Bush—particularly in the Gulf War of 1990–1991 and the Somalia intervention of 1992—provides the best illustration of this faction's approach. In Somalia, the administration used multilateral organizations as a way of permitting action in a humanitarian situation where its expense and danger would otherwise not have been commensurate with American interests. More strikingly, the Gulf War demonstrated that even in cases where the nation's vital interests are endangered, Republican internationalists are willing to act in cooperation with other states—and to scale back maximum American demands somewhat—in order to get the job done at lower cost and risk. Here Bush not only used the UN to legitimate his actions; he also accepted restrictions on American war objectives to sustain a coalition that both paid for the war and reduced the diplomatic risk the United States ran in attacking an Arab, Islamic state. Though not as enamored of cooperative and multilateral approaches as most Democrats, internationalists favor full funding of all the tools of American statecraft and believe that overwhelming American power and skilled leadership can bend international bodies to American purposes.

DEMOCRATS		REPUBLICANS
<u>Idealists</u>	<u>Pragmatists Internationalists</u>	<u>Unilateralists</u>
Left	Centrist	Right

Democratic idealists and pragmatists, Republican unilateralists and internationalists—the struggles of these factions were at the heart of the politics of post–Cold War U.S. foreign policy. Though less often remarked on, cross-party factional cooperation and interparty factional struggles were as common as partisan conflict. Indeed, on most foreign policy issues, the centrist factions, Democratic pragmatists and Republican internationalists, were and are closer to each other than is either to the more extreme faction *in its own party.* Sometimes even the extreme factions, idealists and unilateralists, made common cause across party lines, as on trade issues or when asserting the primacy of domestic over foreign affairs. The voting data presented below attempt to demonstrate these alignments.

Voting Data

Tables at the end of this chapter show how selected members of the Senate and House voted on some of the key foreign policy issues that defined the parties and the factions within them during the late 1990s. Legislators were chosen based on their level of prominence on foreign policy issues, as revealed by press coverage of their views or important party or committee roles. Issues were chosen that reflected major differences between the Clinton administration and congressional Republicans, and particular votes were tallied that seemed to demonstrate either unilateralism or internationalism for Republicans, or idealism or pragmatism for Democrats.

Below are brief explanations of a dozen issues and of why the tallied votes on each are factional indicators.[14] They are grouped into three categories:

TRADE ISSUES
1. Fast-Track Trade Negotiating Authority (Senate, House)
2. Permanent Normal Trade Relations with China (House)

DIPLOMATIC ISSUES
3. UN Arrearages, UN Withdrawal (Senate, House)
4. Foreign Affairs Agency Reorganization (Senate)
5. IMF Replenishment (Senate)
6. Funding the Korean Energy Development Organization (Senate)
7. Taiwan Security Enhancement Act (House)

SECURITY ISSUES
8. Bosnia and the Dayton Accords (Senate, House)
9. Kosovo Diplomacy and War (Senate, House)
10. NATO Expansion (Senate)
11. Chemical Weapons Convention (Senate)
12. Comprehensive Test Ban Treaty (Senate)

Trade Issues

President Clinton consistently campaigned and governed as a believer in the benefits of economic globalization and free trade. That position cut across the Democrats' traditional support from blue-collar workers and organized labor, who feared loss of jobs to low-wage countries overseas, and from environmentalists, who considered developing countries' lax pollution controls an evil in themselves as well as part of their unfair competitive advantage. Action to protect jobs, working conditions, and the environment was, of course, very much in the Democratic tradition of using government to redress inequities and uplift the downtrodden. But idealists tended to be more passionately committed to these causes and to their application overseas as well as at home, whereas pragmatists focused more on the overall benefits freer trade promises across American society in economic efficiency, higher-wage job growth, and lower consumer prices.[15]

Trade liberalization divided Republicans too, though in their case the line did not run down the center of the party but rather split off extreme, populist conservatives like Pat Buchanan and Ross Perot who considered globalization a threat to American sovereignty. Most Republicans supported freer trade as a benefit to U.S. businesses and in line with their laissez faire approach to the government's role—or preferred lack of it—in the economy. It was not surprising, then, that the Clinton administration got the North American Free Trade Association (NAFTA) implementing legislation through a Democratic-controlled House in 1993 via a Republican majority: Republicans voted for NAFTA 132–43, but Democrats voted against it 102–156.[16] Although the administration later got approval for the Uruguay Round of the General Agreement on Tariffs and Trade creating the World Trade Organization by a wider and less divisive margin, it did so only by calling the Democratic-controlled Congress back for a lame-duck session after the 1994 Republican victory.[17]

Case 1: Senate and House Votes on Fast-Track Trade Negotiating Authority

Fast-track authority expired in 1994, but Clinton separated it from approval of the Uruguay Round agreements and did not seek to regain it from the then Democratic-controlled Congress; instead, he made two unsuccessful attempts after the Republicans took over on the Hill. The president made fast track a key legislative goal, so one can take approval of fast-track authority as the Democratic pragmatist position. Opposition to fast track would be an indicator of idealist Democrats, simply because of their concern for the hardship it might cause labor in the United States and also because of poor labor conditions overseas. For Republicans, one would expect internationalists to be free traders (like the elder Bush), but unilateralists to be divided between protectionists (like Buchanan or Perot) and those so ideologically against government interference in the economy that they would be for free trade. On trade, then, one would expect the extremes in each party—idealist Democrats and many unilateralist Republicans—to cooperate against the centrist factions.

Fast track was voted on in the Senate only once in the late 1990s, on a procedural measure (S. 955) of November 5, 1997, that moved the fast-track bill toward a vote.[18] Though both ends of the spectrum blasted the bill, the Senate Finance Committee voted it out with only one member opposing (idealist Kent Conrad) on October 1. On November 4 the Senate invoked cloture to proceed to the bill; and on the fifth, approved S. 955 (86–31). Then it stopped to wait for House action. Looking at this Senate vote, most Republicans of both factions voted for fast track, but the few votes against were mainly from the most extreme unilateralists: James Inhofe of Oklahoma and North Carolina senators Jesse Helms and Lauch Faircloth. Democratic pragmatists were also for fast track, with a few defections. But idealists were mainly against it. So in the Senate the fast track vote is mainly useful for differentiating idealists within the Democratic party, less useful for identifying Republican unilateralists.

In the House, the Ways and Means Committee (chaired by Bill Archer of Texas) approved its version on October 8 by a vote of 24–14 after negotiations between Archer and the Office of the U.S. Trade Representative produced a bill close to the Senate's; only four of the yes votes were Democrats, all of them pragmatists. Republican leaders first said they would require assurances of seventy Democratic votes before they would bring the measure to the floor, but on October 29 they agreed to bring it up before adjournment regardless, and the vote was set for November 7. Clinton made a furious lobbying effort, but still could not get more than forty-odd Democratic votes. To allow him more time, the vote was pushed back into the weekend of November 8–9. But on Monday the tenth, still from eight to twenty-eight votes (probably really ten to twelve) shy of what was needed to pass it, the leadership pulled the bill rather than see it defeated. Therefore there was no vote in the House in 1997, and no further Senate action either.

The 1998 scenario was rather different, in that House Speaker Newt Gingrich and the Republicans brought the bill forward partly as a way of offering farmers some help, partly to entice business campaign contributions, and partly in order to embarrass and split Democrats by forcing them to vote either against their president or against their union backers—all in an election year.[19] Gingrich, though a champion of free trade, forced the bill to a vote even though he knew it would be defeated; while Robert T. Matsui (D-California), the ranking Democrat on the Ways and Means Trade Subcommittee and the floor leader for the bill the year before, now opposed it, saying he wasn't going to let the Republicans use free trade to defeat his Democratic colleagues.[20] The vote was 180–243, on September 25, 1998.

Republicans voted 151–71; Democrats voted 29–171. Looking at this House vote, one finds Democratic idealists solidly against fast track, and Republican internationalists almost solidly for it. Unlike the earlier Senate vote, however, enough pragmatists were pulled by electoral politics to split the group evenly, and unilateralists are also split, with only a slight majority in favor and (as in the Senate vote) many of the most notorious 1994 unilateralists opposed.

Taking both these votes, then, the positional logic sketched above seems to hold. Republican internationalists are the most strongly in favor, and Democratic idealists solidly opposed. Unilateralists in both houses were mainly in favor, but some of the more radical conservatives voted no. The main difference in voting on the two occasions was among Democratic pragmatists, who were mainly in favor in 1997 in the Senate (supporting their president and being farther from the next election), but in the House in 1998 were mainly against (probably since the vote was called by Republicans to embarrass them in an election year).

Case 2: House Vote on Permanent Normal Trade Relations with China

The other big trade vote of the Clinton administration—the House's approval of permanent normal trade relations (PNTR) with China on May 24, 2000—followed similar lines. The overall vote (237–197) was very close to NAFTA's (234–200) but the party division was even more pronounced, with about a quarter more Republicans (and a quarter *fewer* Democrats) voting for PNTR than for NAFTA.[21] Among Republicans, internationalists were solidly in support while unilateralists split; among Democrats intense lobbying by the president was able to persuade most of the pragmatists but only a few of the idealists followed in this study. Of course, some of the positions taken here probably had less to do with trade than with the strategic significance and emotional baggage of China. Unilateralists like Dana Rohrabacher (California), worried about how freer trade might build up China's military capacity, made common cause in the House debate with idealists like Nancy Pelosi (also California), who railed against Chinese human rights abuses.[22] In this instance, then, non-trade issues had the effect of heightening the factional splits that already existed on economic grounds.

The conclusion that can be drawn from these cases is that trade liberalization splits both parties and pits their pro-trade centrist factions against their anti-trade political extremes.[23] Republicans and senators are more likely to be free traders, while Democrats and House members are more likely to be against free trade, but within those parameters the anti-trade forces pull most strongly on idealists and (to a lesser extent) unilateralists, while pro-trade forces pull most strongly on internationalists and (somewhat less) on pragmatists.[24]

Diplomatic Issues

The first three of these issues are the most complex that Clinton and the Congress confronted, since UN arrearage repayment, foreign affairs agency reorganization, and International Monetary Fund (IMF) replenishment were all in play in the same pieces of authorization and appropriation legislation over several years. Votes on these issues are mainly useful in distinguishing unilateralist and internationalist factions in the Republican party. Being opposed to international organizations and skeptical of cooperative diplomacy, unilateralists fought UN and IMF funding but worked for abolition of the United States Information Agency (USIA), the Arms Control and Disarmament Agency (ACDA), and the Agency on International Development (AID), while internationalist Republicans were with most Democrats on the opposite side of all three issues.

Although foreign affairs agency reorganization was an issue during the 104th Congress (1995–1996), the possibility of compromise around it and the UN/IMF issues only appeared after Clinton and the Republican Congress were reelected in 1996. Sometime that winter the president seems to have decided that Republican control on the Hill was more than a passing phenomenon he could outwait. Moreover, he began his second term with a new secretary of state, Madeleine Albright. Albright had for months courted Senator Helms, chairman of the Foreign Relations Committee, and she committed herself to Helms on reorganization during her confirmation hearings. The stage was therefore set in spring 1997 for a number of deals. First, on the same day that Helms released the Chemical Weapons Treaty for a Senate vote (see Case 11), Clinton agreed to a reorganization plan.[25] Next, Helms and ranking Foreign Relations Committee Democrat Joseph Biden (Delaware) negotiated a deal in which Helms agreed to payment of some UN arrearages in return for legislation mandating a variety of UN reforms. Finally, in January 1997 the president had engaged the IMF issue by requesting money in his FY1998 budget for the New Arrangements to Borrow (NAB), an IMF facility designed to support faltering third world currencies.

In the 105th Congress all three issues were caught up in complex negotiations between Republicans, Democrats, and the Clinton administration. Moreover, unilateralist House members led by Christopher Smith (R-New Jersey) insisted on attaching so-called Mexico City language—prohibiting government contributions to overseas family planning groups if they funded or even lobbied for abortion rights—to any and all of them, particularly UN funding. The Mexico City issue often became the deal breaker, since Clinton refused to allow its enactment into law.[26]

Case 3: Senate Vote on UN Arrearages, House Vote on UN Withdrawal

Although unilateralists in both houses moved to cut funding drastically and even to withdraw from the UN and other international organizations as soon as the Republican party captured Congress, real movement on this issue began in early 1997 when Helms and Biden negotiated the deal swapping the payment of UN arrearages that Democrats and Republican internationalists wanted for the UN "reforms" demanded by unilateralists. On June 12, 1997, the Senate Foreign Relations Committee reported out S. 903 (14–4), including the Helms-Biden deal to pay off $819 million of debts to the UN if it agreed, *inter alia*, to reduce the U.S. share of the regular UN budget from 25 percent to 20 percent and the U.S. peacekeeping share from 31 percent to 25 percent, to implement a negative growth UN budget, to allow the U.S. General Accounting Office to audit UN programs, and to accept the $819 million as payment in full for back dues the UN estimated to total about $1.5 billion. (For good measure, the bill also asserted the supremacy of the U.S. Constitution.) Internationalist senator Richard Lugar (R-Indiana) opposed the plan in committee, arguing that the United States owed its UN dues in full and unconditionally, but his amendment to pay the dues over two years instead of three with no strings attached was defeated in committee 12–6.[27]

The full Senate passed the language of S. 903 (which also contained Clinton's plan for foreign affairs agency reorganization—see Case 4) as H.R. 1757 on June 17, 1997. Lugar again proposed an amendment, this time conditioning the arrearage payment only on UN agreement to reduce the U.S. budget share to 20 percent and a certification by the secretary of state that the United Nations had not infringed on U.S. sovereignty. The Lugar amendment was defeated 25–73, mainly splitting Democrats (Republicans voted 4–51, Democrats 21–22).[28] All four Republican votes in favor were from the internationalist faction, while unilateralists were solidly against. Most pragmatists supported Lugar's initiative, while nearly all idealists opposed it. Thus, whatever degree of support there was within each party was heavily skewed toward its centrist faction, supporting the thesis of moderate faction cooperation across party lines against both parties' extremes.

On the House side, the earlier floor debate on H.R. 1757 featured a proposal by Ron Paul (R-Texas) requiring the United States to withdraw from the United Nations outright. The amendment also prohibited appropriation of funds for any UN contribution, as well as the participation of U.S. military personnel in any UN military or peacekeeping operation. It was defeated 54–369 (Republicans 52–171, Democrats 2–197).[29] Although more unilateralists voted against than for this extreme measure, *all* of the yes votes recorded in this study were from unilateralists and especially the most consistent unilateralists, including Tom DeLay (Texas), Dan Burton (Indiana), Duncan Hunter (California), Tom Coburn (Oklahoma), Steve Largent (Oklahoma), Joe Scarborough (Florida), Gerald Solomon (Georgia), and Dana Rohrabacher (California).

As will be seen below, UN arrearage repayment failed in 1997 and even in 1998 (when reorganization and IMF funding succeeded), a victim of House conservatives' insistence on attaching Mexico City language to it and Clinton's refusal to give those restrictions the status of law.[30] In 1999, however, a compromise was worked out in the FY2000 omnibus spending bill. Under threat of the United States losing its vote in the General Assembly from failure to pay its dues, Clinton accepted enactment of the Mexico City language. The president salved his conscience by noting that the law was a spending bill that would expire in ten months, and he also got the power to waive its restrictions at the cost of a $20 million (or 6 percent) cut in the year's $385 million international family planning assistance money.[31] However, to get the UN funds he also had to accept two dozen restrictions on the organization, including the two sets of U.S. contribution cuts, UN acceptance of the money as full payment, and a provision that would withhold 20 percent of the payment if the UN budget rose over the following two years.[32]

Case 4: Senate Vote on Foreign Affairs Agency Reorganization

On April 17, 1997, the same day Helms cleared the Chemical Weapons Convention (CWC) for the floor, Bill Clinton signed off on a reorganization plan that went further than one he had vetoed the previous year. Whereas the plan sent to him by the 104th Congress had demanded elimination of one foreign affairs agency of Clinton's choosing, the president's April 17 plan merged *both* ACDA and USIA into State, along with some of AID's administrative structure.[33]

In the House, Clinton's reorganization plan was incorporated into H.R. 1757, passed by voice vote on June 11, 1997; the bill included Mexico City language. As noted in the prior case, the next day the Senate Foreign Relations Committee reported out S. 903, including (besides the Helms-Biden deal on UN funding) a somewhat stronger version of Clinton's plan that transferred more of AID into State and required that foreign aid be funded through State. The full Senate substituted S. 903's language for that in H.R. 1757 and passed it 90–5 on June 17 (all of the no votes were Democrats, split between the factions). The conference that summer (which merged the authorization and appropriations bills, the latter including Clinton's IMF funding) could not get past the Mexico City issue, on which the House twice voted to insist. In the end, however, the Republican leadership was forced to drop the Mexico City language in order to avoid a repeat of the disastrous government shutdown two years earlier, whereupon the House conservatives refused to allow the reorganization to proceed (as well as UN and IMF funding).[34] "'No give. No give,' said [Tom] Coburn. 'If we don't get something [on Mexico City language], no IMF, no U.N. money, no reorganization.'"[35]

In 1998, Gingrich began by reviving H.R. 1757. In an unusually partisan legislative move, he had House International Relations Committee chairman Benjamin Gilman (New York) reconvene the *Republican* members of the conference committee and got a conference report with no Democrats on board on March 10.[36] H.R. 1757, now labeled the "Foreign Affairs Reform and Restructuring Act of 1998," was scheduled for a House floor vote on March 13, then again on March 18, but it wasn't until March 26 that Gingrich could persuade House unilateralists to hold their noses and vote for the UN money that was included along with the reorganization language. Action then shifted to the Senate, where H.R. 1757 passed 51–49 on April 28 after intense lobbying, this time of *internationalist* Republicans to accept the Mexico City language.[37] Democrats, probably due to Mexico City and Clinton's opposition to the bill, were almost solidly against, and unilateralists were solidly for; but some of the stronger internationalists (John Chafee of Connecticut, James Jeffords of Vermont, Arlen Specter of Pennsylvania, and Olympia Snowe of Maine) joined their Democratic colleagues in opposition. The Senate vote was thus somewhat useful to differentiate Republican factions.

Although Republicans then held the completed legislation six months before sending it to the president, hoping that he would find the IMF and UN funding so attractive that he'd accept the Mexico City language, Clinton vetoed it on October 21.[38] The same day, however, both houses passed the Omnibus Consolidated and Emergency Supplemental Appropriations Act for FY1999, which contained the reorganization language, and Clinton signed it the same day. Finally, after nearly four years of negotiation, pressure, and stalemate, the reorganization deal was done.[39]

Case 5: Senate Vote on IMF Replenishment

Clinton first requested $3.4 billion for the New Arrangements to Borrow in early 1997 as part of his FY1998 budget, but as noted in the prior case the money was knocked out late in 1997 (along with UN funding and foreign affairs reorganization) at conservatives' insistence when the Republican leadership abandoned their Mexico City language in order to get a spending bill past the president.[40] For FY1999, Clinton again requested the $3.4 billion NAB tranche, but added to it a $14.5 billion IMF quota increase, for a total of $17.9 billion. In the House, unilateralists Dick Armey (R-Texas), Tom DeLay (R-Texas) and Jim Saxton (R-New Jersey) led the charge against the Clinton request, arguing that IMF loans just allowed developing countries to avoid tough economic reforms and that the whole procedure violated free market principles.[41] Speaker Gingrich, however, supported IMF funds. Sonny Callahan's (R-Alabama) Foreign Operations Appropriations Subcommittee allowed only the $3.4 billion requested the prior year when reporting out its bill on July 15, and it also attached a series of restrictions on the IMF.[42]

The Senate Appropriations Committee chaired by Mitch McConnell (R-Kentucky), however, put in all of the $17.9 billion when it approved its bill on July 21, with Pete Domenici (New Mexico) warning that failure "to approve these funds could cause the American economy to go down."[43] The full Senate passed the bill on September 2 (90–3), with McConnell arguing for full IMF replenishment to help the recovery of Pacific trade partners and thereby the U.S. economy. Unilateralist Jon Kyl (R-Arizona) proposed that the IMF should receive the funds only if it met a number of requirements that the bill included as merely desirable, but his amendment was tabled 74–19. This vote is an excellent discriminator of unilateralists from internationalists, since except for idealist Robert Byrd, those against tabling Kyl's motion were *all* unilateralist Republicans and constituted a majority of the faction's members followed in this study.[44]

Action now shifted back to the House, where the full Appropriations Committee defeated an amendment by idealist Nancy Pelosi to add the IMF quota increase (22–30) and marked up its bill on September 10. The committee also added the Mexico City language via an amendment by Roger Wicker (R-Mississippi), with a presidential waiver that would limit funds to $356 million/yr., $29 million below current spending. The bill was passed by the full House September 17, with unilateralist DeLay now arguing that "the IMF is an anachronism in today's modern global economy. We ought to be talking in terms of phasing out the IMF."[45]

Despite the rhetoric, however, Republican resistance was being worn down as business and farm groups, worrying about loss of exports to countries hit by the Asian financial crisis, pressed for the IMF credits, while Clinton from his side moved toward the Republican position through a series of proposals regarding IMF reform.[46] Eventually, the differing House and Senate bills were included in the FY1999 Omnibus spending legislation, which gave Clinton the $17.9 billion he asked for (along with foreign affairs agency reorganization).[47] The bill included conditions on the IMF money that Armey hailed as a triumph, but Clinton had scaled them back enough that IMF managing director Michel Camdessus could call them "constructive suggestions that will help us pursue reforms that we have already started."[48]

Case 6: Senate Vote on Funding the Korean Energy Development Organization

The U.S.-North Korean Agreed Framework was laboriously negotiated after the North Koreans overturned the International Atomic Energy Agency (IAEA) inspection regime in their country and threatened to withdraw from the Nuclear Non-Proliferation Treaty (NPT). Finally concluded in October 1994 after several false starts, the Framework provided that Koreans would dismantle their nuclear weapons program in return for foreign construction of two 1,000-megawatt light-water nuclear power reactors and progressive normalization of diplomatic and trade relations with the United States. A multinational private Korean Energy Development Organization (KEDO) was formed to build the reactors with Japanese and South Korean money, and until they could come on line the United States agreed to supply North Korea with heating oil to replace lost energy from the graphite reactors it had promised to shut down.[49]

The deal was anything but a clean end to the nuclear threat from North Korea, and the North continued to take actions which seemed to cast its good faith in doubt and highlighted the potential threat it posed to the West. While the Clinton administration argued that the Agreed Framework was nevertheless the best of a variety of unsatisfying options and far better than a horrific war, Republican unilateralists countered that the administration was doing nothing effective to head off what it had itself called the most serious of all post–Cold War threats to the United States.[50] So the unilateralists began a multiyear effort to require various sorts of North Korean good behavior in return for U.S. money, conditions that, while apparently reasonable in themselves, would certainly have sabotaged the deal.

The most interesting vote on KEDO-related funding occurred in 1996. After zeroing KEDO out entirely in 1995, McConnell's appropriations subcommittee cut Clinton's $25 million request for North Korean oil to $13 million on June 18, 1996.[51] In the full Senate, however, Joe Lieberman (D-Connecticut) introduced an amendment to restore the full amount. It passed 73–27 on July 26, 1996, with Democrats voting yes 46–1 but the Republicans split 27–26 along unilateralist-internationalist lines.[52] Indeed, virtually all the no votes recorded in this study were from unilateralists (who were 5–12 against the funds restoration), with one internationalist and one idealist also voting no.

Case 7: House Vote on the Taiwan Security Enhancement Act

After a failed effort to correct China's abusive human rights practices through economic pressure in 1994, the Clinton administration pursued a policy of "strategic engagement," based on the historic gamble that steadily opening trade and active diplomatic and military relations would eventually lead to Chinese political liberalization. Given their laissez faire economic predilections and business connections, Republicans were not likely to object to a policy based on freer trade; indeed, the annual June renewals of China's most favored trade status carried Congress on Republican votes. But given their Darwinian view of the world, Republicans in general (and unilateralists in particular) were also deeply concerned about the growing power that economic growth was giving China and fearful that its steady military buildup would eventually bring it into conflict with the United States.[53] Being anti-China also appealed to Democratic idealists (who, in addition to their skepticism about free trade, abhorred Beijing's human rights practices), and they often made common cause with socially conservative Republicans (who condemned China's repression of Christians and compulsory abortions). Like trade matters, China was thus an issue ripe for cooperation of both parties' extreme factions against their centrist ones.

Since the United States normalized relations with Beijing in the 1970s, administrations of both parties had maintained a careful ambiguity regarding Taiwan, arming it for defense against military pressure or invasion by the mainland, but accepting China's insistence that there was but one China and limiting governmental relations with the island to unofficial channels. Unilateralists wanted to break that ambiguity, knowing that even a gesture as mild as granting a visa to Taiwan's president for a personal visit to the United States (as the Congress forced the administration to do in 1995) guaranteed a vitriolic reaction from Beijing. Rather than engage China diplomatically on the issue, they pushed legislation that would require

Clinton to recognize Taiwan outright and pledge to defend it against attack.[54] Their most successful effort was the Taiwan Security Enhancement Act, which passed the House 341–70 on February 1, 2000.[55] Written by Helms and DeLay, it would have strengthened U.S.-Taiwanese military ties and given Congress a bigger voice in U.S. weapon sales to the island. With the two Republican factions basically united for this pro-defense and anti-China measure, the vote is somewhat useful in differentiating Democratic idealists (who mainly joined Republicans in their anti-China stance) from Democratic pragmatists (a majority of whom voted against it).

Security Issues

In addition to NATO expansion, two kinds of security issues are surveyed below. One has to do with the use of the American military for humanitarian interventions and peacekeeping; the other deals with the use of treaty law to counter the proliferation of weapons of mass destruction. Unilateralists want the military reserved for fighting and winning America's wars, and idealists tend to be skeptical about the use of military power for any purpose—although some support its use to relieve human suffering overseas. There was thus some possibility for cooperation of the extremes against the centrist factions on the first issue, although it was mainly offset by idealist Democrats' felt need to support their president on overseas military interventions. As to arms control regimes, Democrats of both factions were supportive along with many internationalist Republicans, but unilateralists found treaties worse than useless. Votes on both kinds of issues therefore tend to be useful mainly in distinguishing Republican factions from each other.

Case 8: Senate and House Votes on Bosnia and the Dayton Accords

Though almost all Republicans are uncomfortable voting against anything having to do with U.S. military forces, especially when troops are deployed, unilateralists' distaste for peacekeeping often pushed them to do so. For example, the day before the Dayton Accords ending the Bosnian war were formally signed in Paris and with American Implementation Force (IFOR) peacekeepers already flowing into the region, the House came within eight votes of cutting off funds for the deployment. H.R. 2270 was rejected 210–218 on December 13, 1995. Although Democrats of both factions solidly supported the administration's diplomacy, as did most internationalist Republicans, unilateralists with very few exceptions opposed it: the Republican Class of 1994 voted in favor of the cutoff 64 to 8.

On the same day, the Senate considered a similar funding cutoff introduced by unilateralist Kay Bailey Hutchinson (R-Texas) and strongly supported by unilateralist James Inhofe (R-Oklahoma), who asked, "What greater support could there be for the troops than not sending them into this hostile environment?" S.Con.Res. 35 was rejected 47–52 on an essentially party line vote (Democrats 1–45, Republicans 46–7), but the seven Republicans who prevented its passage were mainly internationalists (McCain, Roth, Lugar, Kassebaum, DeWine, Chafee, and Jeffords). Then the Senate passed S.J.Res. 44 backing deployment 69–30, with nearly all internationalists joining Democrats in favor and nearly all unilateralists voting no.[56]

Once U.S. peacekeepers were in place, unilateralists (and a few idealists) repeatedly attempted to cut off their funding, partly in response to the administration's fudging of the forces' withdrawal deadlines, but also because they simply opposed U.S. involvement in peacekeeping.[57] On March 18, 1998, the House voted on H.Con.Res. 227, to withdraw American troops from Bosnia. Most unilateralists voted in favor, but internationalist Republicans were split on the issue. And while virtually all Democrats opposed the repudiation of the president's Balkan policy, two idealists from Massachusetts joined with their unilateralist colleagues favoring U.S. withdrawal.

Case 9: Senate and House Votes on Kosovo Diplomacy and War

A similar pattern was evident three and a half years later over Kosovo, although this time what began as opposition to peacekeeping ended as opposition to war. On March 11, 1999, while the administration was trying to force Slobodan Milosevic to accept a peace agreement negotiated at Rambouillet, France, unilateralists in the House attempted to undermine the president's coercive diplomacy.[58] H.Con.Res. 42, supporting Clinton's commitment to participate in a post-settlement peacekeeping force in Kosovo, was adopted with just one vote more than a majority (219–191) after an amendment by Tillie Fowler (R-Florida) that would have prohibited the deployment of ground troops to enforce the agreement failed 178–237 (Republicans 169–48, Democrats 9–188; one Independent voted against the amendment). On both votes, unilateralists were overwhelmingly against Clinton's peacemaking efforts and Democrats were overwhelmingly in support. But a strong majority of internationalist Republicans followed in this study bolted their party to support the president's diplomacy, particularly on the Fowler amendment.[59]

Similarly, when the Senate approved S.Con.Res. 21 (58–41), authorizing air operations against Yugoslavia, on March 23, 1999 (the day before the bombing began), most internationalist Republicans joined with Democrats in support while unilateralists were almost unanimously opposed.[60] The House action on S.Con.Res. 21 came on April 28, when the air war had been underway for over a month, civilian casualties were mounting, and Milosevic's surrender seemed nowhere in sight. It was a 213–213 tie, mostly along party lines. Although Speaker Dennis Hastert (Illinois) supported the war, he allowed his unilateralist whips to push their viewpoint; and only the defection of a few, mainly internationalist Republicans saved Clinton from the outright defeat of what unilateralist Roy Blunt (R-Missouri) called "a second Tonkin Gulf resolution."[61] On the same day the House approved H.R. 1569 (249–180), requiring congressional authorization before using ground troops in the war. Forty-five Democrats joined most Republicans to support this assertion of congressional prerogatives, but while unilateralists were overwhelmingly in support of the prohibition, about half the internationalists surveyed here were ready to support the president's use of ground troops as he might think necessary for victory in a war to which the United States was already committed.[62]

Case 10: Senate Vote on NATO Expansion

Interestingly, unilateralists' support for a strong American military does not automatically translate into support for military alliances. Their attitudes toward NATO in the early post–Cold War years, for example, varied according to the relative strength of their views, first, on the threats still faced by the United States, and second, on whether NATO was essentially an alliance or an international organization. Most unilateralists were still worried about the Russian threat and saw NATO as an important facet of American military power, so they were supportive of the alliance. But a few who discounted the Russian threat or viewed NATO more as an international organization than an adjunct to the U.S. military argued that it was a vestige of the Cold War that should now be abolished.[63] While arguments that the United States must lead in Europe were persuasive to internationalist Speaker Newt Gingrich, his colleague from Georgia, John Linder, typified this unilateralist attitude by saying that he was "not the least bit interested in the prestige of NATO."[64]

On April 30, 1998, the Senate overwhelmingly approved the first round of NATO expansion, admitting Poland, the Czech Republic, and Hungary 80–19 (Republicans 45–9, Democrats 35–10). On the same day, it defeated 41–59 a proposal by Senator Warner (Virginia) to impose a three-year delay on the admission of additional new members.[65] In an alignment seen on no other issue surveyed in this chapter, the votes show that the skeptics on NATO expansion came from the left of *each* party, supporters from the right of each. That is, unilateralists and pragmatists were the factions most strongly favoring expansion, while such dissent as there was (revealed more on the Warner proposal than on expansion itself) came mainly from internationalists and idealists. It is understandable that unilateralists would support expansion of a military alliance and that all Democrats would support their president unless they felt compelled to do otherwise. While the opposition alignment is harder to explain, it seems plausible that idealists opposed expansion simply on anti-military grounds, and that internationalists were concerned lest strident Russian opposition to NATO expansion confirm the tendency (so often cited by academic observers) of alliances to beget counter alliances, arms races, and war.[66]

Case 11: Senate Vote on the Chemical Weapons Convention

This is a particularly useful case for distinguishing unilateralist from internationalist Republicans, since the treaty was signed by President George H. W. Bush just before leaving office in 1993 and was therefore as much a Republican internationalist treaty as a Democratic one. Still, Senators Helms and Thurmond vowed in 1995 to block it indefinitely, and they did delay approval three and a half years: from November 1993 when Clinton submitted the CWC until its approval in April 1997.[67]

The treaty was reported out by the Senate Foreign Relations Committee on April 25, 1996, by a vote of 13–5, with all five no votes from unilateralist Republicans.[68] A floor vote was scheduled for September of that year, but had to be postponed when presidential candidate Bob Dole came out against the treaty during the presidential campaign, making it impossible for many Republicans to support it.[69] Unilateralist senators Kyl and Helms were the leading opponents.

In early 1997 Helms wrote Lott that his committee would not release the treaty again until the administration allowed action on Republican foreign policy priorities, including foreign affairs (see Case 4).[70] Helms also insisted on thirty-three reservations to the treaty, called "understandings." Helms and Biden reached agreement on twenty-eight of these and they became part of the resolution of approval, but five were killer amendments that were voted on individually on the floor when the resolution of ratification was approved:[71]

1. no ratification unless the CWC was ratified by pariah or **terrorist** states considered most likely to possess chemical weapons (*deleted 71–29*)
2. no ratification unless **Russia** ratified the CWC, complied with earlier chemical conventions, and ceased all CW activity (*deleted 66–34*)

3. no ratification unless the CIA provides **verification**—that it can detect militarily significant violations in a timely fashion—with "a high degree of confidence" *(deleted 66–34)*
4. U.S. to bar **inspectors** of its chemical plants who were nationals from countries that have sponsored terrorism or violated U.S. nonproliferation laws *(deleted 56–44)*
5. no ratification unless the treaty was renegotiated to drop provisions allowing signatories to obtain chemical defense **technology** and to conduct international trade in chemicals *(deleted 66–34)*

As noted earlier, on April 17, 1997, Clinton signed off on a foreign affairs agency reorganization plan and Helms dropped his objection to a CWC vote. The treaty was approved 74–26 on April 24.[72] All forty-five Democrats voted to consent to ratification of the treaty and to delete all the killer amendments. Of the fifty-five Republicans, twenty-nine voted to approve the treaty, and among those were all the Republican internationalists surveyed here (although five voted to keep one or more killer amendments).[73] A substantial majority of surveyed unilateralists voted no on the treaty and (somewhat redundantly) for all the killer amendments, and of the four unilateralists who voted to approve the CWC, three (Lott, McConnell, and Craig Thomas of Wyoming) also wanted to keep all the killer amendments, essentially negating their approval.[74] The contrast between Republican factions could hardly have been more stark. One final vignette: the implementing legislation was passed by voice vote in the Senate, but Republican leaders in the House attached it to an Iran sanctions bill that Clinton vetoed. The legislation was eventually adopted, along with foreign affairs reorganization and IMF funding, as part of the Omnibus spending bill in late 1998.[75]

Case 12: Senate Vote on the CTBT

This case is also a good one to differentiate internationalists from unilateralists, along with illustrating the radical hostility of unilateralists to national defense through treaties. [76] But unlike on the CWC, the division between Republican factions on this treaty was not between those who voted for and against consent to ratification, but rather between those who supported deferring the vote and those who actively worked for the outright defeat of the Comprehensive Test Ban Treaty (CTBT).

Whereas the CWC was a Bush treaty, it was Clinton who signed the CTBT on September 24, 1996, at UN headquarters in New York (another *bête noire* of the unilateralists). The administration made ratification a major foreign policy goal and submitted the treaty to the Senate about a year later. Helms took no action on it for two years, but on September 1, 1998, the full

Senate voted by only 49–44 to approve funds for the international system being set up to monitor CTBT compliance; the tally was an early warning that the sixty-seven votes needed for approval would be difficult to get. This vote was essentially along party lines (Republicans 7–44, Democrats 42–0), but the few Republicans who voted with their Democratic colleagues were mainly internationalists.

Beginning in the spring of 1999, Jon Kyl led a small group of unilateralists who began collecting commitments against the treaty; they had a blocking third of the Senate by mid-May and forty-two no votes by September. Meanwhile, unaware of Kyl's efforts and wanting to get approval before an October conference in Vienna that was called to urge treaty ratification, the Democrats began baiting the Republicans, demanding a vote. Suddenly, at the end of September, Majority Leader Lott offered an up or down vote in twelve days; and despite strenuous White House efforts to persuade Hill Democrats that the treaty would inevitably be defeated on so fast a timetable, Biden and Minority Leader Tom Daschle (South Dakota) accepted Lott's offer.

Within days the White House and Democrats in Congress realized that they had committed themselves to a vote they could not win. The only way to delay it was either a unanimous consent motion (which could be prevented by just a single unilateralist) or defeat of the procedural motion needed to go to the executive calendar on which the treaty awaited action (which required a simple majority). The Republican leadership successfully characterized the latter possibility as an assault on their majority status, and although twenty-four Republicans (a total of sixty-two senators) signed a letter sponsored by Senators Moynihan and Warner urging that action on the treaty be postponed, the vote to move to executive calendar passed on a strict party line vote on October 13, 1999. Then the treaty itself went down to defeat 48–51: Democrats 44–0 (Byrd voting present), Republicans 4–51. Although most internationalist Republicans voted against approval of the treaty, virtually all of them signed the letter urging postponement; and in addition to the four internationalists who did vote to approve the treaty, four more (Hagel, McCain, Warner, and Cochran) later expressed varying degrees of regret regarding their no votes.[77] Unilateralist Republicans, by contrast, all voted against the treaty, and only two signed the postponement letter.

Conclusion

Voting behavior is admittedly an imperfect indicator of partisanship, to say nothing of foreign policy factionalism. Although votes are tallied in reassuringly hard numbers, they say nothing in themselves about *why* a senator or representative voted as he or she did. Many of the votes surveyed here were on bills containing a variety of provisions that may have pulled members in various directions, and even uncomplicated legislation may be voted yea or nay for reasons having nothing to do with the merits of the issue at hand. Still, votes do provide a kind of shorthand for policy positions, and reliable patterns may emerge across a number of votes even if some are imperfect indicators. Most important, voting behavior may provide a preliminary sense of whether the factions described at the outset of this chapter are comprised of more than an aggregate of views expressed on various issues at various times by various legislative actors, of whether those factions also represent a more or less coherent set of positions taken by individual legislators over time and across a variety of issues.

Many of the votes surveyed here demonstrate the pull of partisanship, but the most interesting ones are those on which factional cohesion was so strong that it broke down the "normal" partisan alignment. For Republicans, these were usually votes on which internationalists voted with Democrats rather than with the unilateralists in their own party. In the House this pattern occurred most strongly on Case 8, the cutoff of funds for Bosnia (H.R. 2770), and Case 9, especially the Fowler amendment prohibiting use of ground troops for peacekeeping in Kosovo. In the Senate it occurred on far more votes, including those for Case 5, IMF funding; Case 6, KEDO oil money; Case 8, Bosnia; Case 9, Kosovo; Case 11, CWC approval; and Case 12, on the letter delaying the CTBT vote. On these Senate cases, too, the percentage of internationalists breaking ranks with their unilateralist colleagues to vote with the opposition party was higher than in the House.

The unsurprising conclusion seems to be that Republican internationalism was considerably stronger in the Senate than in the House. In both bodies, moreover, the Democratic factions were far less cohesive on these issues, the biggest differentiations appearing in the House on Case 7, the Taiwan act, and in the Senate on Case 1, fast track; Case 5, UN arrears; and Case 11, on the three-year delay in additional NATO members. In addition, on the Democrats' side only fast track replicates the Republican pattern of the moderate faction aligning against its own radical faction with a solid opposition party. Otherwise, the patterns of alignment seem different in each case:

> Taiwan (House): idealists uniting with more or less solid Republicans
> Fast Track (Senate): pragmatists uniting with most Republicans

UN arrears (Senate): some idealists with unilateralists, centrists together

NATO delay (Senate): most pragmatists uniting with most unilateralists

One might conclude, then, that Republican factionalism in the late 1990s was considerably stronger than its Democratic counterpart, a logical inference given that the philosophical gulf between unilateralist and internationalists was and is much greater than that between idealists and pragmatists.[78]

Also of interest is the extent to which individual members of Congress appear to be solid in their factional positions. The tables at the end of this chapter offer a scoring of each legislator's factionally deviant votes, that is, the votes cast by each *against* the majority of his or her faction.[79] Thus, the lower the score, the more purely "factional" a member's voting behavior. Particularly among Republicans, the scores seem to match well one's intuitive sense of the positions taken by these legislators over time. It is no surprise, for example, that Faircloth, Helms, Kyl, Ashcroft, Hutchinson, Inhofe, and Nickles are the top unilateralist senators, or that Burton, Coburn, Rohrabacher, Scarborough, Solomon, Blunt, Graham, Saxton, Sensenbrenner, Shuster, Souder, and Spence are the leading unilateralist representatives. Though the distinctions among Democrats are less firmly defined, these too seem to pass the common-sense test, with Byrd, Dorgan, Feinstein, and Harkin being among the leading idealists in the Senate, and Bonior, Dingell, Frank, Gephardt, Kennedy, Markey, and Pelosi capturing those honors in the House.

It can be concluded with some confidence, then, that the factional divisions outlined at the beginning of this chapter did exist in the late 1990s and were reflected on consequential foreign policy issues in the votes of key members of Congress, votes in which factional behavior overrode partisanship. If the key fault lines on foreign policy in the late 1990s did in fact run through the political parties as much as between them, it remains to reflect on what caused the development of such strong intraparty factions and whether they can be expected to continue. Although discussion of the causes for factionalism is necessarily somewhat speculative in nature, it seems likely that three major factors were at work.

First, as argued at the outset, were the changes in the domestic and international environments that forced massive philosophical shifts in the foreign policy thinking of politically active Americans. Domestic changes made the parties more homogeneous and ideological so that their domestic missions became more consequential for members, while post–Cold War developments in international politics and economics ensured that both Republicans and Democrats would face acute dilemmas as they attempted to translate those missions into foreign policy. Even as the parties became more opposed on domestic policy, therefore, they progressively lost philosophical coherence on foreign policy, setting the stage for factional splits.

Against this philosophical background came another change in the international environment that, unlike post–Cold War power shifts and the transformation of the global economy, turned out to be specific to the 1990s: the apparent absence of a serious external threat to the United States.[80] With the threat went the "defining consensus" of the Cold War, and the lack of consensus allowed the impact of divisive internal influences in the policy process to grow dramatically, further weakening the parties' coherence. In addition, in a pattern common to other postwar eras, the absence of a central organizing threat increased the weight of the Congress in the legislative-executive balance of power.

That last development in turn lent importance to the third factor: divided government. For although government split between the parties was more the postwar rule than the exception, the relative weakness of the president in the 1990s made it far more consequential than before. Divided government meant that the key initiator of foreign policy action, President Clinton, knew that he had to get some votes from the opposition party on every issue in order to win. For a weak president, doing so often meant altering his proposals and bargaining tactics to encourage Republican defections in his direction. And to the extent he succeeded with the same people across a variety of issues, he helped create the factions described in this chapter.

Will intraparty factionalism continue to be important in the years ahead? As of this writing, two of these three conditions have changed. September 11 restored Americans' sense of external threat, strengthening the hand of the President and shifting power away from the Congress. And government is now unified, not divided. But neither the philosophical divisions that spring from the very nature of international politics and economics in the post–Cold War era nor the politicization of our political parties have changed, and it seems a fair bet that divided government will one day return. It is also quite possible that the terrorist threat will turn out to have been temporary and manageable, and that within a few years the United States will find itself back in the messy indeterminacy of the post–Cold War era, moving forward to the past. If so, examining the factional roots of statecraft in the late 1990s may turn out to be of more than historical interest.

TABLE 1

SENATE	Score 7.5	1: Fast Track S. 955 11/5/97	Griswold Index on Free Trade				3: UN Arrears Lugar 6/17/97	4: Agency Reorg. H.R. 1757 4/28/98	5: IMF funds table Kyl conditions	6: KEDO H.R. 3540 7/26/96	8: Bosnia S.J.Res. 44 12/13/95	9: Kosovo S.C.R.21 3/23/99
			Isolat-ionist	Free Trade	Interna-tioalists	Interven-tionists						
Republican Unilateralists												
John Ashcroft (Mo.)	0.5	Y	x				N	Y	N	N	N	N
Hank Brown (Colo.)										N	Y	
Sam Brownback (Kans.)							N	Y	Y	Y	N	N
Paul Coverdell (Ga.)	1	Y		x			N	Y		N	N	N
Alphonse D'Amato (N.Y.)										N	N	
Pete V. Domenici (N.M.)	2	Y			x		N	Y		N	N	N
Lauch Faircloth (N.C.)	0	N	x				N	Y	N	N	N	N
Rod Grams (Minn.)	2	Y		x			N	Y	Y	Y	N	N
Jesse Helms (N.C.)	0	N	x				N	Y	against	N	N	N
Kay Bailey Hutchinson (Tex.)	0.5	Y		x			N	Y	N	N	N	N
James Inhofe (Okla.)	0.5	N	x				N	Y	N	N	N	N
Jon Kyl (Ariz.)	0	Y	x				N	Y	N	N	N	N
Trent Lott (Miss.)	1	Y			x		N	Y	Y	N	N	N
Mitch McConnell (Ky.)	2	Y			x		N	Y	N	N	Y	Y
Don Nickles (Okla.)	0.5	Y		x			N	Y	N	N	N	N
Craig Thomas (Wyo.)	2	Y			x		N	Y	Y	Y	N	N
Fred Thompson (Tenn.)	1	Y	x				N	Y	N	Y	N	N
Strom Thurmond (S.C.)	2.5	N				x	N	Y	Y	Y	N	N

TABLE 1 (continued)

SENATE	Score 7.5	1: Fast Track S. 955 11/5/97	Griswold Index on Free Trade				3: UN Arrears Lugar 6/17/97	4: Agency Reorg. H.R. 1757 4/28/98	5: IMF funds table Kyl conditions	6: KEDO H.R. 3540 7/26/96	8: Bosnia S.J.Res. 44 12/13/95	9: Kosovo S.C.R.21 3/23/99
			Isolat-ionist	Free Trade	Interna-tioalists	Interven-tionists						
Republican Internationalists												
John Chafee (R.I.)	0	Y			x		Y	N	Y	Y	Y	Y
Thad Cochran (Miss.)	2.5	Y			x		N	Y	Y	Y	Y	Y
Robert Dole (Kans.)				x							Y	
Slade Gorton (Wash.)	3.5	Y			x		N	Y	Y	N	Y	N
Chuck Hagel (Nebr.)	2.5	Y			x		N	Y	Y			Y
James Jeffords (Vt.)	0	Y			x		Y	N	Y	Y	Y	Y
Nancy L. Kassebaum (Kans.)										Y	Y	
Richard G. Lugar (Ind.)	1	Y			x		Y	Y	Y	Y	Y	Y
John McCain (Ariz.)	1.5	Y		x			N	Y	Y	Y	Y	Y
Gordon Smith (Ore.)	1.5	Y			x		N	Y	Y			Y
Olympia Snowe (Maine)	1.5	N				x	N	N	Y	Y	N	Y
Arlen Spector (Pa.)	0	N				x	Y	N	Y	Y	Y	Y
Ted Stevens (Alaska)	2	Y			x		N	Y	Y	Y	Y	N
John Warner (Va.)	3	Y			x		N	Y	Y	Y	N	Y

TABLE 2

SENATE	Score 3	1: Fast Track S. 955 11/5/97	Griswold Index on Free Trade				3: UN Arrears Lugar 6/17/97	4: Agency Reorg. H.R. 1757 4/28/98	5: IMF funds table Kyl conditions	6: KEDO H.R. 3540 7/26/96	8: Bosnia S.J.Res. 44 12/13/95	9: Kosovo S.C.R.21 3/23/99
			Isolat-ionist	Free Trade	Interna-tioalists	Interven-tionists						
Democratic Pragmatists												
Max Baucus (Mont.)	1	Y			x		N	N	Y	Y	Y	Y
Joseph Biden (Del.)	1	Y			x		N	N	Y	Y	Y	Y
Jeff Bingaman (N.M.)	1	Y			x		Y	N		Y	Y	N
Barbara Boxer (Calif.)	1	N				x	Y	N	Y	Y	Y	Y
Dale Bumpers (Ark.)	1	Y			x		Y	N	Y	Y	Y	
Tom Daschle (S.D.)	0	Y			x			N	Y	Y	Y	Y
Chris Dodd (Conn.)	0	Y			x		Y	N	Y	Y	Y	Y
Russell Feingold (Wis.)	1	N	x				Y	N	Y	Y	N	N
John Glenn (Ohio)	0	Y			x		Y	N	Y	Y	Y	
Daniel Inouye (Hawaii)	1	Y			x		N	N		Y	Y	Y
Robert J. Kerrey (Nebr.)	0	Y			x		Y	N	Y	Y	Y	Y
John F. Kerry (Mass.)	0	Y			x		Y	N	Y	Y	Y	Y
Patrick J. Leahy (Vt.)	1	Y					Y	N	Y	Y	Y	Y
Joseph I. Lieberman (Conn.)	0	Y			x		Y	N	Y	Y	Y	Y
Charles Robb (Va.)	1	Y			x		N	N	Y	Y	Y	Y
Paul Sarbanes (Md.)	1	N				x	Y	N	Y	Y	Y	Y

TABLE 2 (continued)

SENATE	Score	1: Fast Track S. 955 11/5/97	Griswold Index on Free Trade				3: UN Arrears Lugar 6/17/97	4: Agency Reorg. H.R. 1757 4/28/98	5: IMF funds table Kyl conditions	6: KEDO H.R. 3540 7/26/96	8: Bosnia S.J.Res. 44 12/13/95	9: Kosovo S.C.R.21 3/23/99
			Isolat-ionist	Free Trade	Interna-tioalists	Interven-tionists						
Democratic Idealists	3											
John Breux (La.)	1	N					N	Y	Y	Y	Y	Y
Robert C. Byrd (W.Va.)	0	N			x		N	N	N	Y	Y	Y
Kent Conrad (N.D.)	0	N			x		N	N	Y	Y	Y	Y
Byron Dorgan (N.D.)	0	N			x		N	N	Y	N	Y	Y
Diane Feinstein (Calif.)	0	N			x		N	N	Y	Y	Y	Y
Tom Harkin (Iowa)	0	N				x		N	Y	Y	Y	Y
Ernest F. Hollings (S.C.)	0	N	x				N	N	Y	Y	Y	N
Daniel P. Moynihan (N.Y.)	1	Y			x		N	N	Y	Y	Y	Y
Claiborne Pell (R.I.)										Y	Y	
Robert G. Torrecelli (N.J.)	0	N					N	N	Y			Y
Paul Wellstone (Minn.)	1	N	x			x	Y	N	Y	Y	N	Y

TABLE 3

SENATE	10: NATO		11: Chemical Weapons Convention							12: Comprehensive Test Ban Treaty		
	Expansion 4/30/98	3 yr. delay new mem.	Cmte. 4/25/96	Approval 4/28/97	terrorist	Killer Amendments Russia	verification	inspector	techshare	monitor 9/1/98	delay letter	approval 10/13/99
Republican Unilateralists												
John Ashcroft (Mo.)	N	Y	n	N	K	K	K	K	K	N		N
Hank Brown (Colo.)			n									na
Sam Brownback (Kans.)	Y	N								N	x	N
Paul Coverdell (Ga.)	Y	N	n	N	K	K	K	K	K	N		N
Alphonse D'Amato (N.Y.)	Y	N								Y		
Pete V. Domenici (N.M.)	Y	N		Y	D	D	D	K	D		x	N
Lauch Faircloth (N.C.)	Y	N								N		
Rod Grams (Minn.)	Y	N	n	N	K	K	K	K	K	N		N
Jesse Helms (N.C.)	Y	N	n	N	K	K	K	K	K			N
Kay Bailey Hutchinson (Tex.)	Y	Y		N	K	K	K	K	K	N		N
James Inhofe (Okla.)	N	Y		N	K	K	K	K	K	N		N
Jon Kyl (Ariz.)	no vote	N		N	K	K	K	K	K	N		N
Trent Lott (Miss.)	Y	N		Y	K	K	K	K	K	N		N
Mitch McConnell (Ky.)	Y	N		Y	K	K	K	K	K	N		N
Don Nickles (Okla.)	Y	Y		N	D	K	K	K	K	N		N
Craig Thomas (Wyo.)	Y	N	y	Y	K	K	K	K	K	N		N
Fred Thompson (Tenn.)	Y	N	y	N	K	K	K	K	K	N		N
Strom Thurmond (S.C.)	Y	Y		N	K	K	K	K	K	N		N

TABLE 3 (continued)

SENATE	10: NATO		11: Chemical Weapons Convention							12: Comprehensive Test Ban Treaty		
	Expansion	3 yr. delay	Cmte.	Approval	terrorist	Killer Amendments				monitor	delay	approval
	4/30/98	new mem.	4/25/96	4/28/97		Russia	verification	inspector	techshare	9/1/98	letter	10/13/99
Republican Internationalists												
John Chafee (R.I.)	Y	Y		Y	D	D	D	D	D	Y	x	Y
Thad Cochran (Miss.)	Y	N		Y	D	D	D	D	D	N		N
Robert Dole (Kans.)												
Slade Gorton (Wash.)	Y	N		Y	D	D	D	K	D	N	x	N
Chuck Hagel (Nebr.)	Y	N		Y	D	D	D	K	D	N	x	N
James Jeffords (Vt.)	N	Y		Y	D	D	D	D	D	Y	x	Y
Nancy L. Kassebaum (Kans.)			y									
Richard G. Lugar (Ind.)	Y	N	y	Y	D	D	D	D	D	N	x	N
John McCain (Ariz.)	Y	N		Y	D	D	D	K	D	N	x	N
Gordon Smith (Ore.)	Y	N		Y	D	D	D	K	D	N	x	Y
Olympia Snowe (Maine)	Y	Y	y	Y	D	D	D	D	D	N	x	N
Arlen Spector (Pa.)	N	Y		Y	D	D	D	D	D	Y	x	Y
Ted Stevens (Alaska)	Y	Y		Y	D	D	D	D	D	Y	x	N
John Warner (Va.)	N	Y		Y	D	K	K	K	D	N	x	N

TABLE 4

SENATE	10: NATO		11: Chemical Weapons Convention							12: Comprehensive Test Ban Treaty		
	Expansion 4/30/98	3 yr. delay new mem.	Cmte. 4/25/96	Approval 4/28/97	Killer Amendments					monitor 9/1/98	delay letter	approval 10/13/99
					terrorist	Russia	verification	inspector	techshare			
Democratic Pragmatists												
Max Baucus (Mont.)	Y	N		Y	D	D	D	D	D	Y	x	Y
Joseph Biden (Del.)	Y	N	y	Y	D	D	D	D	D	Y	x	Y
Jeff Bingaman (N.M.)	Y	Y		Y	D	D	D	D	D		x	Y
Barbara Boxer (Calif.)	Y	N		Y	D	D	D	D	D	Y		Y
Dale Bumpers (Ark.)		Y		Y	D	D	D	D	D	Y		
Tom Daschle (S.D.)	Y	N		Y	D	D	D	D	D	Y		Y
Chris Dodd (Conn.)	Y	N	y	Y	D	D	D	D	D	Y	x	Y
Russell Feingold (Wis.)	Y	N	y	Y	D	D	D	D	D	Y	x	Y
John Glenn (Ohio)		N		Y	D	D	D	D	D			
Daniel Inouye (Hawaii)	Y	N		Y	D	D	D	D	D		x	Y
Robert J. Kerrey (Nebr.)	Y	N		Y	D	D	D	D	D	Y	x	Y
John F. Kerry (Mass.)	Y	N		Y	D	D	D	D	D	Y	x	Y
Patrick J. Leahy (Vt.)	N	Y		Y	D	D	D	D	D	Y		Y
Joseph I. Lieberman (Conn.)	Y	N		Y	D	D	D	D	D	Y	x	Y
Charles Robb (Va.)	Y	N	y	Y	D	D	D	D	D	Y	x	Y
Paul Sarbanes (Md.)	Y	N	y	Y	D	D	D	D	D	Y		Y

TABLE 4 (continued)

SENATE	10: NATO		11: Chemical Weapons Convention						12: Comprehensive Test Ban Treaty		
	Expansion 4/30/98	3 yr. delay new mem.	Cmte. 4/25/96	Approval 4/28/97	Killer Amendments				monitor 9/1/98	delay letter	approval 10/13/99
					terrorist	Russia	verification	inspector	techshare		
Democratic Idealists											
John Breaux (La.)	Y	N		Y	D	D	D	D	D	Y	x	Y
Robert C. Byrd (W.Va.)	Y	Y		Y	D	D	D	D	D	Y	x	P
Kent Conrad (N.D.)		Y		Y	D	D	D	D	D	Y		Y
Byron Dorgan (N.D.)	N	Y		Y	D	D	D	D	D	Y		Y
Diane Feinstein (Calif.)	Y	Y	y	Y	D	D	D	D	D	Y	x	Y
Tom Harkin (Iowa)	N	Y		Y	D	D	D	D	D	Y	x	Y
Ernest F. Hollings (S.C.)	Y	Y		Y	D	D	D	D	D	Y	x	Y
Daniel P. Moynihan (N.Y.)	N	Y		Y	D	D	D	D	D	Y	x	Y
Claiborne Pell (R.I.)			y									
Robert G. Torrecelli (N.J.)	Y	Y		Y	D	D	D	D	D	Y	x	Y
Paul Wellstone (Minn.)	N	Y		Y	D	D	D	D	D	Y	x	Y

TABLE 5

HOUSE	Score	1: Fast-Track Trade Bill W&M Cmte. 10/4/97	1: Fast-Track Trade Bill House 9/25/98	Griswold Index on Free Trade and Markets Isolationists	Griswold Index on Free Trade and Markets Free Trade	Griswold Index on Free Trade and Markets Internationalists	Griswold Index on Free Trade and Markets Interventionists	2: China PNTR 5/24/00	3: UN withdrawal Paul amendment H.R. 1757 6/4/97
Republican Unilateralists	3.5								
Bill Archer (Tex.)	1.5	Y	Y			x		Y	N
Richard K. Armey (Tex.)	1.5	Y	Y		x			Y	N
Doug Bereuter (Nebr.)	1.5	Y	Y			x		Y	N
Roy Blunt (Mo.)	0.5	Y	Y				x		
Dan Burton (Ind.)	0			x				N	Y
Tom Campbell (Calif.)	1.5	Y	Y		x			Y	N
Tom A. Coburn (Okla.)	0	N	N				x	N	Y
Larry Combest (Tex.)	1	Y	Y			x		Y	Y
Christopher Cox (Calif.)	1.5	Y	Y	x				Y	N
Philip M. Crane (Ill.)	1	Y	Y		x			Y	Y
Tom DeLay (Tex.)	1	Y	Y			x		Y	Y
Benjamin Gilman (N.Y.)	1.5	N	N				x	N	N
Lindsey O. Graham (S.C.)	0.5	N	N				x	N	N
J. D. Hayworth (Ariz.)	1	Y	Y		x			N	N
Duncan Hunter (Calif.)	1	N	N	x				N	Y
John Kasich (Ohio)	1.5	Y	Y				x	Y	N
Ray LaHood (Ill.)	1.5	Y	Y			x		Y	N
Steve Largent (Okla.)	1	Y	Y		x			Y	Y
Bill McCollum (Fla.)	1.5	Y	Y			x		Y	N
Dana Rohrabacher (Calif.)	0	N	N	x				N	Y
Jim Saxton (N.J.)	0.5						x	N	N
Joe Scarborough (Fla.)	0	N	N	x				X	Y
Jim Sensenbrenner (Wis.)	0.5							N	N

TABLE 5 (continued)

HOUSE	Score 3.5	1: Fast-Track Trade Bill		Griswold Index on Free Trade and Markets				2:: China PNTR 5/24/00	3:UN withdrawal Paul amendment H.R. 1757 6/4/97
		W&M Cmte. 10/4/97	House 9/25/98	Isolationists	Free Trade	Internationalists	Interventionists		
Bud Shuster (Pa.)	0.5		N				x		N
Christopher H. Smith (N.J.)	1.5		N				x	N	N
Gerald H. B. Solomon (N.Y.)	0		N				x		Y
Mark Edward Souder (Ind.)	0.5		N	x				N	N
Floyd Spence (S.C.)	0.5		N				x	N	N
J. C. Watts (Okla.)	1.5		Y			x		Y	N
Curt Weldon (Pa.)	1		N	x				Y	N
C. W. Bill Young (Fla.)	1.5		Y				x	Y	N

TABLE 6

HOUSE	Score 3.5	1: Fast-Track Trade Bill		Griswold Index on Free Trade and Markets				2: China PNTR 5/24/00	3: UN withdrawal Paul amendment H.R. 1757 6/4/97
		W&M Cmte. 10/4/97	House 9/25/98	Isolationists	Free Trade	Internationalists	Interventionists		
Republican Internationalists									
John A. Boehner (Ohio)	0		Y				x	Y	N
Sonny Callahan (Ala.)	1		Y			x		Y	N
David Dreier (Calif.)	0		Y			x		Y	N
Newt Gingrich (Ga.)									
Porter J. Goss (Fla.)	0			x				Y	N
J. Dennis Hastert (Ill.)	1		Y		x			Y	N
Henry J. Hyde (Ill.)	1		Y				x	Y	N
James A. Leach (Iowa)	1		Y			x		Y	N
Jerry Lewis (Calif.)	0		Y			x		Y	N
Bob Livingston (La.)	1.5		Y			x			N
Connie Morella (Md.)	0		Y			x		Y	N
Bill Paxton (N.Y.)	0		Y			x			N
John Edward Porter (Ill.)	1		Y				x	Y	N
Christopher Shays (Conn.)	1		Y			x		Y	N

TABLE 7

HOUSE		1: Fast-Track Trade Bill		Griswold Index on Free Trade and Markets				2: China PNTR	3:UN withdrawal
	Score 2.5	W&M Cmte. 10/4/97	House 9/25/98	Isolationists	Free Trade	Internationalists	Interventionists	5/24/00	Paul amendment H.R. 1757 6/4/97
Democratic Pragmatists									
Lee H. Hamilton (Ind.)	2.5		Y			x			N
William J. Jefferson (La.)	1	Y				x		Y	N
Robert T. Matsui (Calif.)	0.5	Y	N			x		Y	N
Jim McDermott (Wash.)	0	Y	Y			x		Y	N
Paul McHale (Pa.)			N				x		N
David R. Obey (Wis.)	0.5		N				x	N	N
Matin Sabo (Minn.)	0.5		N				x	N	N
Charles E. Schumer (N.Y.)	0.5		N				x		N
Ike Skelton (Mo.)	0		Y				x	Y	N
Charles W. Stenholm (Tex.)	1		Y			x		Y	N
John S. Tanner (Tenn.)	1	Y	Y			x		Y	N

TABLE 7 (continued)

HOUSE	Score	1: Fast-Track Trade Bill W&M Cmte. 10/4/97	1: Fast-Track Trade Bill House 9/25/98	Griswold Index on Free Trade and Markets - Isolationists	Griswold Index on Free Trade and Markets - Free Trade	Griswold Index on Free Trade and Markets - Internationalists	Griswold Index on Free Trade and Markets - Interventionists	2: China PNTR 5/24/00	3: UN withdrawal Paul amendment H.R. 1757 6/4/97
Democratic Idealists	2.5								
Howard L. Berman (Calif.)	0		N				x	N	against
David E. Bonior (Mich.)	0		N				x	N	N
Benjamin L. Cardin (Md.)	1		N				x	Y	N
John Conyers (Mich.)	1		N	x				N	N
John D. Dingell (Mich.)	0		N				x	N	N
Barney Frank (Mass.)	0		N				x	N	N
Sam Gejdenson (Conn.)	0		N				x	N	N
Richard A. Gephardt (Mo.)	0		N				x	N	N
Steny Hoyer (Md.)	1		N				x	Y	N
Jesse L. Jackson Jr. (Ill.)	1		N				x	N	N
Joseph P. Kennedy Jr. (Mass.)			N				x		N
Patrick J. Kennedy (R.I.)	0		N				x	N	N
Tom Lantos (Calif.)	1		N				x	N	
Edward J. Markey (Mass.)	0		N	x				N	N
Nancy Pelosi (Calif.)	0		N				x	N	N
Charles. B. Rangel (N.Y.)	1		N			x		Y	N
Fourtney (Pete) Stark (Calif.)	1		N				x	N	N
Pete Visclosky (Ind.)	0		N	x				N	N
Henry A. Waxman (Calif.)	1		N				x	Y	N

TABLE 8

HOUSE	7: Taiwan	8: Bosnia		9: Kosovo Diplomacy and War			
	Security Act H.R. 1838 2/1/00	no funds H.R. 2770 12/13/95	withdraw H.C.R. 227 3/18/98	Fowler amendment 3/11/99	Clinton H.C.R. 42 3/11/99	air ops tie S.C.R. 21 4/28/99	no troops H.R. 1569 4/28/99
Republican Unilateralists							
Bill Archer (Tex.)	N	Y	Y	Y	N	N	Y
Richard K. Armey (Tex.)	Y	Y	Y	Y	N	N	Y
Doug Bereuter (Nebr.)	Y	Y	Y	Y	N	N	Y
Roy Blunt (Mo.)	Y		Y	Y	N	N	Y
Dan Burton (Ind.)	Y	Y	Y	Y	N	N	Y
Tom Campbell (Calif.)			Y	Y	P	N	Y
Tom A. Coburn (Okla.)	Y	Y	Y	Y	N	N	Y
Larry Combest (Tex.)	Y	Y	Y	Y	N	N	Y
Christopher Cox (Calif.)	Y	Y	N	Y	N	N	Y
Philip M. Crane (Ill.)	Y	Y	Y	Y	N	N	Y
Tom DeLay (Tex.)	Y	Y	Y	Y	N	N	Y
Benjamin Gilman (N.Y.)	Y	Y	N	N	Y	Y	Y
Lindsey O. Graham (S.C.)		Y		Y	N	N	Y
J. D. Hayworth (Ariz.)	Y	Y	Y	Y	N	N	Y
Duncan Hunter (Calif.)	Y	Y	N	N	Y	Y	N
John Kasich (Ohio)	Y	Y	Y	Y	N	N	Y
Ray LaHood (Ill.)	Y	Y	Y	Y	N	N	Y
Steve Largent (Okla.)	Y	Y	N	Y	N	N	Y
Bill McCollum (Fla.)	Y	Y	Y	Y	N	N	Y
Dana Rohrabacher (Calif.)	Y	Y	Y	Y	N	N	Y
Jim Saxton (N.J.)	Y	Y	Y	Y	N	N	Y
Joe Scarborough (Fla.)	Y	Y	Y	Y	N	N	Y
Jim Sensenbrenner (Wis.)	Y	Y	Y	Y	N	N	Y

TABLE 8 (continued)

HOUSE	7: Taiwan	8: Bosnia		9: Kosovo Diplomacy and War			
	Security Act H.R. 1838 2/1/00	no funds H.R. 2770 12/13/95	withdraw H.C.R. 227 3/18/98	Fowler amendment 3/11/99	Clinton H.C.R. 42 3/11/99	air ops tie S.C.R. 21 4/28/99	no troops H.R. 1569 4/28/99
Bud Shuster (Pa.)	Y	Y	Y				Y
Christopher H. Smith (N.J.)	Y	Y	N	N	Y	N	Y
Gerald H. B. Solomon (N.Y.)		Y	N				
Mark Edward Souder (Ind.)	Y	Y	Y	Y	N	N	Y
Floyd Spence (S.C.)	Y	Y	Y	Y	N	N	Y
J. C. Watts (Okla.)	Y	Y	Y	Y	N	N	Y
Curt Weldon (Pa.)	Y	Y	Y	Y	N	N	Y
C. W. Bill Young (Fla.)		Y	N	Y	N	N	?

TABLE 9

HOUSE	7: Taiwan Security Act H.R. 1838 2/1/00	8: Bosnia no funds H.R. 2770 12/13/95	withdraw H.C.R. 227 3/18/98	9: Kosovo Diplomacy and War			
				Fowler amendment 3/11/99	Clinton H.C.R. 42 3/11/99	air ops tie S.C.R.21 4/28/99	no troops H.R. 1569 4/28/99
Republican Internationalists							
John A. Boehner (Ohio)	N	N	N	N	N	N	N
Sonny Callahan (Ala.)	Y	N	N	P	P	Y	Y
David Dreier (Calif.)	Y	N	Y	N	Y	N	N
Newt Gingrich (Ga.)							
Porter J. Goss (Fla.)	Y	N	N	N	Y	N	Y
J. Dennis Hastert (Ill.)		Y	Y		Y	Y	Y
Henry J. Hyde (Ill.)	Y	Y	Y	N	Y	Y	Y
James A. Leach (Iowa)	Y	N	N	Y	N	N	Y
Jerry Lewis (Calif.)	N	N	N	N	Y	N	N
Bob Livingston (La.)		N	Y				
Connie Morella (Md.)	Y	N	N	N	Y	Y	N
Bill Paxon (N.Y.)		N	Y				
John Edward Porter (Ill.)	Y	Y	Y	N	Y	Y	N
Christopher Shays (Conn.)	Y	Y	Y	N	N	N	Y

TABLE 10

HOUSE	7: Taiwan Security Act H.R. 1838 2/1/00	8: Bosnia no funds H.R. 2770 12/13/95	withdraw H.C.R. 227 3/18/98	9: Kosovo Diplomacy and War			no troops H.R. 1569 4/28/99
				Fowler amendment 3/11/99	Clinton H.C.R. 42 3/11/99	air ops tie S.C.R.21 4/28/99	
Democratic Pragmatists							
Lee H. Hamilton (Ind.)		N	N				
William J. Jefferson (La.)	Y	N	N	N	Y	Y	N
Robert T. Matsui (Calif.)	N	N	N	N	Y	Y	N
Jim McDermott (Wash.)	N	N	N	N	Y	Y	Y
Paul McHale (Pa.)		N	N				
David R. Obey (Wis.)	N	N	N	N	P	Y	N
Matin Sabo (Minn.)	N	N	N	N	Y	Y	N
Charles E. Schumer (N.Y.)		N	N				
Ike Skelton (Mo.)	N	N	N	N	Y	Y	N
Charles W. Stenholm (Tex.)	Y	N	N	N	Y	Y	N
John S. Tanner (Tenn.)	Y	N	N	N	Y	Y	N

TABLE 10 (continued)

HOUSE	7: Taiwan	8: Bosnia		9: Kosovo Diplomacy and War				
	Security Act H.R. 1838 2/1/00	no funds H.R. 2770 12/13/95	withdraw H.C.R. 227 3/18/98	Fowler amendment 3/11/99	Clinton H.C.R. 42 3/11/99	air ops tie S.C.R.21 4/28/99	no troops H.R. 1569 4/28/99
Democratic Idealists							
Howard L. Berman (Calif.)	Y	N	N	N	Y	Y	N
David E. Bonior (Mich.)	Y	N	N	N	Y	Y	N
Benjamin L. Cardin (Md.)	Y	N	N	N	Y	Y	N
John Conyers (Mich.)	N	N	N	N	Y	Y	N
John D. Dingell (Mich.)	Y	N	N	N	Y	Y	N
Barney Frank (Mass.)	Y	N	Y	N	N	Y	Y
Sam Gejdenson (Conn.)	Y	N	N	N	Y	Y	N
Richard A. Gephardt (Mo.)	Y	N		N	Y	Y	N
Steny Hoyer (Md.)	Y	N		N	Y	Y	N
Jesse L. Jackson Jr. (Ill.)	N		N	N	Y	N	Y
Joseph P. Kennedy Jr. (Mass.)		N	N				
Patrick J. Kennedy (R.I.)	Y	N	N	N	Y	Y	N
Tom Lantos (Calif.)	N	N	N	N	Y	Y	N
Edward J. Markey (Mass.)	Y	N	Y	N	Y	Y	Y
Nancy Pelosi (Calif.)	Y	N	N	N	Y	Y	N
Charles. B. Rangel (N.Y.)	Y	N	N	N	Y	Y	N
Fourtney (Pete) Stark (Calif.)	N	N	N	N	Y	N	Y
Pete Visclosky (Ind.)	Y	N	N	N	N	N	Y
Henry A. Waxman (Calif.)	Y	N	N	N	Y	Y	N

5 Explaining Congressional-Executive Rivalry in International Affairs

The Changing Role of Parties, Committees, and the Issue Agenda

BRYAN W. MARSHALL

Bryan Marshall examines the relationship of the executive and legislative branches from the perspective of individual members of Congress, who for the most part make rational decisions about whether to delegate power to a president in areas that are least important in their efforts to win reelection. This explanation of congressional behavior, based on what Marshall terms a "collective action dilemma," differs strikingly from the more conventional arguments that explain the shifting pendulum between the White House and Congress in terms of the inherent institutional and constitutional advantages enjoyed by the president or in terms of structural, personnel, and ideological changes within the legislature itself. In Marshall's model, members of Congress are willing to delegate powers to the executive branch in areas that do not significantly affect their own constituencies and their chances for reelection. Given the changing foreign policy issue agenda, and especially the growing salience of economic issues that have immediate impact within a legislator's community, the threshold at which members of Congress will act to reclaim authority from the executive branch has been lowered.

Introduction

With the passage of the Iraq war resolution in October 2002, Congress delegated unheralded authority to President George W. Bush, the likes of which had not been seen since 1964 when President Lyndon Johnson was granted wide discretion in Vietnam.[1] The Iraq war resolution not only strengthens the president's hand by legitimizing a policy of preemptive action, but also seemingly undermines Congress's oversight role by conceding any constraints of review once conflict begins and establishes no expiration date for such executive powers.[2] Indeed, one notable scholar, James Lindsay, suggested as much regarding the war resolution, *"Congress voluntarily removed itself from the debate over Iraq and went up into the cheap seats with the reporters and the pundits."*[3] In addition, members of Congress seem willing to concede their most prized check on executive discretion—the power over the purse—in times of war. Regarding this, Senator Joseph Biden Jr. (D-Delaware) said, *"The truth of the matter is that the theoretical notion of the check and balance on the administration through the purse strings in war is ephemeral; it doesn't exist."*[4] And although Congress seemed to embrace the president's recent request to cover war costs on a 2003 supplemental appropriations bill, members were not able to collectively restrain their penchant for pork-barrel spending.[5]

In contrast, President Bush's domestic agenda has been treated quite differently. Despite the war-related boost to the president's high approval rating, Congress cut large chunks from his centerpiece $726 billion stimulus plan. This unceremonious blow to the president's prestige was largely the result of moderate members from his own party led by the Finance Committee chairman, Senator Charles Grassley (R-Iowa). Yet, this was not the only defeat to the president's domestic agenda, as he lost important votes on energy policy (ANWR) and on the nomination of Miguel A. Estrada to the U.S. Court of Appeals just one week earlier.[6] Some observers may have noticed a strong parallel to these policy battles with those of the incumbent president's father. In 1991, George Bush successfully secured a resolution authorizing the use of force to secure Iraq's withdrawal from Kuwait, paving the way for Desert Storm. Then, three months later Congress handed President Bush a stinging defeat on his 1992 budget plan.

Putting these déjà vu-like qualities aside, the contrasting outcomes across the domestic and international arena are part of a more complex phenomenon that has generated intense interest among those studying congressional-executive relations since Wildavsky's assertion of the two-presidencies.[7] There exist a number of explanations for differences in policy influence between the Congress and the president across policy realms. But the most important of these points to the fact that Congress faces an inherently more serious dilemma of collective action in foreign affairs. In this paper, I consider Congress's collective action dilemma as a theoretical lens to view the dynamics of congressional delegation and assertiveness with respect to the president in international affairs. In particular, the empirical analysis assesses the effects of political parties, the foreign policy committees, and the changing issue agenda on presidential success on House international affairs votes from 1953 to 2002.

I begin by highlighting some of the literature explaining presidential influence with Congress. Then, I sketch out how Congress's collective action dilemma in international affairs has been shaped by changes in institutional arrangements as well as the issue agenda to help explain variation in the dynamics of congressional assertiveness vis-à-vis the president over time. Finally, I assess the theoretical argument with data on presidential success in the House of Representatives from 1953 to 2002. The empirical analysis offers a couple of interesting insights. The models of presidential success demonstrate the important impact of congressional committees, parties, and changes to the international affairs agenda. These findings help us to better understand the conditions that affect Congress's willingness to delegate or assert itself in the international realm.

The Pendulum of Power: Presidency-Centered and Resurgent-Congress Explanations

The framers of the U.S. Constitution sought an executive branch with relatively modest powers in legislative affairs. George Washington seemed to fulfill this expectation rather well, sending just a handful of proposals to Congress. In fact, Washington was so compelled by the notion of separation of powers that he refused a House committee's request soliciting his advice.[8] But by design, the U.S. Constitution has invited presidents to compete with Congress over the right to make public policy.[9] Although the executive branch still bears important features envisioned by the founders, the legislative scope of the modern presidency is not one of them. Not only are modern presidents relatively successful at passing their policy priorities, but their proposals also make up a significant share of the congressional agenda.[10]

What causes the pendulum of power to vary back and forth between the Congress and the president? Indeed, explaining the conditions that foster variation in policy-making influence continues to be one of the most significant questions facing scholars studying congressional-executive relations. Spanning several decades, two dominant perspectives have evolved to explain how presidents shape public policy. Much of the early work was presidency-centered. This literature focused on the institutional and legal powers of the executive branch as well as the characteristics of presidential leadership.[11] For example, Wildavsky's two-presidencies argument represented one important addition rooted in this tradition. Applying the presidency-centered approach, scholars have found that presidential influence with Congress stems not only from inherent advantages of the executive branch but also individual skills and discretionary actions.[12]

In contrast, the resurgent-Congress approach focuses more on the legislative environment in explaining patterns of presidential influence. Electoral and institutional changes in Congress had a considerable impact on the policy process that reshaped the landscape for inter-branch conflicts. The focus of this work pointed toward the importance of congressional institutions and especially changes in the ideological makeup of its membership for explaining variation in presidential success.[13]

Both of these perspectives continue to generate valuable insights for understanding congressional-executive relations. Indeed, one such area has been in assessing Wildavsky's two-presidencies argument. According to Wildavsky's thesis, the two-presidencies characterized an important duality of inter-institutional behavior. Presidents dominated in foreign policy, while on domestic issues Congress played a more substantial role. Wildavsky's two-presidencies argument provided a useful framework for understanding the duality of congressional-executive behavior for at least two decades following World War II. His classic study showed the success rate of presidents in foreign and defense policy was nearly twice as high as compared to domestic policy. Moreover, he asserted that when presidents were entirely committed, they had not lost a single foreign policy battle with Congress for the period covered in his study, 1948–1964.[14]

Wildavsky contended that presidential advantage was derived from institutional and informational advantages of the executive as well as widespread public consensus on foreign policy that reflected the Cold War threat. The interconnectedness of foreign policy necessitated that presidents actively engage in all facets of international affairs. Unlike domestic policy, a single foreign policy failure could lead to an array of catastrophic disasters.[15] Wildavsky also suggested that policy preferences were more varied in the domestic arena and therefore more likely to lead to conflict. Moreover, he argued that presidents were successful due to the weakness of other rivals. This seemed an especially accurate description for Congress because of its more narrow focus that revolved around the reelection imperative.

A number of recent analyses find little support for the argument that president's enjoy disproportionate influence over foreign as compared to domestic issues.[16] Accordingly, this appears to suggest the demise of the two-presidencies as a useful model for explaining presidential influence. However, other work has claimed important differences across policy areas still exist.[17] The contrasting findings in the literature attest to the difficulties that persist in answering the two-presidencies question.

Although few would declare Congress's complete irrelevance, congressional weakness appears to be the conventional wisdom for many.[18] In addition, congressional attention to foreign affairs has been criticized for its fleeting duration and for being driven by its newsworthiness.[19] Members of Congress have also recognized their own collective shortcomings, but seem to have little incentive to change. Senator J. William Fulbright concluded that *"With their excessively parochial orientation [members of Congress] are acutely sensitive to the influence of private pressure and to the excesses and inadequacies of a public opinion that is all too often ignorant of the needs, the dangers and the opportunities in our foreign relations."*[20] Historically, even for some of the most powerful statesmen like Senators Fulbright (Arkansas), Church (Idaho), and Percy (Illinois), the tradeoff for pursuing foreign policy over other goals eventually led, at least in part, to their reelection defeat.[21]

To be sure, constitutional, institutional, and political differences persuasively make the case for presidential strength and congressional weakness in foreign policy. But to what extent does this conventional wisdom explain interbranch relations? Does the stylized fact that Congress shirks its foreign policy duties hold up over time and under what conditions? One major problem with assessing the congressional weakness argument is observational equivalency preventing a real distinction between competing hypotheses. For example, if we observe a lack of congressional assertiveness, one might attribute this to Congress's lack of institutional power. However, a lack of congressional assertiveness could also be due to the fact that Congress shares a common set of policy preferences with the president. The former supports the conventional wisdom. The latter suggests Congress does not lack the institutional power to challenge the president, but just the collective incentive to do so. This represents the fundamental distinction for understanding the conditions shaping variation in the balance of power between Congress and the president in foreign affairs.

Thus, I would contend that the conventional wisdom largely misses the true dynamics between Congress and the president in foreign policy.

Certainly, Congress has been able to effectively flex its collective powers across the spectrum of foreign affairs, including war, intelligence, trade, defense, and international aid when it wants to.[22] The answer lies less with the notion of Congress's institutional or constitutional weakness as conventional wisdom suggests. Rather, I argue that Congress rationally chooses to assert itself at times and delegates at other times in the realm of international affairs. To understand this, we need to consider the collective action hurdle Congress faces and how its incentives differ across foreign and domestic policy.

Congress's Collective Action Dilemma: Delegating Authority in International Affairs

Members of Congress have multiple goals.[23] Still, the goal of reelection tends to overshadow the rest. For this reason, Congress seeks to take as much credit for policy making as possible from its constituency in order to achieve reelection.[24] Likewise, members of Congress attempt to avoid the blame associated with the costs of policy making levied against their supportive constituents. Cooperation (or at least tacit consent) between the Congress and the president is a central component, if not a necessary condition, for such lawmaking. Congress delegates much of its policy-making authority internally, collectively organizing itself around the committee system and political parties.[25] In addition, Congress delegates legislative authority externally to the president. As long as the benefits of these institutional arrangements outweigh the costs for the membership, there exists no incentive for Congress to change the status quo system of delegation. In this situation, congressional behavior may be characterized by a seeming lack of legislative attentiveness. Yet, what appears to be weakness is really Congress's rational preference for delegation.

For any principal, the delegation of authority necessarily involves risk. The collective dilemma arises when Congress's institutional agents like its committees, parties, or the president pursue alternative policy goals that make the costs of delegation outweigh the benefits. When this occurs, Congress asserts itself by changing its institutional arrangements and/or challenging the powers delegated to the president. Thus, Congress never totally relinquishes its legislative role to the president or internally to committees or parties. Instead, it just finds a more efficient solution to delegate legislative authority.

Even in the president's strongest sphere—that of war powers—Congress has found a mechanism to balance the risk of delegation in its favor. Despite the grand symbolism associated with the passage of the 1973 War Powers resolution, there remains a relative consensus that its effects on presidential behavior are a far cry from congressional intentions.[26] Interpreted in another way though, the War Powers resolution is consistent with the collective dilemma of delegation. The resolution allows Congress to assert itself in policy making when presidential delegation becomes too costly (or at least to avoid blame) and to claim credit (along with the president) when such delegation is beneficial. Prober makes a similar argument, *"Congress can use the War Resolution to force the president to end an unpopular military operation, or it can criticize presidential failure to comply with the procedural requirements of the resolution when public opinion is supportive or divided. Either way, Congress cannot lose."*[27]

Another important consideration is how issue differences affect Congress's cost/benefit calculation in delegating legislative authority to the president. First and foremost, Congress claims greater and more immediate reelection benefits from domestic policy as compared to foreign policy. That is, members of Congress are primarily motivated to address constituency-level concerns, which tend to be far removed from international politics. Secondly, the cost of congressional oversight in foreign policy is greater than in the realm of domestic policy. In addition, there is a fundamental strategic distinction for exercising legislative authority across issue areas. The greater density of codification and bureaucratic regulation in domestic policy naturally restricts the president's ability to use his delegated powers independently of congressional discretion. The relative lack of such existing biases in foreign policy provides the president with greater latitude to exercise authority.[28] Together, these issue distinctions help to explain why at times the practical management of international affairs has largely fallen to the president, but much less so with domestic policy.

Certainly, one might point out that Wildavsky's argument rang truer during the time of his study than it does today.[29] Yet, even during the height of the Cold War when Wildavsky's thesis seemed the most compelling, his explanation missed the relevance of institutional relationships within the Congress and the structure of member incentives that held those institutions in place. Binder has argued that institutional arrangements not only alter behaviors between Congress and the president, but also affect both the character and frequency of public policies.[30] Indeed, changes in political parties (within and external to Congress), the committee system, and the issue agenda were important, and remain so, in explaining the president's success in foreign affairs. We can now turn to considering how changes in each shaped conditions relevant to Congress's collective action dilemma in foreign affairs and thus get closer to understanding when Congress chooses delegation or assertiveness with respect to the president.

Congressional Reform and Assertiveness: Committees, Parties, and the Issue Agenda

Wildavsky's thesis of the two-presidencies was inspired during a period when Congress had delegated most of its internal legislative authority to committees. Before the 1970s legislative reforms, congressional chairman controlled nearly all policy-making discretion. The seniority system provided committee chairs with property rights over their committees and the policy jurisdictions they oversaw. The seniority system skewed this disparity of power in favor of southern members because of the monopoly hold the Democratic party had in the South.[31] The constituencies of southern members were very supportive of the president's aggressive policy stance designed for the containment of communism. Not only were the president's foreign policy initiatives insulated from congressional challenge because the chairman shared similar policy preferences with the president, but also because those members who might oppose the president's policy preferences (e.g., liberal members) were not in positions of power to mount challenges. So, during this era congressional-executive conflicts were fairly rare in international affairs.

In the context of the pre-reform Congress, the committees primarily responsible for handling foreign and defense policy—House International Relations and the Armed Services Committees—benefited greatly by pursuing the president's initiatives. For Armed Services, the committee's policy jurisdiction over defense spending provided an effective means to win favor with their supporters back home.[32] In contrast, members on House International Relations were less concerned with targeted parochial concerns and instead benefited by having a hand in shaping national foreign policy. Both committees tended to support the president's initiatives and the continued delegation of foreign affairs, albeit for different reasons.[33]

The electoral context members faced also favored delegation of international affairs to the president. On the electoral side there existed little incentive among members of either party to challenge the president in the international arena. A large proportion of member districts were composed of conservative southern Democrats and Republican voters who benefited from the growing military industrial complex and tended to side with the president's escalation of conflict in Vietnam. However, the number of liberal members in Congress was clearly growing in the 1950s and 1960s. The liberals represented primarily northern Democratic voters who were becoming increasingly dissatisfied with support for defense spending, Vietnam, and also on important domestic issues like civil rights. This cleavage in the electorate was reflected in Congress and spurred the movement for institutional reform so that Democratic members could better represent their liberal-oriented districts.

With the institutional reforms of the 1970s, the delegation of legislative authority within Congress was effectively redistributed.[34] Leaving policy-making power in the hands of southern conservative chairmen had become far too costly for the growing number of elected liberal rank-and-file Democrats. Not surprisingly, the conservative chairman became the primary targets of reform. In effect, the majority party sought a more beneficial institutional arrangement for delegating legislative authority, one that enhanced the influence of the liberal rank-and-file. One mechanism the Democratic caucus used to achieve this end was to establish a process that provided for the direct vote on committee chairs.[35] This meant the caucus was better equipped to make chairpersons conform to the collective interests of the party.[36] The procedure was not an empty threat. Several subcommittee and committee chairs were removed from their positions in the 1970s and 1980s. In addition, Armed Services chairman Les Aspin (D-Wisconsin) was threatened with removal when he acted against the Democratic caucus by supporting President Reagan's policies on the M-X missile and aid to Contras.[37]

The party caucus also provided its leadership with seats on the committee-on-committees. This committee gained considerable influence in filling the party's slots on the rest of the committees. Leadership representation on this panel further compelled the party's committee contingents and chairs to be responsive to the collective interests of the majority party. In general, then, the reforms allowed Congress to alter its institutional arrangements for delegation by reducing the authority of committee leaders and increasing the committee system's responsiveness to the collective interests of the majority party. This upheaval in the internal delegation of policy authority also greatly affected the president's ability to dominate foreign affairs. The reforms largely erased the presidential advantage due to shared policy preferences with the powerful committee chairmen. Presidents could now be more easily challenged by the rank-and-file in Congress who were becoming increasingly divided over the direction of international affairs policy.

Changes to the issue agenda represent the last factor in this discussion affecting Congress's collective action dilemma in delegating authority to the president. There have been considerable changes in the type and distribution of issues within the international affairs agenda over time.[38] Some scholars have argued that the rise of congressional assertiveness in foreign policy has been the result of increased congressional interest in economic and trade issues.[39] Members of Congress have found that economic and trade policies have become increasingly relevant to local constituency interests. Not only are these intermestic issues becoming increasingly integrated with domestic concerns, but also the proportion of these issues relative to other issues on the international affairs agenda has grown. With such interests at stake, the cost to the president of congressional delegation has risen, making it less likely for Congress to remain on the sidelines. Thus, congressional assertiveness on this subset of issues has increased.

This argument has sketched out how changes in Congress's institutional arrangements and the issue agenda affect its willingness to delegate authority to the executive in international affairs policy. In sum, I have argued that the institutional reforms altered how policy-making authority was delegated in the House. The House was transformed from a committee-dominated body to one largely dominated and responsive to the political parties. Although I cannot test the underlying theory about Congress's collective dilemma in delegating authority to the president, I can test the arguments indirectly by assessing how these institutional arrangements, as well as changes in the issue agenda, affect congressional assertiveness and thus presidential success over time.

The discussion leads to a couple of expectations for presidential success in the realm of international affairs. The first revolves around the importance of congressional committees. Not only should the support of the most jurisdictionally relevant committees be important to presidential success, but as these committees became more responsive to their respective political parties, we should observe greater partisanship on the committees, and the party conflict should be important for explaining presidential success over time. Secondly, I have argued that congressional delegation of policy-making authority is a rational solution to the collective action dilemma when Congress and the president have similar policy preferences. So, the ideological difference between the House members and the president should be a significant factor in explaining success. More specifically, as the preferences of Congress and the president become more dissimilar, one would expect greater congressional assertiveness and thus less presidential success. Finally, changes to the international affairs agenda also have given members of Congress reason to challenge the president. The growing electoral incentives associated with the increasing proportion of economic and trade issues on the agenda should increase congressional assertiveness and therefore decrease presidential success in this area.

Empirical Analysis: Presidential Success in the House of Representatives, 1953–2002

The data include all floor roll-call votes on the international affairs agenda in which the president took a position between the 83rd (1953–1954) and the 107th (2001–2002) Congress for the House of Representatives. This provides a total of 1,250 votes over the period. The international affairs agenda comprises all votes related to foreign and defense policy issues.[40] The dependent variable in this analysis is presidential success. Presidential success is a dichotomous variable, coded a 1 when the president's position on a House roll-call vote wins and 0 when the president's position fails.

The over time variation in the dependent variable is illustrated in Figure 1. The figure plots the percentage of times the president's position on the House floor vote wins from the 83rd to the 107th Congress. Figure 1 provides a comparison between presidential success on international affairs votes and on the domestic policy agenda. There are a couple interesting patterns in the data. With only a few exceptions, presidential success on international affairs was higher than on domestic policy until the 92d Congress (1971–1972). After the 92d Congress there is a substantial decline in both policy areas. Although presidential success in international affairs tends to remain higher than on domestic policy, the differences between the two have been generally dwindling over time. This trend seems to parallel other findings that suggest the demise of the two-presidencies.[41]

In Figure 2 the data allow us to consider the greater role of political parties and the increasing frequency of partisanship on these same presidential position votes. The figure graphs the percentage of party-unity votes on international affairs and domestic policy for the same time period. A party-unity vote occurs when the majority of both parties vote in opposition to one another. The patterns in Figure 2 emphasize the increasing frequency of partisan disagreement (as measured by party-unity) for presidential position votes in both issue areas over time. For example, party-unity occurred on just over 21 percent of international affairs votes during the 86th Congress (1959–1960) and increased to its highest level of nearly 76 percent by the 104th Congress. On domestic policy, the analogous percentages were 29 percent during the 91st and increasing to over 82 percent by the 107th Congress. In addition, the percentage of party-unity on international affairs votes remained lower as compared to domestic policy until after the 92d Congress. There is an important parallel between the party-unity and the presidential success series. The differences in presidential success between foreign and domestic policies diminished considerably at the same time that there was an analogous change in the patterns of party voting. This tends to support the argument that after the Democratic reforms,

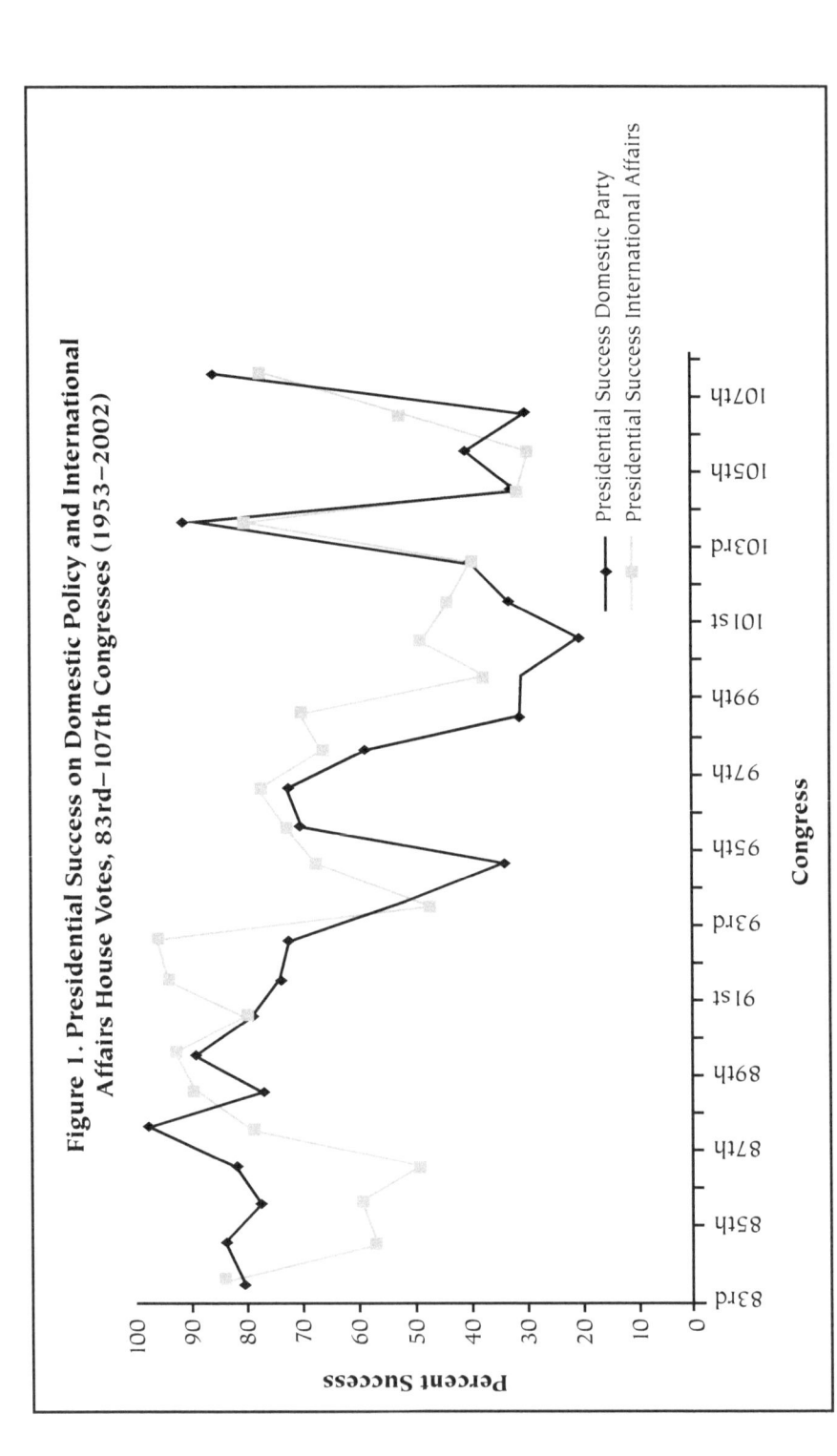

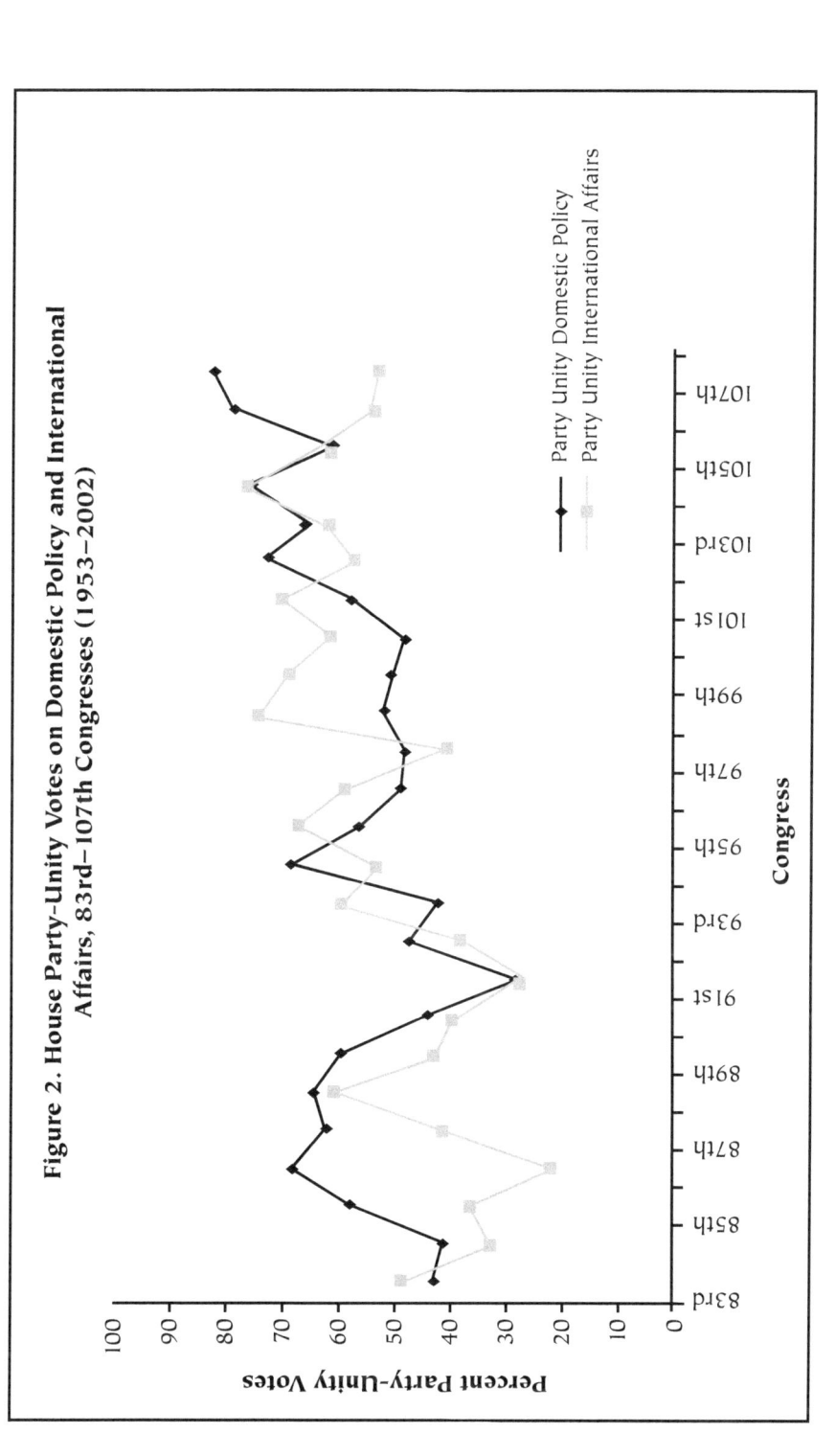

the party rank-and-file members were increasingly able to challenge the president, especially in international affairs. Committee chairs who shared similar preferences over international affairs policy with the president were far less able to protect executive priorities on the floor.

The next two figures illustrate the increasing levels of partisan disagreement on the House Armed Services and International Relations Committees. Figures 3 and 4 plot the percentage of party-unity floor votes on the international affairs agenda for both House committees. The figures also provide the percentage of party-unity on the same votes for the rest of the House to use as a baseline comparison. The patterns in Figure 3 reflect the generally low level of party-unity votes for members of House Armed Services as compared to the rest of the floor. In fact, the percentage of party-unity votes is less than the level found for the House floor for every Congress except the Eighty-sixth. The patterns in Figure 4 also suggest that the level of party-unity votes for the House International Relations Committee tends to be less than the rest of the floor for most of the congresses. Still, the differences in party unity between the International Relations Committee and the floor are much smaller as compared to the differences between Armed Services and the floor. In addition, a comparison in the levels of party unity between Armed Services and the House International Relations Committee suggests that the effects of partisanship on the former were muted for a long period of time. This was less true for the House International Relations Committee. For example, during the 91st Congress, party unity on Armed Services dipped to a mere 5.6 percent but increased to a high of over 61 percent by the 104th Congress. For the analogous period, partisan conflict on House International Relations went from 17 percent to over 74 percent by the 104th Congress.

One important trend found in the previous figures (Figures 1 and 2) was the relationship between partisan disagreement and presidential success. That is, as partisanship in the House increased, there was a general decline in levels of presidential success over time. Similar trends can be observed when gauging floor coalitions among House Armed Services and International Relations Committee members in support of and/or in opposition to the president's position. For example, the results in Table 1 reflect the frequency of two coalition types defining when the two House committees win on international affairs floor votes. The second and fourth columns for House International Relations and Armed Services report the percentage of times a committee majority supports the president's position on the floor and the position wins. In this condition, a committee majority and the president vote together and win. The third and fifth columns

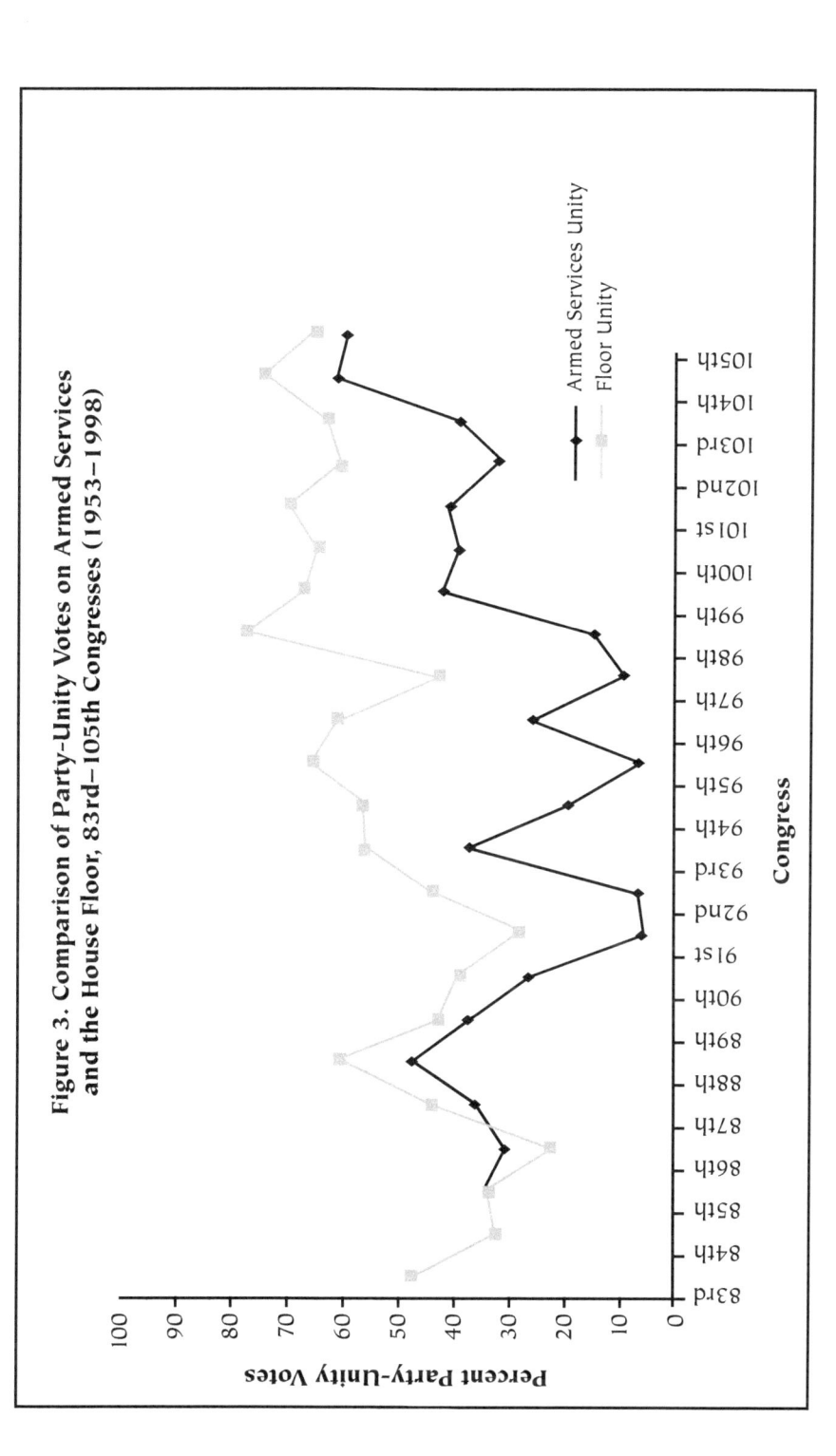

Figure 3. Comparison of Party-Unity Votes on Armed Services and the House Floor, 83rd–105th Congresses (1953–1998)

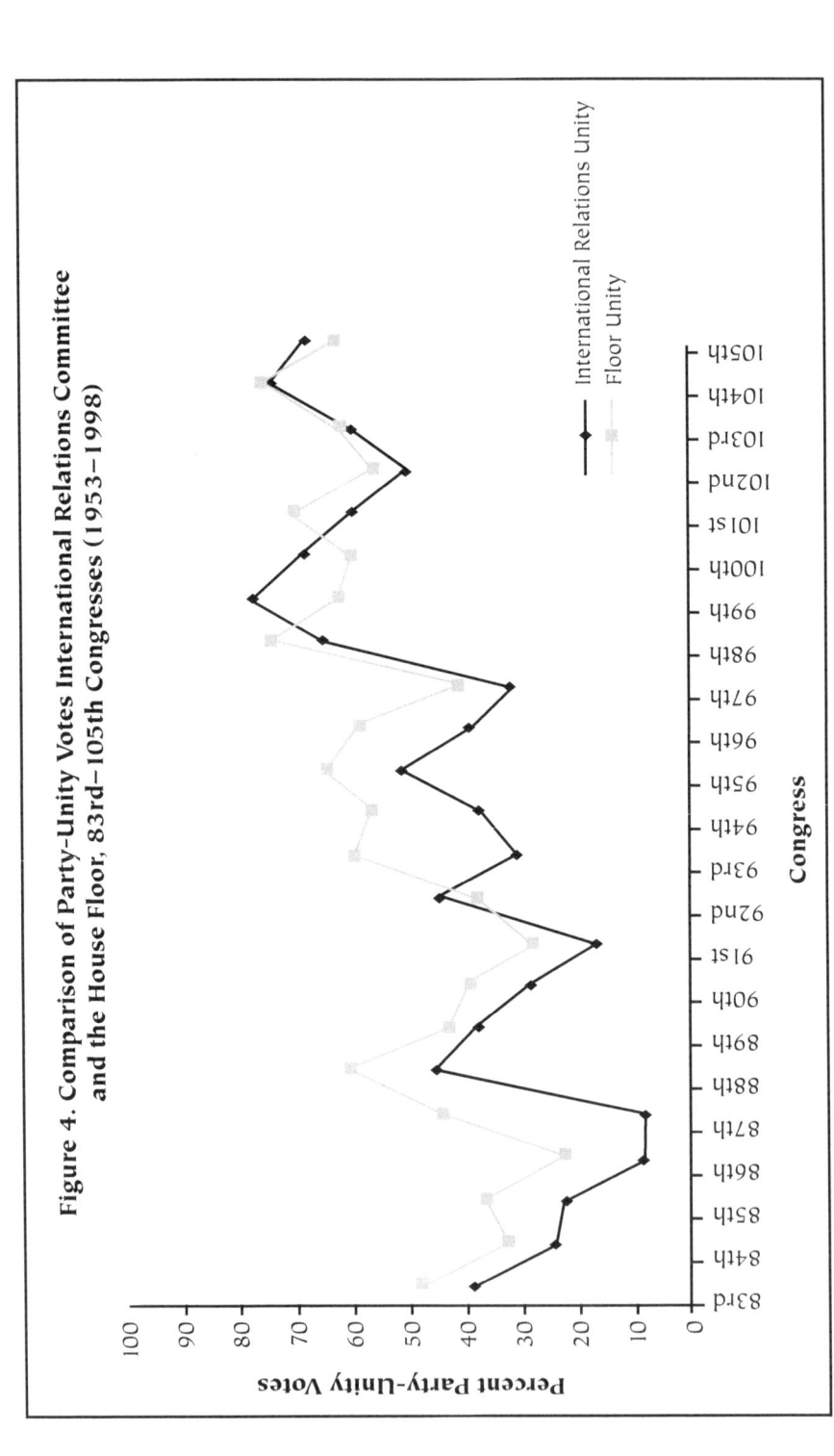

report the percentage of times a committee majority opposes the president's position and the committee wins; or in other words, when the committee wins and the president loses.

The results in columns 2 and 4 from Table 1[42] indicates a large decline for both House committees in the proportion of times the committee majority and the president voted together and won on the floor starting with the Ninety-third Congress. In fact, the proportion of times a majority of International Relations members supported the president's position on a roll-call vote and won dropped nearly in half from 81.3 percent for the Ninety-second to only 42.4 percent for the Ninety-third. The drop was even

TABLE 1: COMMITTEE SUCCESS WITH THE PRESIDENT ON HOUSE INTERNATIONAL AFFAIRS FLOOR VOTES, 83RD–105TH CONGRESSES

Congress	House International Relations Committee		House Armed Services Committee		Presidential Administration
	Supports President and Wins (%)	Opposes President and Wins (%)	Supports President and Wins (%)	Opposes President and Wins (%)	
83rd (1953–54)	76.2	19	71.4	19	Eisenhower I
84th (1955–56)	76	12	72	16	
85th (1957–58)	77.8	13.9	66.7	19.4	Eisenhower II
86th (1959–60)	82.6	13	82.6	13	
87th (1961–62)	97.4	0	92.3	2.6	Kennedy/Johnson
88th (1963–64)	77.5	5	67.5	22.5	
89th (1965–66)	90	5	75	10	
90th (1967–68)	80.4	4.3	69.6	19.6	
91st (1969–70)	88.9	0	66.7	5.6	Nixon/Ford
92nd (1971–72)	81.3	0	87.5	3.1	
93rd (1973–74)	42.4	47.5	33.9	22	
94th (1975–76)	59.4	15.6	50	21.9	
95th (1977–78)	68.6	17.1	27.1	24.3	Carter
96th (1979–80)	74.8	10.4	34.8	20.9	
97th (1981–82)	53.7	27.8	66.7	14.8	Reagan I
98th (1983–84)	44.7	27.6	60.5	5.3	
99th (1985–86)	25.3	59.5	36.7	30.4	Reagan II
100th (1987–88)	36.8	47.1	48.3	28.7	
101st (1989–90)	29	55.1	43.5	34.8	Bush
102nd (1991–92)	31.6	53.9	40.8	48.7	
103rd (1993–94)	66.7	14.8	75.9	16.7	Clinton I
104th (1995–96)	29	58.1	21	62.9	
105th (1997–98)	27	62.2	21.6	67.6	Clinton II
Column Total (N = 1190)	56.1% (n = 667)	29.2% (n = 348)	51.4% (n = 612)	25.1% (n = 299)	

greater for Armed Services, going from over 87 percent for the Ninety-second Congress to only 33.9 percent for the Ninety-third. Similarly, the third and fifth columns for the respective House committees show a significant increase in each committee's propensity to oppose the president's position and win on the floor starting with that same Congress (the Ninety-third). These dramatic changes in the patterns of conflict between committees and the president's position highlight the significance of the reform-era change that reduced the level of control enjoyed by committee chairs, thus allowing greater opposition within the committee and from the party rank-and-file to challenge presidential preferences on the floor.

The final component of the analysis incorporates a multivariate logit model to explain variation in presidential success between the 83rd and 105th Congresses. The dependent variable, presidential success on House international affairs votes, is the same as in the earlier part of the analysis. The logit models are designed to test the impact of institutional arrangements, ideological differences between the president and Congress, and the issue agenda on congressional willingness to delegate authority to the president as measured by success.

As measured previously, the models control for party unity and committee opposition to the president's position for the House Armed Services and the International Relations Committee. The logit model includes a dummy indicator to determine whether economic and trade votes are significantly different with respect to presidential success in international affairs. The analysis also includes a variable capturing the ideological difference between the two institutions. This is measured by the absolute difference between the president's yearly ADA score and the House median score. The argument suggests that larger ideological differences should decrease congressional willingness to delegate authority to the executive and should therefore lead to less presidential success.

In addition, the analysis includes control variables that have been used in previous work explaining presidential success.[43] For example, the model includes two dummy indicators, one for divided government and another for the period of Cold War consensus (1953–1973). The expectations here are that there should be greater presidential success during the height of the Cold War and there should be significantly less presidential success under divided government. Finally, the analysis includes a variable measuring the Gallop monthly approval rating of the president one month prior to when the vote was taken. The approval measure allows one to assess the extent that a president's public prestige can assist him in marshaling winning coalitions in Congress.[44]

TABLE 2: EXPLAINING PRESIDENTIAL SUCCESS ON HOUSE INTERNATIONAL AFFAIRS VOTES, 1953-1998

Independent Variables	MODEL 1		MODEL 2	
	β /s.e.	ΔPr	β /s.e.	ΔPr
Presidential Approval	.001	0	.007	.02
	(.006)		(.009)	
Divided Government	-1.028***	-.21	-.872***	-.13
	(.172)		(.245)	
Cold War Threat (1953-73)	.833***	.18	-.136	.02
	(.195)		(.262)	
Economic & Trade Issues	-.664***	-.16	-.686**	-.13
	(.196)		(.305)	
Ideological Difference House	-.014***	-.05	-.015*	-.04
Median & President (ADA)	(.005)		(.008)	
Party Unity Armed Services	-1.093***	-.25	-.722***	-.13
	(.147)		(.203)	
Party Unity International Relations	-.536***	-.11	-.238	-.04
	(.146)		(.219)	
Armed Services Majority	——		-3.567***	-.64
Opposition			(.308)	
International Relations Majority	——		-4.027***	-.71
Opposition			(.317)	
Constant	2.291***		5.399***	
	(.364)		(.611)	
	N = 1180		N = 1180	
	χ^2 = 202 (p < .000)		χ^2 = 220 (p < .000)	

*Indicates statistical significance at (p < .10), ** at (p < .05), and ***at (p < .01). Standard errors in parentheses are robust.

The results of two logit models explaining presidential success on House international affairs votes from 1953 to 1998 are provided in Table 2. The first model (Model 1) offers a number of interesting results that are consistent with expectations. For example, when the respective party membership on House Armed Services and the International Relations Committees opposed each other on a floor vote, the likelihood of presidential success decreased significantly. In fact, the values on the right-hand side under Model 1 show that when a party-unity vote occurs the probability of presidential success drops by .25 and by .11 for Armed Services and International Relations, respectively. The results in Model 1 also indicate that the ideological difference (as measured by ADA scores) between the president and Congress significantly decrease the probability of presidential success by .05 (or 5 percent). Even more, the model shows that the effects of economic and trade issues are significantly different from other issues on the international affairs agenda. Consistent with the discussion, an economic and trade vote significantly reduced the probability the president's position would win by .16.

In addition, the effects of some of the control variables were found to be important in explaining presidential success. The effects of divided government were significant and decrease the probability of success in international affairs by .21. Also, Model 1 indicates that during the height of the Cold War threat (1953–1973), presidents succeeded significantly more on international affairs votes than afterward. In contrast, the level of presidential approval was found to have no important effects on the likelihood of presidential success on foreign affairs votes.

The results of Model 2 (from Table 2) include two additional variables that capture when majorities of the House Armed Services or International Relations Committees respectively vote in opposition to the president's position. The results of the second model are mostly similar to the first, but there are a couple noteworthy findings. For example, the effects of Armed Services opposition and the effects of International Relations opposition significantly reduce the likelihood of presidential success on international affairs votes.[45] In addition, the Cold War variable no longer achieves statistical significance in explaining presidential success. Although far from conclusive, the null effects of the Cold War in the second model may hint that Congress's institutional arrangements (e.g., committees) were an important reason, maybe even more important than the foreign policy consensus characterizing this period that Wildavsky and others had emphasized.[46]

Conclusion

In the wake of the 1970s congressional reforms, there were significant changes in the role of committees and of political parties in Congress. Certainly, the empirical results suggest that the president's ability to successfully pass international affairs legislation in the U.S. House became a significantly different and more difficult proposition over time. The theory articulated here suggests that this can be explained at least in part by Congress's collective action dilemma when it chooses to delegate legislative authority through institutions and/or to the president. The reformers' attack against the power of chairpersons signaled that the old form of congressional delegation had become too costly for a sizable number of members.

Moreover, the loss of agenda control began a long and sustained demise in the president's ability to successfully get his policy priorities adopted on the floor. The analysis demonstrates the rise in partisan conflict on the heels of the Democratic reforms of the 1970s. At the same time as the significant rise in partisan conflict, there was a sizable decrease in the level of presidential success. In addition, the analysis suggests the important impact the reforms had in structuring committee behavior on the floor of the House. Conflict between Armed Services and International Relations majorities rarely occurred on presidential position votes prior to the Ninety-second Congress. But, after the reforms removed the advantages shared by committee chairs and the president, congressional conflict began to characterize presidential initiatives in foreign affairs. In effect, the reforms represented a stark change in the way the House chose to delegate its legislative authority.

The logit analysis was designed indirectly to assess the argument regarding how institutional arrangements and changes in the foreign policy issue agenda affect Congress's choice to delegate or assert legislative authority in the realm of international affairs. According to the theory, each of these features conditions Congress's collective action dilemma in delegating authority to the president. The logit models do offer a systematic test regarding the importance of party conflict, committees, and agenda change on presidential success. The results demonstrate the relatively large and significant effects of partisan and committee opposition as well as the impact of ideological differences on presidential success. Moreover, the analysis shows that Congress seems more willing to challenge the president on economic and trade issues. The probability of presidential success on this subset of issues was substantially smaller as compared to other issues on the international affairs agenda. Indeed, the issue-specific differences found here parallel the findings and assertions advanced by Ralph Carter's analysis in this volume. Consistent with the theory and expectations then, each of these factors seems important for understanding congressional delegation at times and its choice of assertiveness at others.

Scholars have recently concluded that the two-presidencies model no longer offers leverage for understanding congressional-executive relations.[47] The evidence presented here shows that the gap in presidential success across domestic and foreign affairs has decayed significantly in the House from 1953 to 2002. Although the two-presidencies remains an important question, the focus of this analysis has not been on explaining the gap or its disappearance, but rather on explaining changes in the president's success on international affairs votes. The argument here suggests the more important question is to better understand the conditions in which Congress chooses delegation to the president over asserting its own legislative authority in foreign affairs. There is a persuasive argument for presidential strength and congressional weakness as emphasized by Wildavsky and many others, who in one way or another embrace conventional wisdom. But, this perspective is only half of the story for understanding congressional-executive interactions. Understanding presidential success in the realm of international affairs is less about Congress's institutional weakness. Rather, the answer lies more about understanding the conditions that shape Congress's collective action dilemma in delegation and its incentives to challenge the president in the international arena.

6 Which Dancer Leads?

Foreign Trade Policy Making and Divided Government

RALPH G. CARTER

Ralph Carter notes the growing importance of congressional action affecting foreign trade, especially under conditions of divided government when different parties control the White House and one or both houses of Congress. Two patterns emerge. First, across all cases, as the degree of divided government increases, the percentage of congressional wins increases, as do the number of joint wins. Gridlock tends to develop if one house—especially the House of Representatives—is in opposition hands. But if both houses are in opposition hands, gridlock is less common and joint wins decrease, probably because Congress feels itself to be in a stronger position. Second, when only disputed cases are considered, under divided government when both houses are in opposition, Congress wins 38 percent of the time, the president 35 percent. Joint wins are least likely (26 percent, as opposed to 39 percent for unified government and 42 percent when the opposition controls only one house). The logic is that if consultation does not lead to early policy agreement, both sides dig in their heels and resist compromise.

Introduction

Like the art of dance, the legislative process involves choreography.[1] Due to the multiplicity of partners, the choreography may be stark or subtle, simple or intricate, cooperative or confrontational, or fast or slow. However, it is difficult to excel if all partners seek to lead the dance, and the phenomenon of divided government complicates matters for the dancers. If different political parties control the presidency and at least one chamber of Congress, there can easily be a struggle for leadership of the legislative process. Given the prevalence of divided government in recent years, this pattern of contested leadership could have significant impacts on U.S. policy making, both in terms of domestic and foreign policy.

The making of foreign trade policy provides an interesting illustration of the impact of divided government. Foreign trade is a classic case of intermestic policy.[2] To some observers, it is just another type of foreign policy and, as such, features a stronger role for the president than for Congress. To others, foreign trade policy making has more in common with domestic policy, thereby favoring Congress in the potential leadership role. This study examines the impact that divided government has on the executive-congressional relationship in foreign trade policy making. What impact does divided government have on the vital question of who wins?

Foreign Trade Policy Making and Divided Government

The Madisonian model of checks and balances makes passing important legislation difficult under any circumstances.[3] Whether institutional or idiosyncratic, there are multiple and different obstacles that must be overcome for legislation to go from introduction to enactment as a public law.[4] When the opposition political party to the president controls at least one chamber of Congress, considerations based on partisanship can add another potential check on the policy-making process. Such circumstances can lead to legislative gridlock.[5]

Beyond gridlock, divided government can produce other detrimental effects. The addition of partisan conflicts to the normal institutional ones may require additional time and effort in order to negotiate a policy position mutually acceptable to both the White House and Capitol Hill. The result can be a policy process marked by a slower pace and the possibility of diluted or lowest-common denominator outputs.[6] At the very least, it becomes easier to oppose important legislation in the context of divided government.[7] Domestically, some see negative impacts of divided government on important areas like environmental policy,[8] taxation policy,[9] and the deficit spending.[10]

Nevertheless, concerns about divided government may be overblown. Divided government is only one factor in the broader executive-legislative relationship; also important are presidential leadership skills, public opinion and other public inputs, and the ideological composition of the Congress at that time.[11] As Leroy Rieselbach notes, "Partisanship (embodied in divided or unified government), the responsiveness of government to electoral considerations, the character of congressional organization, and the quality and commitment of presidential leadership conspire in distinctive ways to create a policy process prone to delay and deadlock."[12] Thus, delay and deadlock are not solely the product of divided government.[13]

Several studies have shown that divided government does not seem to detract from legislative productivity.[14] Voters do not seem particularly troubled by divided government, as they keep voting for presidents and legislators of different parties. While who controls a congressional chamber is very important to the legislators who comprise it, it may be less important in the context of dealing with the administration. After all, a wide variety of legislation must be passed every year, regardless of divided or unified government.[15]

Each year, some of that legislation involves foreign trade. When considering the process by which foreign trade policy is made, two crucial questions arise in the literature. Does Congress actually play a meaningful role in foreign trade policy making, or is this arena the preserve of the president and administration? If Congress does play a meaningful role, to what types of factors does Congress respond in making its foreign trade decisions? The literature offers a mixed picture regarding these two questions.

The Congressional Role in Foreign Trade Policy Making

An important role for Congress in foreign trade policy making seems guaranteed by the Constitution, as Article 1, Section 8 grants Congress the sole power "To regulate Commerce with foreign Nations." The congressional role in setting tariffs and promoting exports was strong in the period from the end of the Civil War until the 1930s.[16] However, the congressional role in foreign trade policy making changed with the disastrous 1930 Smoot-Hawley tariff bill. By ratcheting tariffs up sharply, this congressional response to the Great Depression actually made the global depression worse.[17] Realizing its members could not resist the demands of organized interests demanding protection, Congress responded in 1934 by delegating the setting of country-specific tariff levels to the executive branch with the Reciprocal Trade Agreements Act.[18] According to the foreign policy literature's conventional wisdom, with this delegation of power Congress's meaningful role in foreign trade policy making largely ended. This viewpoint argues that Congress now delegates trade policy making to the executive branch, with the congressional role being reduced to a largely symbolic one.[19]

This viewpoint illustrates the metaphor of a carefully choreographed dance. It begins with organized interests harmed by others' trade practices appealing to Congress for help. Members of Congress then react with howls of outrage directed at countries accused of unfair trading practices or those that resist the "leveling" of playing fields. Pressed on by constituents who fear economic harm, members of Congress hold hearings, bash the foreign villains, and promise dire vengeance. They do this knowing that the president will use their outrage to negotiate concessions from the offending state, with the final result being a further step toward a global free trade regime. Members of Congress look like they are ardently championing the interests of their constituents, and presidents get the commitment to freer trade they desire. Politically, everyone wins. Congress looks like it is leading the dance, but it is really the president who leads.[20] According to the conventional viewpoint, this works out well for members of Congress, as they actually prefer the final political responsibility for trade policy outcomes to be borne by the executive branch.[21] They do not want their openness to constituency input to lead them down the road to another global depression, but they do not want important constituents to think their legislators do not care about their needs.

According to the foreign policy literature's conventional wisdom, another example of such a choreographed dance concerns trade promotion authority, better known as the "fast-track" procedure. This procedure is seen as another example of significant congressional delegation of power to the executive branch. Congress makes it easier for presidents to negotiate trade agreements, and then Congress is not allowed to change them. It must vote "yes" or "no."[22]

However, there are good reasons to challenge this conventional viewpoint in the foreign policy literature regarding foreign trade policy making. To many observers, the congressional role in foreign trade policy making can neither be ignored nor minimized. To begin, Congress is constitutionally bound to play an important role via legislation.[23] The United States is "the only major industrial country where the ultimate authority over international commerce rests with a separate legislative branch."[24] Moreover, the Constitution's separation of powers creates a number of other important institutional roles for Congress—such as oversight of the executive, the role of institutional dissent, and on and on.[25]

The way Congress works helps it to play a meaningful role in foreign trade policy making. Scholars have long noted that members of Congress are most comfortable dealing with the politics of structural issues,[26] and foreign trade policy making falls neatly into this structural policy category.[27] According to the "new institutionalism" literature, Congress often makes its policy imprints indirectly through its control of processes and procedures.[28] Consider, once again, fast-track trade procedures. As noted earlier, the conventional wisdom in the foreign policy literature sees this as a delegation of congressional power to the president. However, the way fast-track actually works *ensures* a significant congressional role. First, fast-track requires consultations by the president both with members of Congress and with executive branch agencies, that must report to relevant congressional committees, before the negotiating process with other governments ever begins. Second, members of Congress must be appointed to the diplomatic negotiating team. Third, fast-track authorization can be revoked by Congress if its members feel the president has not adequately consulted with them during the negotiations. Fourth, any resulting legislative proposal must go through mandatory "mock markup" sessions conducted by the House Ways and Means and Senate Finance Committees thirty days *before* being formally submitted to Congress. Finally if after clearing all these points of substantive congressional access the bill still does not meet congressional expectations, Congress can vote it down.[29] In short, despite the appearance of delegation, Congress plays a major role in shaping the substantive policy results of a fast-track procedure.

Recent studies have confirmed this significant congressional role in foreign trade policy making. A study of congressional foreign trade behavior from 1985 to 1995 showed that Congress played an active role in 78 percent of the cases in that era and got all or part of its policy desires enacted in 84 percent of the cases.[30] Another study covering the 1985–1996 period found similar congressional dominance of the overall process. The congressional role was particularly strong, vis-à-vis the administration, when the trade policy debates involved product-specific as opposed to country-specific issues.[31] This strong congressional role can be expected to continue; "as trade becomes more central to the well-being of the economy, the Congress, which is more immediately accountable to the workers and communities affected by trade decisions, will inevitably demand a greater role in trade matters."[32] Based on these studies, it is hard to argue that Congress does not play a meaningful role in foreign trade policy making. Both branches of the federal government cooperate and compete to set trade policy, and the congressional role should not be minimized just because Congress, at times, prefers less direct means to accomplish its trade goals.

Policy-Making Influences in Congress

The nature of the issues involved in foreign trade guarantees an important congressional role. Trade policy involves classic intermestic issues[33] that arouse powerful interests in society.[34] The conventional view in the trade policy literature is that interest groups dominate the congressional consideration of trade policy. Even if the president is viewed as having the "first-mover" leadership role in forging a liberal trade policy, if he does not take sufficient advantage of this role, protectionist interests will mobilize in Congress, and Congress will respond to them.[35] These powerful interests include skilled labor and large corporations.[36] Both these groups want protection from foreign competition and/or the promotion of their exports abroad. These groups are consistently important, and their political importance is magnified if they are clustered in geographic proximity where they can reinforce each other.[37] Whether one is talking about the 1890s, the 1930s, or the 1990s, the impact of organized interests virtually dictates that members of Congress will engage in *significant* foreign trade policy making.[38]

However, is Congress responsive solely to interest groups? According to one expert, Congress may be seen as "neither held captive by pressure groups nor dominated by the executive branch."[39] The impact of partisanship must also be considered. One study found that, from 1877 to 1934, parties played an important role in mediating the impact of interest group demands on government. It also found that parties played a substantial role in affecting tariff levels.[40] More broadly, partisanship has long been seen as a very important factor in congressional-executive interactions.[41] More recently, Congress became a sharply more partisan institution in the 1980s, and foreign policy making became much more partisan and ideological as a result.[42] Thus partisanship extended into the foreign trade arena as well. A study of the 100th Congress (1987–1988) found that partisanship was the strongest factor in explaining congressional trade policy making.[43] Given the role that partisanship plays in Congress, both ideologically and in terms of structural control, the impact of parties must be considered on foreign trade policy making.

Foreign Trade and Divided Government

So the research question is posed: how does divided government affect the executive-congressional relationship in the making of foreign trade policy? According to some researchers, divided government may have little or no role. David Karol concludes his study by saying that divided government has no *consistent* effect on trade policy outcomes.[44] However, that is not to say that divided government is not important. He finds that divided government favors protectionist interests in government, whether in Congress or the White House. He also finds that divided government makes it harder for a free-trade oriented president to be successful with Congress.

Common sense suggests that divided government would make it harder for presidents to get their way in foreign trade policy making. In addition to any idiosyncratic or personal reasons to oppose the president's position, partisanship would provide another reason for opposition party members to object to the administration's proposals. In a more direct test of the impact of divided government, one study found that, from 1890 to 1990 Congress delegated less authority and less discretion to the president in foreign trade policy under divided government than under unified government. Thus, divided government mattered significantly over that one-hundred-year-long period, by creating "a more constrained bureaucracy, with less flexibility to respond to changing circumstances, and in greater conflict with its political supervisors."[45] Another examination focusing on trade policy in the post–World War II period found that Congress put more restrictions on presidential foreign trade policy-making authority under divided government than under unified government, and it found that "U.S. trade policy is significantly more protectionist under divided than under unified government in the postwar era."[46]

Other foreign policy studies suggest the importance of partisanship and divided government. Since the end of World War II, Congress has become more assertive over time in challenging the administration's positions across a wide variety of foreign policy issues.[47] Again since at least the 1980s, congressional foreign policy making has taken on a more ideologically partisan nature as well.[48] These two factors combined should lead to more congressional victories over the president under divided than under unified government.

Methodology

TRADE POLICY AND THE PERIOD UNDER STUDY

Robert Pastor defined trade policy as "the sum total of actions by the state intended to affect the extent, composition, and direction of its imports and exports of goods and services."[49] The working definition of trade policy used here is the identification of cases involving policies that have a direct impact on U.S. imports and exports. Generally speaking, trade policies found here tend to deal with specific products or industries (such as protection from imports or promotion of exports), efforts to regulate trade with specific countries (such as most-favored-nation/normal-trade-status cases, free trade agreements, or the imposition of economic sanctions), or the administration of trade policy (such as the granting of "fast-track" authority, funding the Export-Import Bank, etc.).

Some trade policy-making cases were found in omnibus trade bills. As these included a number of very different trade issues that at other times would be considered as separate bills, such omnibus trade bills were disaggregated into their major substantive components that were then coded as individual trade policy-making cases in their own right. For example, the 1988 Omnibus Trade Bill comprised seventeen separate trade policy cases, involving issues such as country-specific tariffs, product-specific tariffs, multilateral tariffs, product-specific export restrictions, country-specific trade sanctions, product-specific export promotions, and so forth. To be comparable to other trade legislation for the time frame under study, each of these relevant sections of an omnibus trade act was coded as a distinct case of foreign trade policy-making behavior.

In recent years, divided government has been far more common than unified government. Accordingly, one has to go back in time to ensure some meaningful inclusion of unified government for comparison purposes. Consequently, the period of time under study is the twenty-four-year period from 1977 to 2000. That period includes the unified governments of the 95th and 96th Congresses (featuring Democratic Congresses with Democratic president Carter, 1977–1980), the divided governments of the 97th through 99th Congresses (featuring Democratic control of the House and Republican control of the Senate and White House under President Reagan, 1981–1986), the divided governments of the 100th through 102nd Congresses (featuring Democratic Congresses with Republican presidents Reagan and Bush, 1987–1992), the unified government of the 103rd Congress (featuring a Democratic Congress with Democratic president Clinton, 1993–1994), and the divided governments of the 104th through 106th Congresses (featuring Republican Congresses with Democratic president Clinton, 1995–2000).

The data source used is a series of *Congressional Quarterly* publications.[50] In these, a total of 357 trade policy-making cases (those directly affecting imports and exports) are identified and coded. Methodologically, it is important to note that these cases represent the *universe* of major trade activities for this period and not a sample thereof.

CODIFYING TRADE POLICY OUTCOMES

In addressing the central question of "who wins trade policy debates," four output categories are possible. In some cases, both the president and Congress agree on the issues at hand. Such cases of *policy agreement* lack contentiousness; there is no opposition to the proposal. The dynamics of the decision process may be active, as was the case in the 1985 U.S.-Israel Free Trade Area case. Both members of Congress and the president were active and enthusiastic about this new policy initiative, and they agreed on the policy desired. However, policy agreement may be the result of one branch being active and the other being indifferent. Such was the case with the 1986 extension of Most Favored Nation (MFN) status to Romania. President Reagan made the proposal and, since members of Congress essentially did not care, they agreed with his request.

When Congress and the president disagree over the desired policy output, three possibilities arise. Congress may prevail, the president may prevail, or both may win partial victories. As an example of the first case, in the 1985 agricultural export programs authorization bill Congress prevailed, despite repeated veto threats by President Reagan. Reagan had promised to veto any agriculture export bill costing more than $50 billion. Congress challenged him by passing one costing $52 billion, and Reagan backed down, reluctantly signing the bill "despite his misgivings about many key provisions, including a $52 billion price tag."[51] Thus this outcome was coded as a *congressional win*.

Cases of presidential victories (or a *presidential win*) were most starkly seen when a presidential veto was upheld, as in the textile import cases of 1985 and 1988. In instances like the South African sanctions case of 1988, the threat of a presidential veto was enough to cause Congress to accede to presidential desires. However, presidential victories need not involve the threats of vetoes. In 1988, the president submitted to Congress an executive agreement regulating the exports of U.S. nuclear materials to Japan. Despite objections from members of the Senate Foreign Relations and of the House Foreign Affairs Committees, the president won approval of the agreement when the Senate failed to overturn it. Since both chambers would have had to reject the agreement to invalidate it, the House never acted following the Senate decision, and the case featured a presidential win output.

Finally in cases when both branches could claim some sort of victory, the case was coded as a partial victory or *joint win* for each. The 1986 Export-Import Bank authorization extension is a good example. The president wanted the bill to include a $300 million package of "tied aid"— which combined loans and grants to make U.S. exports more attractive to purchasers. Long adverse to grants rather than direct loans, Congress authorized the requested $300 million but added two important limiting conditions. Only $100 million of it could actually be used for tied aid and then only if the chairman of the Export-Import Bank certified to Congress that those funds were not needed for the bank's direct loan program. Thus the president got a commitment for the tied aid funding he wanted, but Congress cut the desired amount by two-thirds and put a potentially important restriction on its use. Since each branch got part of what it wanted, the output was coded as a joint win.

The present data set builds on one compiled for another study.[52] That prior data set includes all the foreign trade cases from 1985 to 1996. They were initially coded by one author, with the coding results reviewed the other. Any disagreements regarding case coding were resolved through discussion. The cases from 1977 to 1984 and 1997 to 2000 were added to that prior data set and coded in the same manner by the present author.

Findings

Two hypotheses are tested. They are:

> Hypothesis$_1$—Congressional victories over the administration in foreign trade policy making should be higher under conditions of divided government than under conditions of unified government.
> Hypothesis$_2$—This increase in congressional victories should be greater when both chambers are controlled by the opposition party to the president than when one chamber is controlled by the opposition party.

In Table 1 I show the frequencies of the trade outputs from 1977 to 2000 under conditions of unified and divided government. It compares the frequencies for the dependent variable across three possibilities: unified government, divided government with one congressional chamber controlled by the opposition party, and divided government with both congressional chambers controlled by the opposition party. For the sake of convention, the Chi-Square, Cramer's V, and statistical significance are reported, but these are not meaningful in this analysis. Since the findings are based on the universe of foreign trade policy-making cases for this period and not on a sample thereof, statistical significance is meaningless and the relationship measures are less important than the actual frequencies found. Importantly, *the frequencies move in the expected directions.* Presidential wins are less likely as the opposition party gains in institutional strength. Presidential wins are more likely under unified government, less likely when the opposition party controls one chamber of Congress, and even less likely when the opposition party controls both chambers of Congress (26 percent to 25 percent to 24 percent, respectively). Congres-

TABLE 1. FOREIGN TRADE OUTPUTS BY TYPE OF PARTISAN CONTROL OF GOVERNMENT

Foreign Trade Outputs	Unified Government	One Chamber Opposition Party Control	Two Chamber Opposition Party Control
Presidential Wins	28 (26%)	25 (25%)	36 (24%)
Joint Wins	31 (29%)	35 (35%)	27 (18%)
Congressional Wins	20 (19%)	23 (23%)	39 (26%)
Policy Agreement	29 (27%)	18 (18%)	46 (31%)
Total	108 (101%*)	101 (101%*)	148 (99%*)

* = Rounding Error
Chi-Square = 12.450 with 6 degrees of freedom
Cramer's V = .132
Significance = .053

sional wins increase even more as the situation moves from unified government to one chamber controlled by the opposition party to both chambers controlled by the opposition party (19 percent to 23 percent to 26 percent, respectively). Thus, the findings in Table 2 support both hypotheses. Divided government makes a difference in congressional wins in foreign trade policy making.

An interesting finding in Table 1 concerns the joint win outputs (when both the president and Congress get partial policy victories). These outputs are most likely when one chamber of Congress is controlled by the opposition party (35 percent) and least likely when a president faces a Congress with both chambers controlled by the opposition party (18 percent). It appears that when the situation shifts from one chamber controlled by the opposition to both chambers controlled by the opposition, some of the instances that otherwise would have led to joint wins shift instead to congressional wins (26 percent as opposed to 23 percent under one chamber control) or to instances of policy agreement (31 percent as opposed to 18 percent under one chamber control by the opposition).

Finally, the cases that are most interesting politically are those in which there is some contention between the branches. Table 2 displays the frequencies when the instances of policy agreement are deleted from the analysis. When contention is present, congressional victories increase sharply as opposition party control of Congress increases. When cases of policy agreement are deleted, the percentage of congressional wins goes from 25 percent under unified government to 28 percent when one chamber is controlled by the opposition party, and up to 38 percent when both chambers

TABLE 2. CONTENTIOUS FOREIGN TRADE OUTPUTS BY TYPE OF PARTISAN CONTROL OF GOVERNMENT

Foreign Trade Outputs	Unified Government	One Chamber Opposition Party Control	Two Chamber Opposition Party Control
Presidential Wins	28 (35%)	25 (30%)	36 (35%)
Joint Wins	31 (39%)	35 (42%)	27 (26%)
Congressional Wins	20 (25%)	23 (28%)	39 (38%)
Total	79 (99%*)	83 (100%)	102 (99%*)

* = Rounding Error
Chi Square = 7.010 with 4 degrees of freedom
Cramer's V = .115
Significance = .135

are controlled by the opposition party. Thus not only are both hypotheses confirmed again, but when considering only contentious cases, the impact of divided government on the likelihood of congressional victories in foreign trade policy making is even greater. Yet counterintuitively, the percentage of presidential wins is actually the same for unified government and when both chambers are controlled by the opposition party.

Discussion

The findings demonstrate that divided government makes a notable difference in foreign trade policy making. As opposition party control of Congress strengthens, the percentage of congressional wins increases, and when instances of policy agreement are deleted from the analysis, the percentage of congressional wins increases dramatically. Across all cases, presidents get a smaller percentage of wins when moving from unified government to opposition party control of one chamber to opposition party control of both chambers.

Yet counterintuitively when instances of policy agreement are deleted, presidential wins are just as likely when both chambers are controlled by the opposition party as under conditions of unified government. In contentious cases when both chambers are controlled by the opposition party, presidential wins are almost as likely as congressional wins (35 percent to 38 percent, respectively).

Based on these findings, two patterns seem clear. First across all cases, as the degree by which the government is divided increases (going from one chamber controlled by the opposition party to both chambers controlled by the opposition party), the percentage of congressional wins increases. Thus *divided government matters in terms of who wins*. The explanation of this finding is fairly straightforward. Foreign trade involves "intermestic" policy. Legislators typically deal with foreign trade as they would any other domestic policy issue. They ask: "What does this mean to my constituents?" For years, the American public has shown their greatest concern for those foreign policy issues that might affect the economy or their own jobs.[53] Consequently, there are electoral imperatives for legislators to act on foreign trade issues. Thus as a considerable part of the literature suggests, Congress already has good electoral reasons to play a strong role in foreign trade policy making, and divided government just gives members of Congress another reason to be willing to challenge the policy positions of the president.[54]

Beyond outright presidential or congressional wins, there are several interesting findings when all cases are considered. Joint wins (or partial victories for each branch of the federal government) are an interesting category of foreign trade outputs. It appears joint wins can be achieved in very different ways. On the one hand, they may be produced through accommodation. As one would expect, there seems to be a greater willingness by each branch of government to accommodate at least some of the policy wishes of the other when each branch is controlled by the same party. Table 1 suggests this pattern. Here, partisanship may lead to logrolling-type dynamics in foreign trade cases where both the president and members of his party in Congress get at least part of what they want.

On the other hand, a very different picture is portrayed when the opposition party controls one chamber of Congress. In these instances, the percentage of joint wins increases sharply (to 35 percent). In these cases, joint wins may be the output of an acrimonious process, whereby the opposition party members dig in their collective heels and hold out for at least something that can be called a partial victory. According to congressional staffer Pete Rose, "Around here, who wins often comes down to who's stubborn longer."[55] When the opposition party controls one chamber of Congress and faces both the presidency and the other chamber controlled by the other party, those opposition party members may hunker down in a siege mentality, holding out for whatever they can get and thus producing noticeably more joint wins. During the time period under study, in every case in which one chamber is controlled by the opposition party, that chamber is the House of Representatives. That fact may contribute to this pattern. A House controlled by the opposition party may be more prone to hunker down in such a siege mentality, holding out for whatever it can get, than a Senate controlled by the opposition party. After all, representatives are never more than twenty-four months away from facing their constituents in their reelection campaigns. With six-year terms, opposition party senators may be more willing to make concessions to the administration, on the presumption that they can later "make it up" to any offended constituents or that those constituents will have forgotten about the issue by the time reelection rolls around.

Yet when a president faces a Congress in which both chambers are controlled by the opposition party, an interesting finding is not present. *Partisan gridlock does not appear to develop*, at least in foreign trade policy making. Because Congress is in a stronger position, joint wins decrease and congressional wins increase, as one would expect. Perhaps counterintuitively, *instances of policy agreement dramatically increase;* in fact, policy agreement becomes the most frequent output. The most likely explanation for this behavior is based on the role of "anticipated reaction" on the part of the administration. Facing a Congress totally controlled by the opposition party, presidents know winning is much harder. Thus they may try to anticipate what members of Congress want and build that into their foreign trade initiatives. This is certainly the case, for example, under the fast-track procedure. If this dynamic is more prevalent when presidents face Congresses with both chambers controlled by the opposition party, such behavior falls into the "lead them where they already want to go" executive branch approach in foreign trade policy. More study is needed to understand the political dynamics that produce more instances of policy agreement under conditions of extremely divided government. Perhaps both institutions are eager to avoid political gridlock in such cases, given the high political salience of foreign trade issues.

The second broad pattern is seen when instances of policy agreement are deleted and only contentious cases are considered. Then Congress wins most often (38 percent) but presidential victories are not far behind (35 percent). In this most stark version of divided government, we see the "polarized politics" of the 1980s and 1990s.[56] When they control both chambers and policy agreement is not to be found, opposition party members dig in their heels and fight for a policy victory. So too do presidents, who do not wish to concede their leadership role over an issue they see as more "foreign" than "domestic." These "fight-it-out" dynamics are heightened due to the "greater homogeneity within the parties and the greater polarization between them."[57] In these cases, the achievement of compromise solutions (i.e., joint wins) is *least* likely (26 percent compared to 39 percent for unified government and 42 percent for opposition party control of one chamber). So *for contentious cases, not only does divided government matter, it matters even more.*

Conclusion

Divided government makes a notable difference in foreign trade policy making. Its effects are seen across all cases, and it is most notably displayed when instances of policy agreement are deleted from the analysis. Thus in terms of foreign trade policy making, divided government matters.

In the case of foreign trade, the "fault lines" are easy to see. One problem is institutional. Presidents look at foreign trade as both an end and as a means in foreign affairs. Beneficial foreign trade patterns benefit the U.S. economy, and foreign trade can be an instrument of statecraft used to advance other foreign policy goals. Thus presidents have an institutional incentive to want to lead the dance in foreign trade policy making. Members of Congress are more likely to see foreign trade policy making as another instance of domestic policy making, something that directly affects local constituent groups. To the extent that foreign trade matters become congressionally defined as "jobs" issues, they rise in importance, becoming the kind of "hot button" issues with voters that can potentially cost a member of Congress reelection.

In the context of divided government, ideological differences create another "fault line," by widening the gulf between Capitol Hill and the White House. Democrats often view foreign trade issues from a "bottom-up" perspective, where "doing the right thing" typically involves the protection of labor or of the environment or the promotion of human rights (see the NAFTA and China trade debates, for example). Republicans often view foreign trade issues from a "top-down" perspective, where "doing the right thing" typically involves promoting free trade and letting market forces both determine winners and losers and reallocate capital efficiently. Such ideological differences exacerbate the institutional differences noted above. The increased partisanship seen in Congress (and particularly in the House of Representatives) since the 1980s just makes this hurdle more difficult to overcome.

The good news is that these patterns tend to change over time. As Richard Fleisher and Jon Bond point out, there have been cycles of heightened and diminished partisanship before.[58] The "polarized politics" that emphasize "why don't you agree with me?" at some point will be replaced by processes that emphasize "why can't we just get along?" One wonders what the stimulus will be that changes the direction of the pendulum's swing. How damaging will the effects of partisanship have to be before both presidents and legislators look beyond it? That answer is presently unknown.

The other good news is that foreign trade policy making goes on. The findings here do not indicate partisan gridlock. Even under the worst conditions of divided government, either the two chambers tend to agree on policy or one of the two chambers prevails over the other. There is no indication that important foreign trade policy gets held up in a partisan purgatory. For better or worse, issues get decided, and movement on the governmental agenda proceeds.

Thus just as partisanship matters in domestic policy making, divided government produces a notable difference in foreign trade policy making as well. As fictional President Bartlett on the NBC television show *The West Wing* says, "Important decisions are made by those who show up." In these cases, voters determine who shows up,[59] and voters' tendencies to choose presidents and legislators of opposing parties affect who wins and who loses in the foreign trade policy-making arena.[60]

7 Long-Term Trends in Congressional Foreign Policy Behavior

Explaining Variations in Contention in the U.S. Senate in the Past and in the Future

MARIE T. HENEHAN

Marie Henehan reminds us that any nation's foreign policy is shaped by events beyond its borders as well as the vagaries of its internal politics. Focus on the "life cycle" of issues reveals a sequence of events which begins with the recognition of a new problem or the acknowledgment that an existing policy has failed, followed by a national debate over the determination of a new policy, and culminating in the emergence of a new defining consensus that places the issue in perspective and delegates responsibility for the implementation of policy. The legislature is likely to be most active in the second stage—the debate over a new policy—although the executive branch has considerable influence, especially in times of crisis or if the issue is tied to national security. Henehan notes that two other arguments have been advanced to explain high levels of congressional activity—divided government, when one or both houses of Congress are in opposition hands, and the tendency for Congress to be more active in times of peace—but concludes that the argument that Congress plays a more active role during the debate phase of the issue cycle offers greater explanatory power.

Introduction

Predicting the future of congressional behavior on foreign policy can be an exercise in futility. As recently as the spring of 2001, Randall Ripley summarized America's foreign policy situation thus: the Bush administration had practically no foreign policy agenda, Congress had none, individual members of Congress, even those with influence, had only idiosyncratic interests, the public was uninterested in foreign affairs as long as the United States was not threatened by major conflict, and no international challenges were visible.[1] Everything he said was accurate given the contingencies, but the attacks of September 11, 2001, changed the situation. He did indicate that a confrontation would be a major challenge to an administration without a plan, and that coordination between the two branches would be unlikely. In fact, he speculated that having to respond to terrorism was a likely scenario, but that the administration had no plan or vision to implement. Of course, as he also says, it is impossible to predict crises by their nature, yet crises have a huge impact on foreign policy and on the roles of the president and Congress.

Lacking a crystal ball, the best we can do is to look at patterns of behavior and develop theoretical understandings of past behavior so that we have at least a notion of the conditions under which congressional behavior will change. The key to doing this is in identifying the factors that trigger changes in congressional behavior on foreign policy. Crises such as the attacks of 9/11 or Pearl Harbor can change attitudes enough to change behavior and policy. Whether one party controls both branches of government or there is divided government will affect the support the president achieves from Congress on his foreign policy. Whether or not the country is at war can also affect the presidential-congressional relationship. However, in this chapter, the focus will be on the role of the most salient issue of a given era, the critical issue in foreign policy, in shaping the behavior of the U.S. Senate. It is hypothesized that these issues play the most important role in congressional behavior on foreign policy, and that other factors play comparatively less important roles. While the critical issue theory of congressional foreign policy behavior cannot predict when crises will arise, it can be an aid for understanding why Congress is assertive at some times and acquiescent at others and what future conditions will make these shifts likely. Much of the discourse about the attacks of 9/11 implied that the world fundamentally changed on that day, but this is not really true. Predictable patterns of institutional behavior have followed what was an unpredicted event.

The Critical Issue Explanation of Congressional Behavior on Foreign Policy

The critical issue theory of congressional behavior on foreign policy holds that the most important factor in shaping congressional assertiveness and acquiescence is the life cycle of critical foreign policy issues. While domestic politics have a role in foreign policy behavior, the most important issues in history that shape U.S. foreign policy have had their source in the international environment. Consistent with Peter Gourevitch's notion of the second image reversed, this theory holds that events, crises, and relationships at the global level intrude on domestic institutions, often setting the foreign policy agenda from the outside.[2] When a new critical foreign policy issue emerges in this way, there is a domestic debate over it, involving not only Congress and the president, but also the public, the press, and interest groups. Normally, several alternatives are considered, and then a policy is hammered out. Congress is active in the debate at first, but once an overall policy response to the issue is chosen, Congress becomes more quiescent, presumably having participated in the choice of policy, and takes a back seat to the executive, which has a natural role in implementing policy. This process is not so much a matter of executive dominance as executive implementation of a policy on which there has been a previous debate.

The importance of critical issues is reflected in the fact that they are usually linked to national security interests. They tend to "gobble up" more minor issues, so that policy responses to minor issues are often shaped by the direction of the policy response to the critical issue. For example, during the Cold War, decisions on foreign aid to poor countries were shaped more by whether the target governments were anti-communist than by their need. In the current era, the very same type of policy is more likely to be justified in terms of preventing terrorism. Also, because of both the salience of critical issues and the tendency to couch the issues in terms of broad interests of the nation, a consensus eventually emerges on the policy response. For example, such a consensus produced the bipartisanship that was so touted during the early Cold War, but it has existed in other eras as well.[3] Aided by the consensus, the longer a policy on a critical issue stays in place (as long as the critical issue does not get resolved and the policy does not produce a major failure) the less scrutiny there is of the policy.

Implementation of the policy thus proceeds apace until one of three things happens: a new issue supplants the old, as anti-communism emerged to replace the debate over internationalism; the issue is resolved, as with the issue of anti-communism, which simply removed itself from the agenda with Mikhail Gorbachev's policy decisions and the emergence of reform throughout the "second" world; or the policy response to the critical issue fails, as in Vietnam. In the last case, the policy is reversed and the issue is revisited in debates in Congress and society. If the critical issue is not resolved, it stays on the agenda, but the response to it is reconsidered.

Elsewhere, I have argued that there have been three critical issues and one major policy failure since 1898: imperialism, involvement in Europe, anti-communism, and the failure of containment in Vietnam.[4] Each critical issue raises fundamental questions about values and choices in the face of threat or interests, so it produces significant debate in the country. Different options are considered as part of the debate until one wins out. The economic disruptions of the 1870s and 1880s gave rise to the three options of territorial imperialism, informal commercial expansion, or complete isolation and self-sufficiency. President Cleveland was dead set against involvement in Cuba and President McKinley resisted it, but Congress pushed with resolutions on Cuba until McKinley finally handed Spain an ultimatum in 1898. In the policy of going to war against Spain, imperialism and self-sufficiency were both rejected, and with the establishment of an indigenous Cuban government under the restrictions of the Platt amendment, informal neocolonialism emerged as the chosen policy.

The country followed the path of neocolonialism in Latin America (plus one formal colony in the Philippines) coupled with a fairly isolationist posture toward Europe until Wilson took the United States into the Great War. After the war, debate ensued over whether to follow his internationalist dream or return to isolation. This critical issue was encompassed in the debate on the Versailles treaty in 1919. The defeat of the treaty confirmed isolationism as U.S. foreign policy through the debates over the Neutrality Acts and up until the attack on Pearl Harbor.

Pearl Harbor and U.S. involvement in World War II put an effective end to any notion that the United States would be isolationist. However, even with a turn toward internationalism, it was not immediately obvious what sort of internationalist posture would be adopted toward the Soviet Union. Being naturally hostile to communism because it is a capitalist country, the United States was already ill-disposed to be friendly toward the Soviet Union, but when the USSR emerged from World War II with superpower status, the need to respond to the issue of communism became the critical foreign policy issue. This time, the policy choices were accommodation, associated with Henry Wallace; rollback, later associated with General McArthur's adventuristic actions in Korea; and containment, as formulated by George Kennan in the Mr. X article.[5] Passage of the Truman Doctrine signaled the ascent of containment as the policy response to Soviet communism.

Once a policy is chosen in response to a critical issue, as long as the policy is working, a period of bipartisanship emerges and executive implementation proceeds apace. This can be disrupted if the policy fails, as did the policy of containment in Vietnam, causing the policy to be debated anew and reversed. Because Vietnam was seen as a mistake, Congress acted not only to end U.S. involvement in Southeast Asia, but with the War Powers resolution to attempt to prevent a similar debacle in the future. Thus, there was not only renewed activity in Congress, but an era of congressional assertiveness.[6]

The Impact of Critical Issues

From the above understanding of critical issues and major policy failure, four key years can be identified as likely to produce assertiveness in Congress. The critical issue years are 1898, 1919, and 1948, and the policy failure year is 1968. If the theory is correct, it should be the case that indicators of congressional activity and disagreement will be high following these years. This can be tested by observing congressional behavior on foreign policy over time. The Senate was chosen for the study because of its more significant role in foreign policy. The indicator of activity is the number of roll calls on foreign policy taken by the Senate each year, and the indicator of disagreement within the Senate is the number of close votes (45 percent to 55 percent or closer) on foreign policy taken each year.

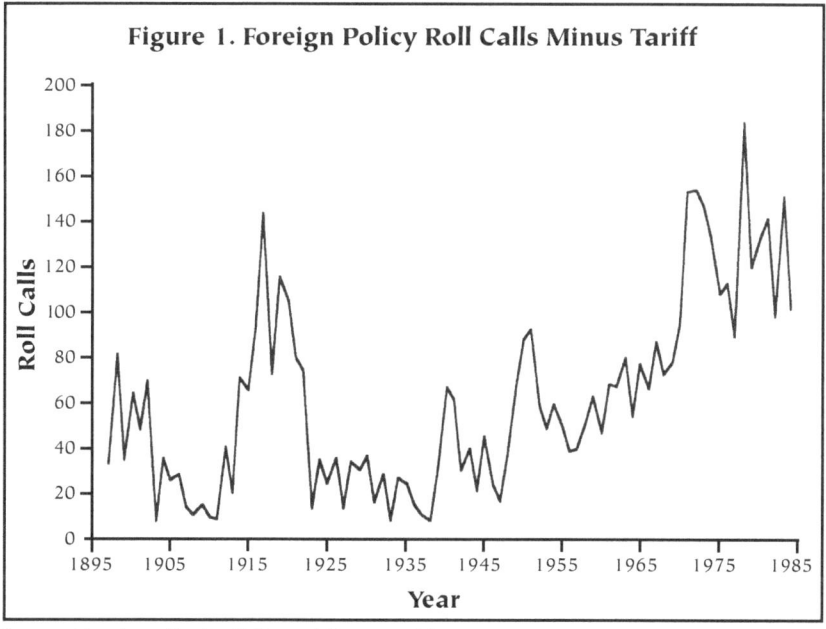

SOURCE: Henehan, *Foreign Policy and Congress*, 94.

Visual inspection of the graph in Figure 1 of all foreign policy votes, except for tariff,[7] indicates that it is the case that activity increases with the advent of critical issues and with a major failure related to a critical issue. The level of activity (i.e., number of roll calls) in the Senate is high in 1898/1900/1902, 1919–1920, 1949–1951, and shows the most activity from 1971 to 1974. The first time period, corresponding to the critical issue of imperialism, is characterized by not only resolutions on Cuba, but also votes on Hawaii and the Philippines and on the Panama Canal. The debate over the Versailles treaty in 1919 and 1920 produces the second-largest number of votes taken on a single issue in the entire eighty-eight-year period. The post–World War II period did not produce immediate contention the way the Versailles treaty did, owing largely to FDR's having learned from Wilson's mistakes. Incorporating senators into the decision-making process on the United Nations forestalled and defused potential contention over the postwar order. Thus, there is not a high level of activity in 1945. However, the question of how to respond to Soviet communism was very real.

Although the indicator of number of roll call votes does not show a high level of activity on the first policy implementation of containment, the Truman Doctrine, this aid package was not passed into law without the airing of concerns on the part of the leadership, and, more important, not without a very strong argument on the part of the Truman administration in the person of Dean Acheson. The initial reaction of congressional leaders was that this was unnecessary spending on what was a British responsibility.[8] Acheson's shrewd packaging of the policy as an antidote to communism needed to protect American security forged a historic consensus on the issue of responding to communism.[9] In fact, his characterization of the moment, "No time was left for measured appraisal," shows the extent to which the administration recognized what it would take to win over Congress to not just one aid package, but to a whole approach to the communist threat.[10] It was only Republican senator Arthur H. Vandenberg's advice to Truman to make a speech to the nation couching the need for aid to Greece and Turkey in terms of the nation's security that assured the proposal's passage in Congress.[11]

Thus, it would be a mistake to conclude that Congress was a rubber stamp on containment. After the relatively easy passage of the Truman Doctrine, there were high levels of roll call activity from 1949 to 1951 reflecting debates over the extent and nature of the aid to be given under the Marshall Plan. On NATO, again Vandenberg paved the way for bipartisan agreement on the concept of containment, but there was still a twelve-day debate on the floor over concerns about future military assistance programs.[12] Vandenberg himself responded to questions about the congressional role by pointing out that without the substantial consultation that took place before the proposals came to a vote, the policy would not have worked. Bipartisanship was not "a carbon copy process," rather it was a "meeting of minds."[13] Thus, there was a role for Congress in choosing the policy of containment, and the constitutional prerogative of Congress in authorizing and appropriating money was exercised in its implementation.

There are other periods of high levels of roll call activity besides the four predicted times, but these are not related to critical issues. The peaks in 1917 and 1940–1941 are composed mostly of votes on war mobilization, and the spike of activity in 1979 is on the Panama Canal treaty. These three cases are instances of senatorial activity, but not of contention over critical issues. The critical issue theory holds that either the advent of a critical issue or a policy failure on a critical issue is a sufficient condition for an increase in activism, but not a necessary condition. Other factors can also increase activity.

However, contentious behavior is particularly associated with critical issues—one can observe disagreement within the Senate by looking at close votes. Peaks in the critical issue and policy failure years should dominate a graph of close votes (those with a margin of 10 percent or less). Figure 2 shows that the four predicted dates are the highest in disagreement: 1898/1900/1902, 1919–1920, 1949–1951, and 1971–1974.[14] Also, it is significant that each set of peaks is a multiyear period, owing to the complexity of the issues.

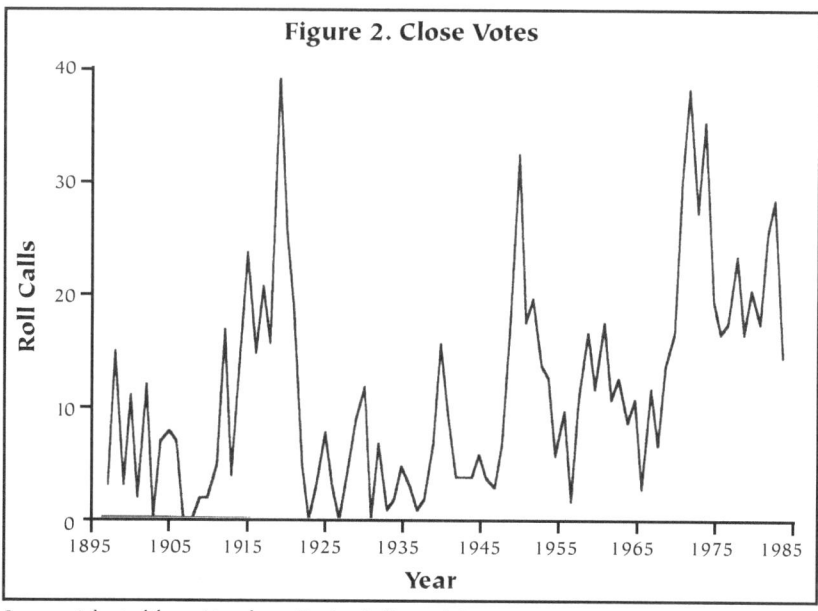

SOURCE: Adapted from Henehan, *Foreign Policy and Congress*, 112.

Mere visual inspection, however, is prone to imprecision and differences in interpretation, so a Box-Tiao impact analysis was conducted to measure the extent and duration of the impact of each of the issues. There were insufficient data points prior to 1898, so only the second and third critical issues (1919 and 1948) and the policy failure (1968) were tested. The first step is to conduct an Autoregressive Improved Moving Average (ARIMA) analysis to identify the characteristics of the series. Since the existence of a trend in the data is relevant to the analysis, the trend was not removed, so the models are AR, MA models, accounting for auto-regression and moving averages. The existence and extent of a trend were measured by a trend dummy variable and a trend function variable. The trend dummy identifies the existence of a trend, and the trend function measures the trend before and after the impact. The second part of the analysis is the impact analysis, which shows whether the impact of the critical issue or policy failure is abrupt or gradual and temporary or permanent.

In Table 1 I show that the Treaty of Versailles has a statistically significant abrupt and temporary impact on the level of activity. The significant omega (1.124) shows that the impact is very large, and the nonsignificant trend dummy shows that the upward shift is not a trend. This confirms that there was a significant level of debate over the Versailles treaty, and that once it was resolved (Wilson was defeated), debate waned and Congress

TABLE 1. THE IMPACT OF THE INVOLVEMENT-IN-EUROPE CRITICAL ISSUE

Impact year: 1917
ARMA model (4, 2)
Abrupt and temporary impact

Variable	coefficient	std Error	T-Stat	significance
constant	-.034	.085	-.399	.691
AR(1)	.209	.143	1.46	.149
AR(2)	-.351	.054	-6.519	.000*
AR(3)	-.599	.092	-6.543	.000*
AR(4)	.345	.091	3.788	.000*
MA(1)	-.741	.103	-7.181	.000*
MA(2)	1.298	.112	11.615	.000*
Trend dummy	.001	.002	.625	.534
Omega	1.124	.431	2.609	.011*

AIC = 181.313   BIC = 201.420
Q = 13.564   .258
*statistically significant at p < .05

SOURCE: Henehan, *Foreign Policy and Congress*, 99.

pursued isolationist policies. Isolationism was so dominant that even such a strong president as FDR was not able to dislodge it when he wanted to support the British in the war. He had to wait for the attack on Pearl Harbor to shift opinion. On December 7, 1941, opinion on U.S. involvement in Europe shifted definitively toward internationalism and it has never shifted back.[15]

The findings for the next critical issue, anti-communism, also show an abrupt, temporary impact (see Table 2). The omega is not quite as large, but it is .984 and significant. This time the trend dummy is significant, although very small. This is tapping the fact that the number of roll calls on foreign policy is also gradually increasing independent of the critical issue.[16] In other words, after 1948, there are two patterns: a peak in activity and disagreement due to the impact of the critical issue, and the beginning of a long-term trend in increased activity produced mainly by votes on the issue of foreign aid.

Table 3 shows that the failure of containment in Vietnam produced not only asignificant increase in activity, but a permanent (at least, more long-lasting than the others) stepwise increase. In this case, there is not only a significant omega (.930) indicating an abrupt impact and a significant trend dummy (.028) showing a strong trend, but a significant trend function statistic, which shows that there is a significant difference between the trend before 1968 and after.[17]

TABLE 2. THE IMPACT OF THE ANTI-COMMUNISM CRITICAL ISSUE

Impact year: 1948
ARMA model (0,3)
Abrupt and temporary impact

Variable	coefficient	std Error	T-Stat	significance
constant	-.025	.023	-1.109	.272
MA(1)	-.627	.127	-4.952	.000*
MA(2)	-.045	.139	-.326	.746
MA(3)	-.596	.133	-4.485	.000*
Trend dummy	.001	.000	3.037	.003*
Omega	.984	.407 2	.417	.019*

AIC = 181.587 BIC = 194.992
Q = 19.069 .162
*statistically significant at p < .05

Source: Henehan, *Foreign Policy and Congress*, 100.

TABLE 3. THE IMPACT OF THE FAILURE OF CONTAINMENT IN VIETNAM

Impact year: 1968
ARMA model (2,1)
Abrupt and permanent impact

Variable	coefficient std	Error	T-Stat	significance
constant	5.184	.397	13.043	.000*
AR(1)	-0.509	.124	-4.105	.000*
Ar(2)	0.521	.119	4.368	.000*
MA(1)	1.156	.092	12.557	.000*
Trend dummy	0.028	.008	3.707	.000*
Omega	0.930	.340	2.740	.008*
Trend function	-0.044	.013	-3.492	.001*

AIC = 188.749   BIC = 204.388
Q = 23.104   .059
*statistically significant at p < .05

Source: Henehan, *Foreign Policy and Congress*, 100.

These findings confirm that the predicted increases in activity and disagreement do occur after the entry of a critical issue to the agenda, and that the spurts in disagreement are the most significant over time. The pattern of behavior on critical issues and the major policy failure shape the overall pattern in the data, confirming the importance of critical issues.

The Roles of Divided Government and War

Recognizing the role of critical issues in foreign policy can be helpful in assessing competing explanations for variations in congressional assertiveness. Two alternative hypotheses are that Congress will be more assertive when it is controlled by the opposite party from the presidency and that Congress is acquiescent during war and assertive after war. Each is plausible, but they have less explanatory power than the critical issue explanation.

At first blush, it would seem obvious that Congress as an institution, or one or the other chamber, will be more likely to resist a president's program when the president is of the opposite party. Democrats such as Thomas Eagleton (D-Missouri) and Edward Boland (D-Massachusetts) were more hostile than most Republicans to Nixon's and Reagan's foreign policies, respectively. During the Clinton administration, Thomas Campbell (R-California) provided the voice of constitutional prerogative from across the aisle. Is there evidence that congressional opposition to presidential foreign policies is more likely under divided government?

Observation of the pattern produced by the three critical issues and the one failure in Figures 1 and 2 does show that Versailles and Vietnam produced a great deal more activity and contention than imperialism and the initial response to communism. Presidents Wilson and Nixon were both faced with a hostile Senate/Congress that was all the more hostile because it was led by the opposite party. Nevertheless, the critical issue was still dominant—partisan opposition developed into bipartisan opposition on the merits of the issue. Democrats in the Senate jumped ship as Wilson became more rigid in his demands for support for the League, and Republicans withdrew their support for Nixon with the revelation of the smoking gun.[18] Perhaps a tentative conclusion is that divided government increases the *magnitude* of the increase in activity and disagreement within Congress when it does arise.

This leaves open the question of whether there is a systematic relationship between divided government and assertiveness. In other words, are activity and disagreement likely to be higher under divided government and lower under unified government? There is certainly anecdotal evidence that the relationship is not systematic. First, there are eras of divided government that do not have high levels of activity and disagreement, such as the Eisenhower administration. Second, there are periods of unified government with high levels of contention. For example, while contention over Vietnam did not reach great heights until the Nixon administration, there was sufficient dissensus to move Johnson to decide not to run for a second term. Third, the Truman administration was able to forge a bipartisan consensus on containment during the divided government of the 80th Congress, keeping the number of votes on the floor in 1947 and 1948 very low. With the return to Democratic control of Congress in 1949, the level of activity and disagreement actually went up (mostly regarding military aid under NATO and the Marshall Plan). Also, in addition to the familiar bipartisan support by individual members of an established policy, there are plenty of examples of individuals opposing presidents of their own party on the basis of Congress's constitutional prerogatives. For example, Republican Jacob Javits was an original sponsor of the War Powers resolution that was vetoed by Republican president Nixon, and Democrat Lee Hamilton raised the same constitutional issues during the Clinton years as during the administrations of his Republican predecessors. Thus, there is not a strong, obvious correlation between party and support for the president's foreign policy.

The job of political parties is to formulate platforms mostly on domestic policy. Rarely, if ever, does foreign policy determine the outcome of a presidential election. The exception of Vietnam only highlights the strength of bipartisanship in both directions—bipartisan support for Nixon in 1972 and bipartisan opposition in 1974. Members of Congress support a president's foreign policy less on the basis of party platform and more based on their sense of the national interest, patriotism, simple policy agreement, or assessment of their constituents' support. In the case of an imminent use of force, even if the policy seems ill-conceived, members may be loath to create the impression of weakness through disunity, to cut off funds to troops in the field, or to risk creating a constitutional crisis if the president is determined to act in any case.[19] Likewise, opposition is often based on nonpartisan considerations, such as institutional prerogatives. For example, Senator Robert A. Taft (R-Ohio) said he would have supported Truman's decision on Korea if asked, even though he was in the opposing party, but he maintained that, without the authorization of Congress, there was no legal authority for Truman's action.[20]

According to the critical issue theory, critical foreign policy issues come onto the agenda from the international arena and usually have a dimension related to security or grand strategy. Such issues are likely to cut across party lines. If critical issues are more important than divided government, there should be a relationship between the years in which critical issues arise and the highest levels of activity and disagreement on foreign policy in the Senate. If divided government is an accurate predictor of contention in the Senate, there should be a relationship between years with divided government and years with high levels of activity and disagreement. Table 4 shows a cross tabulation between the predicted critical issue years of 1897–1898, 1917–1920, 1947–1950, and 1968–1973 and the highest peaks in activity and disagreement. The *phi* for critical issue years and activity is .634 (statistically significant at $p < .05$), and for disagreement it is .397 (also statistically significant at $p < .05$). However, the *phi*'s for party control by activity and disagreement show no relationship: .177 and .175 (nonsignif-

TABLE 4. PARTY CONTROL VERSUS CRITICAL ISSUES

	peaks in activity (phi)	peaks in close votes (phi)
Critical issue years with one-year lag	.634*	.397*
Party control	.177	.175

*statistically significant at $p < .05$

Source: Henehan, *Foreign Policy and Congress*, 152.

icant), respectively.[21] Thus, while divided government might increase the level of activity and disagreement in the Senate when there is already contention over a critical issue, it is not correlated with contention in general. Contention goes up with the advent of critical issues.

Of course there are other indicators of contention besides roll calls, and the behavior of the president can be affected by his assessment of the likelihood of opposition in Congress. For example, on the issue of a North Atlantic Treaty, the Truman administration avoided submitting a treaty to a Senate controlled by the opposition, while assiduously working with Republican senator Vandenberg to assure Republican support—even to the point of excluding Democrat Tom Connally from the process.[22] Careful case studies and studies with other indicators of congressional behavior should be combined with aggregate analyses to assess the relative strength of the two variables.

Some evidence from case studies that congressional reactions to presidents' foreign policies are often not purely partisan is offered by Ryan Hendrickson's study of the use of force in the Clinton administration. While there is evidence of partisanship in the Democrats' attempts to protect Clinton from congressional opposition in the cases of Somalia, Haiti, and Kosovo and in Republicans' opposition to the Somalia policy, there were cross-party cleavages on constitutional prerogatives and policy agreement.[23] For example, the concerns of Representative Thomas Campbell (R-California) were explicitly constitutional and not partisan or based on his position on the policy. In the case of Bosnia, many Republicans supported him due to their opposition to Clinton's policy, and most Democrats opposed him, but, on other issues, for example, Haiti and Somalia, he was joined by Democrat Russ Feingold (D-Wisconsin) on concerns over constitutional war powers.[24] Other Republicans supported the president (or at least did not oppose him) because they were interested in other issues (such as the budget: Newt Gingrich [R-Georgia]) or were protective of the president's role (such as presidential candidate Bob Dole [R-Kansas]).[25] Thus, the role of partisanship is weaker in foreign policy than in domestic politics—there is more policy agreement across parties on foreign policy and one's position on the issue of constitutional prerogatives cuts across parties. With that much division in the opposition party, it is not surprising that divided government cannot by itself account for the major increases in contention.

The other commonly held view is that war is the key variable. This perspective holds that Congress yields to the president during wartime and then reasserts itself after the war. The most recent case of such a resurgence could be the increase in activism in the 1990s. No longer restrained by the exigencies of the Cold War, members could flex their policy-preference muscles and test out new ideas.[26] Hrach Gregorian used the classic case of congressional deference to Wilson in World War I followed by not only assertiveness, but a rousing defeat of the Versailles treaty after the war, to generalize that Congress is always acquiescent during war and resurgent after.[27]

However, this is not empirically the case. Congress was activist *before* the Spanish-American War, passing resolutions on Cuba and pushing a reluctant President McKinley to finally present Spain with an ultimatum. With Vietnam, the assertiveness did not wait until the end of the war, but took place *during* the war in order to bring it to an end. As for the Cold War, the assertiveness on Vietnam took place during the Cold War, the era known for congressional resurgence was the 1970s (with congressional investigations on Chile and blocking intervention in Angola), and certain institutionalized checks stayed in place throughout the eighties.[28] And yet, as active as Congress was in the 1990s in the wake of the Cold War, President Clinton was able to use force abroad in a major way six times with limited or little input from Congress.[29] The largest action, Kosovo, relied on NATO for support and justification, and avoided the United Nations and the U.S. Congress. Although some would say that Congress said no to the war over Kosovo,[30] there was a contradiction between the votes against the use of troops and air and missile strikes on the one hand, and the votes against a declaration of war, against withdrawal of troops, and in support of increased spending on the other hand, indicating the absence of a unified opposition.[31] This was not the "resurgent Congress" of the 1970s. Thus, there is no clear correlation between assertiveness and the postwar period.

To confirm the lack of correlation, a cross tabulation was run between war years and peaks in activity as well as years in which wars ended and peak years. The results are in Table 5. Interestingly, there are small signifi-

TABLE 5. WAR VERSUS CRITICAL ISSUES

	peaks in activity (phi)	peaks in close votes (phi)
Critical issue years with one-year lag	.634*	.397*
War endings		
one year after	.056	.077
two years after	.082	.113
last year of war plus two years	.236*	.212*
War years	.222*	.213*

*statistically significant at $p < .05$

SOURCE: Henehan, *Foreign Policy and Congress*, 152.

cant findings for war years and two years after wars, but not for shorter time lags. Nevertheless, the largest *phi* is .236, which is much smaller than the *phi*'s for critical issues.

The weakness of the findings on party control and the role of war indicate that they are less powerful explanations for congressional assertiveness than critical issues. If the critical issue theory provides a good explanation for the increases in activism in 1898, 1919, 1949, and 1971, then what does it tell us about the immediate post–Cold War period, the implications of the issue of terrorism, and what the future holds for the role of Congress in foreign policy?

Conclusion: Congress and Foreign Policy—Now and in the Future

With the above findings as a foundation, the critical issue explanation can serve as a means to a more theoretical understanding of recent patterns in congressional behavior and an aid in discussing likely developments in the future. Following the dismantling of the Vietnam policy, Congress became very assertive in a number of areas. Because the critical issue of anti-communism was not resolved, even though the Vietnam policy was reversed, there remained the dilemma of how to stop communism without getting involved in a quagmire or violating democratic or constitutional principles. Such contradictions and disagreements led to the Reagan administration's covert policy uncovered in the Iran-Contra affair. If the Vietnam policy had not been discredited, the policy of aiding the Contras might not have had to be kept secret, and indeed it could well have involved direct U.S. military intervention. As it was, the response to communism limped along without a consensus, symbolized by the various Boland amendments passed in the 1980s. This critical issue never was resolved; Gorbachev unilaterally took it off the agenda by opting out of the Cold War.

With the fall of the Berlin Wall in 1989, the Cold War was officially over. The critical issue was removed from the agenda, and there was no major failure at that time to react to. In fact, some saw the end of the Cold War as an American success. What is significant about the era that followed is that no single overarching critical issue emerged to shape debate over policy. This is the reason that congressional foreign policy in the 1990s is characterized by contention but not by coherence or direction.[32] Terry Deibel not only highlights this phenomenon, but documents the fact that there are intraparty as well as interparty splits on foreign policy, producing several different potential directions that policy could take. He raises the question of whether or not this factionalism will become a permanent feature in the foreign policy stances of members of Congress if the terrorism issue is successfully handled.[33]

The critical issue theory would say that the factionalism emerged due to the lack of a new critical issue. Terrorism was a problem in the nineties, but it was not critical until it produced an attack on the mainland of the country. The events of 9/11 very likely made terrorism the new critical issue. Because the country was attacked, Congress fell behind the president nearly unanimously. However, the war with Iraq and its aftermath have revealed chinks in the consensus. In the public, an antiwar movement emerged even before the war began, and those organizing the movement began to address the general principle of responding to issues with violence. There was less opposition in Congress, but it was not entirely absent. As widely as Dennis Kucinich was dismissed as a hopeless candidate for the presidency, it is still significant that there was a consistently antiwar person on the dais.

Finally, the critical issue reveals patterns that aid in making tentative predictions about the future. The pattern of strong consensus after 9/11 followed by some questioning of policy over Iraq is not unlike what happened with the Truman Doctrine and the Marshall Plan. The Truman Doctrine passed quickly and overwhelmingly, but the Marshall Plan was subjected to much more scrutiny. Congress does not have to oppose a policy to participate in shaping it. There can easily be a trend from overwhelming support in the immediate aftermath of 9/11, to minor criticisms of the war on Iraq, to more searching analyses of the Bush administration's unilateralist approach. The debate phase could well be under way now. On the one hand, the Republican successes in the midterm elections and the relatively quick and successful war in Iraq would indicate that more members of Congress are likely to support Bush than before, and a consensus could emerge on a unilateralist militarist approach to foreign policy. On the other hand, concerns about the $87 billion price tag for reconstructing Iraq together with continuing casualties have the potential of triggering a reassessment of the policy specifically and the go-it-alone doctrine generally.

Just as in 1964 Senator Wayne Morse saw the possibility that a policy that would "bog down thousands of American boys in Asia" could bring down an administration,[34] there is also some possibility that current policy could run into a failure that would lead to a reopening of debate and reversal of the policy. The United States is in a very strong position to do what it wants on the world scene because of its power. However, while the more powerful side in a war usually wins, it does not always win. The more military adventures the United States pursues, the larger the statistical likelihood that one will fail, like Vietnam. Thus, the critical issue theory would guess that the era of drift is over, debate over how to handle terrorism has ensued (largely over whether the response should be unilateral or multilateral), a consensus is likely to be hammered out, and that the response to terrorism will dominate foreign policy as long as it appears to be successful.

8 Seeing Things in Perspective

DONALD R. KELLEY

Introduction

Offering meaningful conclusions about the vital and ongoing political life of the nation is always risky; the debate is never ended, and the battle is rejoined for each new president and Congress, for each new issue, and for each new iteration of the broader global reality within which the struggle occurs. The best one (with proper modesty) can hope to do, as Senator Fulbright would have put it, is "to see things in perspective." That has been the goal of this undertaking: to offer a snapshot in time of the relationship between the executive and legislative branches on the formation of American foreign policy, framed and informed by the intellectual and political realities that characterize the post–Cold War, post–September 11 world.

Some parts of that reality seem unchanging. Because of the constitutional realities of divided power, the struggle is endemic and endless. Whatever else may be said about the wisdom of the balance of powers created by the founding fathers, it must be acknowledged and probably celebrated that it has produced an irresolvable struggle over just about every aspect of American politics, including our relations with the rest of the world. Like Euclidian geometry, the study of American foreign policy must begin with an unchallenged axiom, in this case that struggle is inevitable, and that such struggle will involve the interrelated but nonetheless distinct issues of *what* policy will be and *who* will make it. The necessary corollary of that conclusion is that all such struggles are best understood as complex *nested games,* that is, encounters in which all players operate in multiple arenas, each of which defines goals, rewards, and sanctions. In this setting, the calculus of decision therefore factors in not only the interactions of the players and their institutional venues (the legislature vs. the executive branch, for example, or the State Department vs. the CIA) but also the decisional processes internal to each player (for example, which is more important to me, the content of a particular policy or my party's control of the Senate, and how am I cross-pressured by the criteria imposed by other relevant arenas?).

But if some factors are constant, there also is a transient dimension that affects the outcome of the inevitable struggle. Every battle over *what* American foreign policy will be and/or *who* will make it occurs, as we note in chapter 1, "within a broader political, cultural, and intellectual context." That context changes, albeit usually within predictable parameters. That change is the legitimate focus of most studies of the politics of American foreign policy, and it guides the inquiries contained in this volume.

The Cultural and Intellectual Context: What We Think Determines What We Do

Action does not occur in a vacuum; it takes place within a cultural and intellectual context—we have termed them "conventional wisdoms"—which produces a "defining consensus" that gives order to the universe, or at least the part of it that shapes foreign policy. Such consensus is vital, since it both frames the issues within intellectual and partisan parameters acceptable to the major players and defines the rules of engagement for the inevitable, if now structured, struggles over what occurs within those parameters.

For the most part, the creation of such conventional wisdoms occurs in predictable, if sometimes unsettling ways. As Marie Henehan points out, understanding the issue cycle is critical to comprehending both the role of such "wisdoms" and how they are created or rejected. Issue cycles define the trajectory of problem-solving activity, beginning with the recognition of a new issue, moving through the characterization of the problem and the search for answers, and ending with the emergence of what we have termed a "defining consensus." They typically begin in one of two ways. They may be initiated by a defining event—the sinking of the *Lusitania*, Pearl Harbor, September 11—and produce a debate about how the nation should respond. The more traumatic the defining event, the more likely that the executive branch will be dominant in formulating the initial response and influencing the subsequent debate. Alternatively, they may begin with the perceived failure of an existing policy, usually resulting in an anguished debate in which the executive and legislative branches are more evenly matched, although neither is likely to be monolithically positioned on one or another side of the issue. Both will produce new and complex "nested" decisions, that is, broadly shared if not precisely articulated decisions about the general directions of policy and the relative role of the players. The broader the agreement, the more likely that routine matters will be relegated to the realm of implementation, to be performed within certain discretionary parameters by various agencies of the executive branch. Conversely, the less encompassing the agreement, the narrower the discretionary parameters within which the executive branch may operate, the greater the level of congressional oversight, and the more likely that the initial debate over *what* and *who* may be reopened.

Two caveats are in order concerning the real power of such conventional wisdoms. The first deals with their inherent ambiguity and their ability to evolve, even while seeming to remain constant. Even unchallengeable shibboleths such as the Cold War mindset contained many variations both on the true nature of the enemy and the choice of policies to confront it, and it evolved over time as the bipolar Cold War of the immediate post–World War II era morphed into the multilateral Cold War of the seventies, eighties, and nineties. Subtle but still important partisan issues also persist within such consensus; if the definition of democracy requires a degree of "contention," as the theorists usually describe it, then politicians must have something to "contend" about, and it breaches common sense to argue that such divisiveness would totally exclude the nuances of even the most commonly accepted foreign policy priorities. By definition, consensus suggests something less than unanimity, and the game of politics lies in sorting out the details.

The second caveat reminds us of the ephemeral nature of victory and defeat, at least as defined by the conventional wisdom of the day. The writing of revisionist history is a favorite activity of scholars and public officials alike, and what may be thought to be success or failure at one moment is subject to an almost Orwellian process of "re-thought." In the Soviet era, Russian historians frequently lamented the inherent dangers of their profession by saying that the past was dangerous to predict, and while extreme, the observation has resonance to the extent that the "truths" that stand at the core of any conventional wisdom are subject to future invalidation. The "truth" of the Munich analogy or of the inherent expansionism of communism, to name but two, has been both functional and dysfunctional, depending on the moment of their application.

In moments of transition, inherently contradictory elements may coexist within the same conventional wisdom. Arguably this is now a part of the current American dilemma of developing a new post–Cold War, post–September 11 mindset. Two unchallengeable facts stand in seeming contradiction: (1) the hegemonic power of the United States, at least in conventional military terms, and the more disputed consensus that such power will be used either multilaterally or unilaterally, as befits the nature of the challenge and the predilections of the current leadership; and (2) the unassailable reality of an increasingly interdependent world, measured in terms of economics, the environment, the rising salience of issues such as human rights and the status of women, the presence of virtually instantaneous worldwide communication, and the spread of ubiquitous global culture. Reconciling these elements of cognitive dissonance may depend either on the events, metaphors, and myths that eventually come to be most widely held, or on the eventual choice of one element of such dualism as more important than the other. Or, in the terms of nested games, reconciliation may depend on the relative political power of those forces and institutions that hold a particular point of view. In the abstract, at least, how the final conventional wisdom will emerge cannot be determined. As in all nested games, it will depend on the players' preferences and strategic choices.

The Institutional Context: Domestic Politics

If ideas and conventional wisdoms matter, so do institutions. People think, but when they organize to undertake collective action, they create institutions that acquire both the virtue of routinization and the liability of inertia. It is within such institutions that the nested struggles described above occur, and it is in the subtle evolution of their sense of mission and their interrelationships that the invitation to struggle will be answered.

Not surprising, all of our authors have dealt in one way or another with the institutionalized struggle over the formation of American foreign policy. And equally unsurprising, they have found that even the most seemingly fixed institutions change over time, sometimes because of purposeful efforts to redefine their role or the rules of the game of politics, sometimes because the individual members utilize and exploit them for differing purposes, and sometimes because the larger international milieu within which they operate changes.

A number of our contributors have noted the impact of the purposeful reforms of the committee system in the 1970s, which undercut the tenure and power of committee chairs (and, in partisan terms, of long-term southern Democrats who held views sympathetic to a hard-line interpretation of the Cold War and the dominant role of the president in foreign and defense policy) and made the Congress more responsive to the rank-and-file membership of the House and Senate. These reforms had two mutually reinforcing consequences. First, as noted, they weakened and deinstitutionalized the early Cold War consensus about both the need to resist communism and the mechanisms through which such a policy was to be implemented. This opened and then substantially widened the partisan divisions on foreign policy questions, both animating and legitimizing a broader debate about the nature of the defining consensus. Second, they reanimated the debate about the powers of the presidency and the legislature in defining foreign policy. With the close link between committees dominated by senior party leaders and the president broken, rank-and-file members of both houses were freer to raise more fundamental questions not only about the substance of policy but also about more essential constitutional issues.

It also is hardly surprising that all of our contributors noted the impact of increasing partisanship over the last decade. In part because of the more permissive atmosphere for debate, and in part because of the absence of a defining consensus that would establish the parameters if not the details of policy, partisan identity has rushed into the void. But there are caveats and nuances. One of the most important caveats concerns the continuing impact of divided government, that is, when the White House is held by one party, and one or both houses of Congress are under control of the other. Whatever the mixture, divided government usually compromises the power of the president. To be sure, there are many nuances of such compromise. Presidential influence may be issue-specific, waxing and waning in relationship to the policy interests of either or both houses. Or divided government may simply lead to closer consultation between the opposite ends of Pennsylvania Avenue, producing compromises earlier on in the policy process that reflect a win-win situation for the president and Congress. Or cautious chief executives may work under self-imposed restrictions, submitting to Congress only those policies that are sure of passage.

One of the more interesting nuances in partisanship has been presented by Terry Deibel, who notes the importance of factionalism *within* parties. Defined probably best as schools of thought rather than ideologies, these factional identities speak both to the style of American diplomacy—Republican *internationalists* as opposed to *unilateralists,* for example—and to the extent to which a party's philosophy may be applied—Democratic *idealists* versus *pragmatists*. Policy alignment therefore was just as likely to occur along factional as well as party lines, especially in the absence either of an issue or strong presidential leadership that cuts across the factional subidentities. While Deibel's research presents a particular snapshot in time of the Clinton administration, the broader point is well taken. Parties are never monoliths, and it is not surprising that their internal divisions correspond to both their own broader worldviews and to the tactical dimensions of their implementation.

Most of our commentators also noted the increasingly ideological nature of the foreign policy debate. To be sure, ideology, or what passes for it in the context of American politics, always has been present to some degree. But in recent years, the litmus test of ideological correctness has become more important. This, of course, merely reflects the increasingly ideological nature of domestic politics. In the absence of clear party identities, ideological labels have become all the more significant, both as battle cries to capture the more conventional labels of Republican or Democrat, and as reference points through which to win support from a general voting public that increasingly eschews party identity.

Further insight into the politics of the executive-legislative relationship is offered in Bryan Marshall's argument that congressional delegation of authority to the executive branch should be viewed as a collective action dilemma in which individual members of the House of Representatives (and implicitly the Senate, although it is beyond his present research) delegate authority to the president only so long as it is rational to do so. Rationality, in this context, is defined in terms of optimizing the ability of individual members to strengthen their prospects for reelection by claiming credit for successful policy and avoiding blame for failure. Only when the political costs of delegation outweigh the benefits is it rational for legislators to revise the current patterns of delegation. The changing issue agenda, and in particular the increasing importance of economic issues that affect domestic constituencies, further complicates the task of choosing a politically rational level of delegation; the more closely international issues strike home, the greater the potential risks of incorrectly assessing an optimum level of delegation.

Nested Games and the Domestic Context of Foreign Policy

The domestic institutional milieu within which American foreign policy is debated and implemented offers a rich and nuanced setting in which nested games can be played out in the context of conflicting venues and overlapping issues. The very nature of nested games lends itself to such a complex institutional setting. Whatever else the founding fathers did in creating divided power and checks and balances, they certainly established an institutional environment in which nested games could be played out in the context of conflicting branches and levels of government, each informed and animated not only by the inevitable personal and partisan dimensions of political life but also by the conflicting jurisdictions and prerogatives of different institutions.

Seen in this context, most of the elements of the executive-legislative relationship reveal dimensions of such "nesting," both in terms of the multiple and usually conflicting perspectives of the individual players (that is, the normal sort of nested game) or in terms of deciding whether a dispute is primarily about the *substance* of a particular policy or about the issue of *who makes the decision* (that is, a game of institutional design). Our contributors have described numerous instances of the complex interplay of such questions. For example, the growing importance of international economic issues has raised the ante for most legislators, in part because such intermestic issues reach deeply into the constituencies of lawmakers and in part because they mobilize a wide assortment of interest groups and other stakeholders who have immediate concerns with the substance of such policies. They animate disputes about the substance of a particular economic policy—how will a particular trade agreement affect industries in my bailiwick, encouraging exports or losing jobs to foreign workers—and about how power will be allocated between the executive and legislative branches—how much power will the president have to conclude "fast-track" trade agreements, for example. The increasing partisanship of foreign policy decisions also complicates the nesting of such decisions, both for individual legislators who must sort out increasingly salient party or factional pressures and in the larger institutional context, which is confronted with the question of whether a particular issue should prompt a more serious game of institutional design or simply be decided by playing out a normal, albeit now more complex, nested game.

The nested game approach also yields insights into the policy cycle analysis of executive-legislative interaction. The initial phases of the policy cycle inevitably will invoke strong components of the institutional design game; by definition, new issues raise fundamental questions about who gets to define the issue, and, once defined, who becomes involved in designing and implementing the response. No matter how seemingly crisis-driven, the initial question of *how* to respond inexorably is tied to the more protracted issue of *who* gets to decide policy both now and in the future and how the initial determination of these issues will affect the long-term allocation of power and resources. Conversely, later phases of the policy cycle occurring after the initial definition of the issue and allocation of responsibilities will invoke the more conventional sort of nested game in which policy makers choose among their own priorities. That said, it remains possible that there will occasionally be efforts to reopen the question of institutional design, either because individual legislators find it difficult to resolve contradictions within their own priorities and wish to redefine the issue in ways that reduce the conflict, or because institutional actors who lost out in the first round wish to replay the game in the hope of improving their relative power and influence.

The impact of the events of September 11, 2001, on the nesting of foreign policy games is, as yet, unclear. It certainly can be argued that the American fixation with homeland security and the pursuit of terrorists through a unilateral forward strategy have created a new form of (mostly) bipartisan conventional wisdom, much as did the first decade of the Cold War. To the extent that such consensus persists, and to the extent to which tactical policy choices—*who* constitutes the primary threat, and *how* to battle them—seemingly are consistent with the broader objectives, then the new consensus will create a clear set of benchmarks against which policy makers can measure their own priorities. In simple terms, the clearer and more widespread the agreement on the essential goals and tactics of American foreign policy, the easier for legislators to resolve the conflicting signals and priorities that are inherent in any nested game.

This suggests two further observations about the relationship between nested games and policy outcomes. First, in the face of widespread consensus about the central core of the new conventional wisdom—the presence of a terrorist threat, however defined, and the need to be proactive in responding to it—other concerns and priorities are likely to shrink in salience. Simply put, party or intraparty factional identity, or ideological orientation, should diminish in importance, at least for a time. To be sure, they will never completely zero out in the calculation, but they will be viewed through a lens created by the larger consensus. Conversely, the perceived threat of terrorism will add another profoundly intermestic issue to the equation. As several of our contributors have noted, the growing importance of economic issues in the 1980s and 1990s changed the way in which legislators viewed foreign policy issues and their need to influence them; what policy was and, in many cases, who made it now reached deeply into their own districts, and political survival dictated that they now play a more proactive role in the formulation of any foreign policy decision that had economic consequences for their constituents. In a similar fashion, the question of terrorism is seen as profoundly close to home; few Americans were actually in lower Manhattan, in Arlington, or in a Pennsylvania farm field on the morning of September 11, and few are at real risk of falling victim to terrorism. But that is not the point. *Perceived* risk was the important issue, and the chilling thought that they or a loved one *could* be a victim is what will enter into the political equation, affecting the way in which all other foreign policy (and many domestic) issues are resolved, and changing the internal compass of every elected official who must balance out the conflicting priorities of a nested game.

September 11 also altered the nested game of institutional design, that is, the determination of *how* decisions are to be reached. Change came in two ways. First, the institutional playing field was substantially altered by the creation of the Department of Homeland Security or by the addition of terrorist-related functions to other agencies. In a setting in which power and influence are measured by the size of one's budget or the scope of one's turf, such restructuring changes the nature of the playing field, empowering newly created or elevated agencies and altering critical issues such as access to the White House and congressional leadership. Second, the crisis nature of the perceived terrorist threat, as well as the subsequent military actions in Afghanistan and Iraq, shifted the institutional balance in favor of the White House. Not surprising, the power both to define the nature of the threat and to initiate action against whatever forces were seen as its incarnation fell to the president, at least in the early days of America's new war on terrorism. Consequently, the role of the legislature diminished to that of willing handmaiden or timid critic, at least until the growing costs of the Iraqi occupation began to take their human and political toll. To be sure, such movement in favor of the executive branch was no more dramatic than that which had occurred at other times of crisis, and the legislative response was equally foreshadowed by past experience. What is significant is that both kinds of nested games—the conventional game in which players had to reconcile their own conflicting priorities, and the game of institutional design in which the rules of engagement were subject to reinterpretation—were simultaneously in play to a greater degree than had been present since the end of the Vietnam War.

The Institutional Context: The International System

In the broader context, the formulation of American foreign policy also occurs within the intellectual and institutional framework of the international system. The dualism linking domestic and external factors can never be fully disconnected. What happens in the international milieu shapes how a nation perceives and responds to the world. Undue preoccupation with the nation's domestic political life inevitably diminishes recognition of the significance of the international setting in shaping foreign policy.

But even if we willingly accept the admonition to take the broader international context into account, how do we conceptualize it in terms of our analysis of the formation of American foreign policy? Marie Henehan again offers a useful point of departure in arguing that the policy cycle frequently determines the relative impact of international versus domestic factors. At both the beginning and end of the cycle, international factors potentially carry great weight. Events beyond a nation's borders frequently compel it to deal with crises, threats, or opportunities, thus forcing it to begin a new policy cycle. At the beginning phase of the cycle, new issues must be recognized and defined. The stakes are immense, affecting not only the creation of a new conventional wisdom that will shape the interpretation of the nation's priorities but also defining the political and institutional relationships that spell out the rules of engagement. In the terminology of nested games, both conventional and institutional design games are simultaneously in play; the former occurring in the minds of all the key players, who must sort out their own priorities, and the latter taking place throughout the larger institutional milieu to define the relative allocation of power and influence for the foreseeable future.

The international milieu also has exceptional impact at the end of the policy cycle, especially if previous policies are perceived to have ended in failure. To be sure, success—especially if defined in military terms—prompts the usual kudos for all involved and confirms the correctness of both the content of policy and the wisdom of the policy process (and the policy makers) that produced it. Having "won," policy makers must simply adjust their own conventional wisdoms and policy procedures to deal with the new reality created by their victory. But failure involves a different set of imperatives. Responsibility must be assessed and blame meted out, and in political terms these activities exact costs both for individuals and institutions.

Henehan's arguments certainly offer instructive insights about America's responses to the end of the Cold War, its increasing immersion in a sometimes friendly and sometimes hostile global economy, and the events of September 11. In all three cases, the catalysts for change came from the international system, albeit in different form. The end of the Cold War caught America, and most of the rest of the world, by surprise. That the threat of world communism in general and of the Soviet Union in particular should evaporate so quickly was hardly foreseen in the spring of 1985 when a largely unknown Mikhail Gorbachev took power in Moscow. Whatever his intentions for domestic reform and redefinition of the role of Soviet power in the world, Gorbachev set in motion a series of eventually unstoppable events that brought about the collapse both of a powerful adversary and of an ideology. That left Americans free to proclaim "victory," legitimating, at least in the minds of the Reagan and Bush administrations, both the American version of how the world should work and the institutional arrangements at home that had produced such victory. But it also left a void in terms of the new direction of American policy. As Henehan's analysis would suggest, that void produced a debate among a widened circle of actors. Questions over whether, or how much, to invest in the stabilization of democracy in the former communist nations, whether to define American objectives in terms of the discovery of new foes (China, as a growing regional power, or Islamic fundamentalism as a more generic global force hostile to American interests headed the lists), or whether to retreat into a preoccupation with domestic economic and social needs were joined at all levels of the executive and legislative branches and by stakeholders and commentators in the private sector. Two aspects of these discussions are relevant to our purposes. First, the executive and legislative branches participated in the debates on a relatively even footing, and both were influenced by private interests who had a stake in the outcome. Even allowing for the tendency for the legislature to be more aggressive under divided government—Republicans controlled one or both houses of Congress for six of Clinton's eight years in office—the struggle to define American foreign policy was remarkably evenly matched. Second, little was actually decided. Philosophical commitments to the support of democracy in former communist states translated at best into limited financial assistance and increasingly qualified endorsement of leaders like Boris Yeltsin, and no one quite sorted out or prioritized the threats facing America. With little real pressure to create a new defining consensus or to deal with the political costs of coming to such agreement, America's political leaders debated, but did not decide.

The changing nature of the global economy also compelled American policy makers to cope with a new reality. The detailing of those realities do not require reiteration in this study. But it is appropriate to note how deeply they affected both the content of American policy and, perhaps more important for our purposes, how they changed the roles of the executive branch, the legislature, and organized economic interests in the formulation of that policy. For reasons noted above, concerned legislators sought to affect foreign policy decisions that had economic impact on their constituents. Across the political and institutional spectrum, both the perceptions of the individual players and the nature of the institutional relationships shifted to take account of the new reality that economic issues now were increasingly transcendent. Yet even with such increasing activism, the respective roles of the legislative and executive branches were played out in predictable fashion. For the most part, Congress focused on the delineation of policy-making procedures, while the White House seemed more concerned with substantive issues.

It is also important to note the impact of the changing international institutional milieu within which American foreign policy operates. To be sure, a nation's foreign policy always functions within an institutionalized framework, even at the international level; comprehensive entities such as the United Nations are complemented by a growing number of international organizations that perform an assortment of regulatory or advisory functions. Significant for our purposes, however, is the rapid expansion of such organizations over the last quarter century. The increasing number of international or supranational organizations has changed the institutional milieu within which American foreign policy must be crafted and implemented, and the increasing (although, to be sure, often resisted) encroachments of such entities into the once sovereign space of the nation-state have altered the domestic political costs of interacting with an increasingly interdependent world. Just as we have noted the intermestic nature of economic issues and the way in which such penetration has altered both the calculations of individual policy makers and the relative roles of Congress and the presidency, so too we must acknowledge that the permeability of national borders on other issues such as human rights, the environment, or criminal justice will inevitably compel domestic political leaders and the institutions through which they govern to adjust to the change. If all politics is local, then the growing assortment of international entities whose mandates and (sometimes) formal powers transcend once impermeable national boundaries will inevitably change the definition of local.

Most dramatically, the morning of September 11, 2001, illustrated how rapidly and profoundly a new policy cycle can be initiated by events rooted in the international system. Few moments have so forcefully captured the nation's attention and animated its fear and outrage, and few have so profoundly illustrated the extent to which a nation's policy agenda can be shaped by forces beyond its borders. That said, two realities must be acknowledged. The first addresses America's previous experience with terrorism. While nothing on the scale of the attacks of September 11 had occurred before, the public had witnessed a gradual escalation of terrorism at home and abroad, manifested in attacks on American embassies abroad or an earlier attempt to bomb the World Trade Center in 1993. What America acquired on September 11 was not just another more extreme example of such action but also—and perhaps more important for our purposes—a new and clearly defined enemy: Muslim extremism in general and al-Qaeda in particular. The enemy now had a name and a face, and even, so it seemed, an address to which we could send our response. The presumptive clarity of that perception informed and motivated the creation of a new conventional wisdom about the threats facing the nation and led the crafting of new institutions such as the Department of Homeland Security to meet the challenge.

The second reality is that politics is still politics. As with all of the conventional wisdoms in the past, eventually the new reality would come to incorporate some aspects of the political life of the old. The new consensus soon yielded to disputes about how to define the enemy and where to find him. And these questions would soon raise, even if only in retrospect, further questions about whether or not initial choices had been correct. As noted, politics is still politics, and in a democracy it must generate disputable issues, no matter how nuanced. The point is that even the most striking new realities imposed from whatever source must eventually be processed by a set of conventional wisdoms and domestic political institutions that, while malleable, are not completely elastic. Some things remain constant, no matter the source of the issue, and these draw the parameters of the struggle over foreign policy even if they do not map the entire terrain of the battlefield. And that brings us back to our point of departure. As Corwin reminded us, the American constitution offered at best an "invitation to struggle" over the origins and content of foreign policy. What our studies in the volume have hopefully revealed is the complexity of that struggle, framed by enduring and yet flexible institutions, informed and defined by the conventional wisdom of the day that melds certain unchanging habits of thought in the way Americans think about the outside world and how to respond to it with their contemporary perception of the problems of the moment.

Contributors

RALPH G. CARTER

Ralph G. Carter is a Professor of Political Science at Texas Christian University in Fort Worth, Texas. He received his Ph.D. from Ohio State University. He is author of *Contemporary Cases in U.S. Foreign Policy: From Terrorism to Trade,* and he has contributed numerous articles to *Politics and Society, PS: Political Science and Politics, Congress and the Presidency,* and *International Trade Journal.*

TERRY L. DEIBEL

Terry L. Deibel is Professor of National Strategy in the Department of National Security Policy at the National War College. He received his Ph.D. from the Fletcher School of Law and Diplomacy. His government service has included the Office of Management and Budget, the Executive Office of the President, and the Department of State's Bureau of Politico-Military Affairs, and his academic affiliations have included the School of Foreign Service, Georgetown University, the Carnegie Endowment for International Peace, and the Center for Strategic and International Studies. His books include *Clinton and Congress: The Politics of Foreign Policy; Presidents, Public Opinion, and Power: The Nixon, Carter, and Reagan Years;* and *Containment: Concept and Policy,* edited with John L. Gaddis. He has contributed to *Foreign Affairs, Foreign Policy, International Security,* and the *Washington Quarterly.*

MARIE T. HENEHAN

Marie T. Henehan is a Senior Lecturer and Research Associate in the Department of Political Science at Colgate University. She received her Ph.D. from Rutgers University. She is author of *Companion to International Relations:*

Major Concepts, Terms, and Thinkers, coauthored with John A. Vasquez, and *Foreign Policy and Congress: An International Perspective.* Her articles have appeared in *Journal of Peace Research, Legislative Studies Section Newsletter,* and *Comparative Foreign Policy Notes.*

GARY R. HESS

Gary R. Hess is a Distinguished Research Professor of History at Bowling Green State University. He received his Ph.D. from the University of Virginia. His books include *Sam Hagginbotham of Allahabad: Pioneer of Point Four to India; America Encounters India; America and Russia: Cold War Confrontation to Coexistence; United States' Emergence as a Southeast Asian Power, 1940–1950; Vietnam and the United States: Origins and Legacy of War; The United States at War, 1941–1945;* and *Presidential Decisions for War: Korea, Vietnam, and the Persian Gulf.*

DONALD R. KELLEY

Donald R. Kelley is Professor of Political Science and Director of the Fulbright Institute of International Relations at the University of Arkansas. He received his Ph.D. from Indiana University. His more recent books include *The Clinton Riddle: Perspectives on the Forty-Second President,* co-edited with Todd Shields and Jeannie Whayne; *After Communism: Perspectives on Democracy,* editor; and *Politics in Russia and the Successor States.* He has published in the *American Political Science Review, Journal of Politics, American Behavioral Scientist,* and *Soviet Studies.*

BRYAN W. MARSHALL

Bryan W. Marshall is Assistant Professor of Political Science at the University of Missouri, St. Louis. He received his Ph.D. from Michigan State University. His published works have appeared in *Social Science Quarterly, Politics and Policy, Congress and the Presidency, Political Research Quarterly, Journal of Legislative Studies,* and *American Review of Politics.*

BERT A. ROCKMAN

Bert A. Rockman is Professor and Director of the School of Public Policy and Management at the Ohio State University. He received his Ph.D. from the University of Michigan. His most recent book, with Joel Aberbach, is *In the*

Web of Politics: Three Decades of the U.S. Federal Executive. His other books include *The Clinton Legacy*, co-edited with Colin Campbell; *Do Institutions Matter? Government Capabilities in the U.S. and Abroad*, co-edited with R. Kent Weaver; and *The Leadership Question: The Presidency and the American System*. His articles have appeared in the *American Political Science Review, Journal of Politics, American Journal of Political Science, British Journal of Political Science, Comparative Political Studies, Legislative Studies Quarterly, Public Administration Review,* and *Journal of Public Administration Research and Theory.*

Notes

Chapter One: Answering the "Invitation to Struggle" by Donald R. Kelley

1. Edward S. Corwin, *The President: Office and Powers, 1787–1957* (New York: New York University Press, 1957), 171.
2. George Tsebelis, *Nested Games* (Berkeley and Los Angeles: University of California Press, 1990), 1–17.
3. Samuel Huntington, *The Third Wave: Democratization in the Late Twentieth Century* (Norman: University of Oklahoma Press, 1991).
4. Samuel Huntington, *The Clash of Civilizations and the Remaking of World Order* (New York: Simon and Schuster, 1996).
5. Francis Fukuyama, *The End of History and the Last Man* (New York: Free Press, 1992).

Chapter Two: The President, Executive, and Congress: The Same Old Story? by Bert A. Rockman

1. These include, also, J. W. Fulbright, *Old Myths and New Realities* (New York: Random House, 1964); J. William Fulbright, *The Arrogance of Power* (New York: Vintage Books, 1966); and several books after leaving the Senate, including J. William Fulbright and John Charles Daly, moderator, *The Future of the United Nations: A Round Table Held on November 6, 1976* (Washington, D.C.: American Enterprise Institute for Public Policy Research, 1977); J. William Fulbright, *The Crippled Giant: American Foreign Policy and Its Domestic Consequences* (New York: Random House, 1972); and with Michael Glennon and a foreword by J. William Fulbright, *Constitutional Diplomacy* (Princeton, N.J.: Princeton University Press, 1990).
2. Potter Stewart was an associate justice of the United States Supreme Court. The reference was to the definition of pornography, a definition elusive to the Court and in the law. Justice Stewart, known for his moderate ways, thus opined in essence that pornography was subjective, but with enough subjective agreement "it" could be banned.

Chapter Three: Authorizing War: Congressional Resolutions and Presidential Leadership, 1955–2002 by Gary R. Hess

1. The war resolution against international terrorism, which passed Congress with only one dissenting vote on September 14, 2001, differed from these five resolutions in that it accepted that the United States was at war as a result of the terrorist attacks three days earlier. This led to acknowledgment of the principle that the commander-in-chief's power included responsibility for defending the nation against attack: "the President has the authority under the Constitution to take action to deter and prevent acts of international terrorism against the United States." This was not part of the other resolutions. At the same time, the 2001 resolution accepted the necessity of a military response overseas: "the President is authorized to use all necessary and appropriate force against those nations, organizations, or persons that he determines planned, authorized, or aided the terrorist attacks that occurred on September 11, 2001 . . ." As that open-ended wording indicates, the resolution had an element of "prior authority" in that it left to the discretion of the president determination of the targets of U.S. military force. Thus, the resolution provided authorization principally for the military campaign against the Taliban in Afghanistan, but also for smaller military operations against terrorism. See *Congressional Record*, September 14, 2001, H5638; *New York Times*, September 14–15, 2001.

2. Dwight D. Eisenhower, *Mandate for Change* (Garden City, N.Y.: Doubleday, 1963), 82.

3. Robert A. Divine, *Eisenhower and the Cold War* (New York: Oxford University Press, 1981), 55–56.

4. Eisenhower, *Mandate for Change*, 466.

5. Alexander L. George and Richard Smoke, *Deterrence in American Foreign Policy: Theory and Practice* (New York: Columbia University Press, 1974), 285–87.

6. Memorandum of Conversation, January 20, 1955, *Foreign Relations of the United States* [FRUS] 1955–1957, vol. 2 (Washington, D.C.: Government Printing Office, 1986), 55–68; Memorandum of Conversation, January 19, 1955, ibid., 46–49; Memorandum of Conversation, January 19, 1955, ibid., 50–52.

7. *Public Papers of the Presidents of the United States: Dwight D. Eisenhower, 1955*, 207–11; hereafter *PPP*. An earlier draft of the speech, prepared by the Department of State, was notably briefer and gave less attention to the importance of congressional support and also specified a termination date of the resolution of June 30, 1956, or earlier at the discretion of the president; Eisenhower eliminated the reference to a specific date and left termination incumbent on the president. See Draft Message from the President, January 20, 1955, FRUS 1955, 2:83–85.

8. Arthur M. Schlesinger observes that prior authorization for warfare had been considered by the Executive on a few occasions between 1799 and 1858, but Congress had declined to sanction it. Schlesinger, *The Imperial Presidency* (New York: Houghton Mifflin, 1973), 18–23, 56–58, 160.

9. Stephen A. Ambrose, *Eisenhower: The President,* vol. 2 (New York: Simon and Schuster, 1984), 232.

10. Phleger cited in Walter LaFeber, *America, Russia, and the Cold War, 1945–1996,* 8th ed. (New York: McGraw Hill, 1997), 166.

11. Joint Resolution by Congress, January 29, 1955, FRUS 1955, 2:162–63.

12. Divine, *Eisenhower and the Cold War,* 65–66.

13. Eisenhower to Gruenther, February 1, 1955, and Eisenhower to Churchill, February 10, 1955, FRUS 1955, 2:189–93, 259–61.

14. George and Smoke, *Deterrence in American Foreign Policy,* 287–88.

15. Divine, *Eisenhower and the Cold War,* 61.

16. Ibid., 61–66.

17. Ray Takeyh, *The Origins of the Eisenhower Doctrine: The U.S., Britain, and Nasser's Egypt, 1953–57* (New York: St. Martin's Press, 2000), 142–59; George and Smoke, *Deterrence in American Foreign Policy,* 316–22.

18. Memorandum of Meeting, January 1, 1957, FRUS 1955–1957 (Washington, D.C.: Government Printing Office, 1991), 12:432–37; Eisenhower, *Waging Peace* (New York: Doubleday, 1965), 179; Ambrose, *Eisenhower,* 2:381–82. For background on the resolution, see Memorandum of Dulles-Eisenhower Conversation, December 8, 1956, FRUS 1955–1957, 12:395–96; Memorandum of Dulles-Knowland Conversation, December 8, 1956, FRUS 1955–1957, 396–407; Hoover to Murphy, December 10, 1956, FRUS 1955–1957, 398; Murphy to Dulles, December 15, 1956, FRUS 1955–1957, 410–12; Memorandum by Dulles, December 18, 1956, FRUS 1955–1957, 413; Memorandum of Dulles et al. conversation with Eisenhower, December 20, 1956, FRUS 1955–1957, 415–17.

19. *PPP: Eisenhower,* 1957, 6–16; *New York Times,* January 6, 1957.

20. Divine, *Eisenhower and the Cold War,* 91–92; George and Smoke, *Deterrence in American Foreign Policy,* 325–28; Cecil V. Crabb, *The Doctrines of American Foreign Policy* (Baton Rouge: Louisiana State University Press, 1982), 166–71.

21. Fisher, *Presidential War Power,* 108.

22. Smoke and George, *Deterrence in American Foreign Policy,* 321–25.

23. 103rd *Congressional Record* (1957), 3120.

24. Ibid., 3121–23.

25. Cited in Crabb, *Doctrines of American Foreign Policy,* 171.

26. Philip J. Briggs, "Congress and the Middle East: The Eisenhower Doctrine, 1957," in *Dwight D. Eisenhower: Soldier, President, Statesman,* ed. Joann P. Krieg (New York: Greenwood, 1987), 256–65.

27. Department of State, *Policy in the Middle East,* 45–47; Divine, *Eisenhower and the Cold War,* 92–93.

28. *New York Times,* March 5–11, 1957.

29. *PPP: Eisenhower,* 1957, 177–78.

30. LaFeber, *America, Russia, and the Cold War,* 189. Eisenhower's commitment to cooperation with Congress continued with his appointment of Congressman James P. Richards to head a special mission to Middle Eastern countries to explain the Eisenhower Doctrine and to report back to the president; Fisher, *Presidential War Power,* 110.

31. Rostow to Rusk, February 13, 1964, FRUS 1964–1968, vol. 1: Vietnam, 1964 (Washington, D.C., 1992); Bundy to Johnson, May 22, 1964, ibid., 349–51; Draft State Dept. Resolution, May 24, 1964, ibid., 356–58; Bundy to Johnson, May 25, 1964, ibid., 374–77; Summary of Honolulu Meetings, June 2, 1964, ibid., 428–33; Summary of White House Meeting, June 10, 1964, ibid., 487–92; Bundy to McNamara, June 15, 1964, ibid., 500–516; State Department Memorandum, June 15, 1964, ibid., 516–18; Randall Woods, *Fulbright: A Biography* (New York: Cambridge University Press, 1995), 347–49.

32. Edwin E. Moise, *Tonkin Gulf and the Escalation of the Vietnam War* (Chapel Hill: University of North Carolina Press, 1996), 82–207.

33. NSC Meeting Notes, August 4, 1964, FRUS 1964–1968, 1:611–13; Leadership Meeting Notes, August 4, 1964, ibid., 615–21. At a White House staff meeting the next morning, when one member questioned the logic of a resolution that used an attack on U.S. forces to justify maintenance of freedom throughout Southeast Asia, "Bundy jokingly told him perhaps the matter should not be thought through too far. For his own part, he welcomed the recent events as justification for a resolution the administration had wanted for some time." Later, discussing the meeting with congressional leaders, "Bundy commented that 'leadership' was a funny word in this case, in that there was little Congressmen could do in the way of leading in a situation in which the President's role was so primary." See: White House Staff Meeting Record, August 5, 1964, ibid., 631–32.

34. *PPP: Johnson*, 1963–64, 2:927–28.

35. Johnson also referred to the precedent of the Cuba resolution, passed by Congress on October 3, 1962. This resolution had language similar to the two earlier resolutions, but it differed from the prior authorization resolutions in a number of ways. It had not been formally requested by President John F. Kennedy, who claimed in September 1962 sufficient authority as the commander-in-chief to deal with the unfolding situation in Cuba; he did state that he would be "glad" to have the resolutions and in announcing the naval "quarantine" of Cuba, he based his action on "the authority entrusted to me by the Constitution as endorsed by the resolution of the Congress." The Cuba resolution is thus described by Louis Fisher as an expression of congressional sentiment, not a formal congressional authorization to use military force, and, as a result, it had no provision for its termination. Fisher, *Presidential War Power*, 111–13.

36. *PPP: Johnson*, 1963–64, 928; *Department of State Bulletin*, August 24, 1964, 260–63.

37. Woods, *Fulbright*, 353–55; Daniel Westerfield, *The President, the Congress, and the Question of War* (Westport, Conn.: Praeger, 1996), 82–85; *Congressional Record Senate*, August 6, 1964, 18132–416; *New York Times*, August 6–8, 1964.

38. John Hart Ely, *War and Responsibility: Constitutional Lessons of Vietnam and Its Aftermath* (Princeton, N.J.: Princeton University Press, 1993), 19–30.

39. Cited in Woods, *Fulbright*, 475.

40. Westerfield, *War Power*, 8–9, n. 9.

41. Woods, *Fulbright*, 572–74; Ely, *War and Responsibility*, 32–35.

42. Michael J. Glennon, *Constitutional Diplomacy* (Princeton, N.J.: Princeton

University Press, 1990), 87–122; Cecil V. Crabb Jr. and Pat M. Holt, *Invitation to Struggle: Congress, the President, and Foreign Policy,* 4th ed. (Washington, D.C.: Congressional Quarterly Press, 1992), 144–46; Fisher, *Presidential War Power,* 128–61, 191–97; Westerfield, *War Power,* 85–115.

43. George Bush and Brent Scowcroft, *A World Transformed* (New York: Knopf, 1998), 371–72.

44. Ibid., 371.

45. *PPP: Bush,* 1991, 1:13–14.

46. Ibid., 1:20.

47. Gary Hess, *Presidential Decisions for War* (Baltimore, Md.: Johns Hopkins University Press, 2001), 188–89.

48. Ibid., 191–95.

49. *PPP: Bush,* 1991, 1:40.

50. This summary of the 2002 resolution is based on coverage in the *New York Times,* August 16, September 3, 5, 6, 9, October 1–11, 2002, and the *Washington Post,* August 26, September 8, October 9–11, 2002.

Chapter Four: Intraparty Factionalism on Key Foreign Policy Issues: Congress versus Clinton, 1995–2000 by Terry L. Deibel

1. The views expressed here are the author's and do not necessarily reflect the official policy or position of the National War College, the National Defense University, the Department of Defense, or the U.S. government.

2. Samuel Huntington argued at the time that this shift had overcome all sense of the national interest, and he advocated a moratorium on foreign policy until some cohesiveness returned. See "The Erosion of American National Interests," *Foreign Affairs* 76 (October/November 1997): 28–49.

3. For a more complete description of these factions and the events that divided them, see Terry L. Deibel, *Clinton and Congress: The Politics of Foreign Policy,* Headline Series No. 321 (New York: Foreign Policy Association, fall 2000). Some parts of this chapter are condensed or borrowed from that monograph.

4. In a *Washington Post*/Henry J. Kaiser Foundation/Harvard University poll conducted in the summer of 1998, Republicans and Democrats split sharply on the issue of whether "the federal government 'should do everything possible to improve the standard of living of all Americans,'" or whether "that is not the government's responsibility, and that 'each person should take care of themselves [sic].'" Democrats agreed with the first statement 64 percent to 34 percent, while Republicans agreed with the second 59 percent to 39 percent. It was among the strongest differentiating indicators of partisanship found. Dan Balz, "Picking Up Votes in a Maze of Ideals," *Washington Post* (October 5, 1998): A8.

5. The "classic congressional foreign policy maneuver," according to former representative Lee Hamilton (D-Indiana), is that "we get the domestic political advantage, but the president gets the responsibility." Helen Dewar, "Congress Approves Move of U.S. Embassy to Jerusalem by Mid-1999," *Washington Post* (October 25, 1995): A22.

6. It is instructive in this context to reflect on why the Clinton administration moved inexorably toward NATO expansion while most academic experts in the country (except those who had served in office) opposed it. One possibility is that the officials were profoundly influenced by the Eastern Europeans, who pushed NATO membership upon them almost as a moral duty after years of communist domination, whereas the academics had the luxury of considering only theories of alliance formation and counter formation.

7. Ronald Reagan does not, in my view, break this pattern. Though a conservative, his actions in office were far less right wing than his public persona. See Terry L. Deibel, "Reagan's Mixed Legacy," *Foreign Policy* 75 (summer 1989): 34–55.

8. Note that a similar calculus applies between the two houses of Congress: the House will be more extreme and ideological than the Senate, because the Senate has more responsibilities under the Constitution than the House (e.g., treaty and ambassadorial approval) while most House members are elected from smaller districts. In addition, the House is more affected by public opinion of the moment, being entirely rather than only a third elected every two years, and therefore more likely to reflect a temporary and extreme mood of the public.

9. For a brief overview of the feckless early Clinton statecraft, see David Halberstam, *War in a Time of Peace* (New York: Scribner, 2001).

10. Remarks by the President to the Nixon Center for Peace and Freedom, Mayflower Hotel, March 1, 1995.

11. On the day he was elected Speaker of the House, Bob Livingston put it this way: "'That's what being Republican is all about, . . . valuing independence and human dreams, and knowing that if government gets too big, or takes too much of the family income that those dreams begin to fade, and freedom dwindles.'" Guy Gugliotta and Juliet Eilperin, "House Embraces Livingston," *Washington Post* (November 19, 1998): A32. Above all, the Republican party is the party of the triumphant American individual, the self-made man whom Robert Reich identifies as one of four enduring American myths. The Democrats are more about one of Reich's other myths, that of the benevolent community. See his *Tales of a New America* (New York: Random House, 1987).

12. Stephen S. Rosenfeld put it this way: "Here is the foreign policy divide in the Republican Party. Conservative as it may appear, the Kissinger-Reagan-Bush-Baker-Scowcroft brand of internationalism—the more-or-less enlightened presidential brand—is visibly more outward-looking, cooperation-minded and realistic than the Dole-Helms/House Republican brand currently enjoying a congressional run." "Bob Dole's World View," *Washington Post* (March 3, 1995): A25.

13. "Helms, Lott and other GOP conservatives want the administration to forgo further international agreements and concentrate on building a missile defense system to shield the U.S. against threats from such nations as Iran and North Korea." Thomas W. Lippman, "Support for Test Ban Treaty May Be Lacking," *Washington Post* (September 3, 1998): A6, A7.

14. The votes in the tables are numbered to coincide with the case numbers in the text and the portions of the text noting the votes are underlined for easier identification.

15. "The Politics of Trade," *Economist* (October 23, 1999): 27–28.

16. David E. Rosenbaum, "House Backs Free Trade Pact in Major Victory for Clinton after a Long Hunt for Votes," *New York Times* (November 18, 1993): A1, A20.

17. David E. Sanger, "Senate Approves Pact to Ease Trade Curbs; A Victory for Clinton," *New York Times* (December 2, 1994): A1, A22.

18. The data for the next two paragraphs on 1997 fast track legislating comes from "Clinton Loses 'Fast Track' Trade Bill," *1997 Congressional Quarterly Almanac* (Washington, D.C.: Congressional Quarterly, Inc., 1998), 2:85 to 2:88; "Lawmakers Again Reject President's Attempt to Regain Fast-Track Trade Authority," *1998 Congressional Quarterly Almanac* (Washington, D.C.: Congressional Quarterly, Inc., 1999), 23:3 to 23:9; Paul Blustein, "'Fast Track' Trade Plan Pits White House against Top Congressional Democrats," *Washington Post* (March 22, 1997): A11; Peter Baker, "Clinton Opens Push for New Trade Pacts," *Washington Post* (August 24, 1997): A10; John F. Harris, "Clinton at the Center of Another Cliffhanger," *Washington Post* (November 10, 1997): A1, A6; John F. Harris and Peter Baker, "Clinton Neglected to Sell 'Fast Track' to U.S. Public," *Washington Post* (November 12, 1997): A4. Voting data from appendixes to Daniel T. Griswold, *Free Trade, Free Markets: Rating the 105th Congress,* Trade Policy Analysis No. 6 (Washington, D.C.: CATO Institute, February 3, 1999), 15–31.

19. Data in this paragraph is largely based on the articles in "Lawmakers Again Reject President's Attempt to Regain Fast-Track Trade Authority."

20. "Two Free Traders Helped Set Back 'Fast Track,'" *Congressional Quarterly* (October 3, 1998), reprinted in *1998 Congressional Quarterly Almanac* (Washington, D.C.: Congressional Quarterly, Inc., 1999), 23–28.

21. Eric Schmitt and Koseph Kahn, "House, in 237–197 Vote, Approves Normal Trade Rights for China," *New York Times* (May 25, 2000): A1, A10.

22. David E. Sanger, "Rounding Out a Clear Clinton Legacy," *New York Times* (May 25, 2000): A1, A10.

23. Daniel T. Griswold has done an intriguing study of fifteen votes on free trade and export subsidies in the 105th Congress that align well with these findings. He focuses squarely on whether a member favors a laissez faire approach to trade and exports or government intervention in both. Hence, in his scheme, the extremes are occupied by *free traders* (logically Republican) at one end who oppose governmental action either to restrain trade or to grant export subsidies, and *interventionists* (logically Democrats) at the other who want government to interfere by restraining trade and also by providing subsidies to exports. Economic *isolationists* are then defined as those who are against both free trade and subsidies (that is, they advocate that government interfere to stop trade but not to grant subsidies), while economic *internationalists* (defined as the Clinton position) are those who want free trade but with subsidies to help the United States compete (and who, like his isolationists, are inconsistent in their attitude toward government intervention, being

for it in the form of subsidies but against it in the form of interference with trade).

Comparing these economic categories with my factional ones (see tables at the end of this chapter), it appears that both free traders and isolationists tend to be mainly Republican and often unilateralists—especially the isolationists, who are overwhelmingly unilateralists in both houses (though a few are idealists). (Both groups, it will be recalled, oppose subsidies, but they take opposite positions on trade.) However, these groups are small parts of their chambers, each comprising only 6 percent to 14 percent of the membership. By contrast, pro-subsidy, pro-trade economic internationalists (Clinton's position) are more than half of the Senate, and in both houses they tend to be from the centrist factions in both parties, that is, they are either Republican internationalists or Democratic pragmatists. In the House, more than half the members are pro-subsidy, anti-trade interventionists, and they are more likely to be Democrats than Republican, and somewhat more likely to be from the factional extremes of both parties. In fact, virtually all Republican interventionists are, like their isolationist and free trade colleagues, unilateralists, though a Democratic interventionist is only somewhat more likely to be an idealist than a pragmatist. It is also worth noting that in both houses, unilateralists are much less cohesive on (and therefore defined by) these economic issues than any of the other three factions. Daniel T. Griswold, *Free Trade, Free Markets*.

24. Representative Barney Frank (D-Massachusetts) divides members into three groups on trade issues: *isolationists*, skeptical of all international bodies and of free trade (no doubt much the same as our most conservative unilateralists); *trickle downers*, who favor free trade and markets and oppose regulation of the global economy (much like Griswold's free traders, who tend to be all Republicans and also mainly unilateralists); and *international New Dealers*, who care passionately about lifting labor standards and wages in the United States and globally (probably idealists). E. J. Dionne Jr., "The Trade Battle," *Washington Post* (January 26, 1999): A19.

25. Stephen Barr and John F. Harris, "Administration Considers Moving Foreign Affairs Agencies to State Department," *Washington Post* (March 23, 1997): A14.

26. Mexico City language had been in effect during most of the Reagan and Bush administrations, but only as an executive order, one that Clinton rescinded as soon as he was inaugurated.

27. "State Department Authorization Stalls," *1997 Congressional Quarterly Almanac* (Washington, D.C.: Congressional Quarterly, Inc., 1998): 8:35 to 8:36.

28. Ibid., 8:36.

29. Ibid., 8:35.

30. "Clinton Wins Backing for IMF Funds, Loses Effort to Repay U.N. Debts," *1998 Congressional Quarterly Almanac* (Washington, D.C.: Congressional Quarterly, Inc., 1999): 2:45 to 2:56.

31. Helen Dewar, "Dispute Imperils U.S. Vote at U.N.," *Washington Post* (October 28, 1999): A10; Eric Pianin and John F. Harris, "Impasse Ends on

U.N. Dues," *Washington Post* (November 15, 1999): A1, A8; "Foreign Aid Compromise Is a Success for Clinton Team," *Congressional Quarterly Weekly* (November 20, 1999): 2791–94.

32. Colum Lynch, "Holbrooke's Tough Sell on U.N. Debt," *Washington Post* (November 17, 1999): A2.

33. "State Department Authorization Stalls," 8:33.

34. Ibid., 8:32 to 8:36.

35. "Foreign Aid: GOP Relents on Abortion," *1997 Congressional Quarterly Almanac* (Washington, D.C.: Congressional Quarterly, Inc., 1998), 9:43.

36. Gingrich not only reconvened the conference without Democrats, he even replaced internationalist Jim Leach with unilateralist Dan Burton when the former refused to sign the Mexico City language and said, "I would like to have as much of the U.N. money as rapidly as possible."

37. "Anti-Abortion Language Dooms State Department Bill, U.N. Debt Repayment," *1998 Congressional Quarterly Almanac* (Washington, D.C.: Congressional Quarterly, Inc., 1999): 16:3 to 16:7.

38. "Anti-Abortion Language Dooms State Department Bill," 16:7 to 16:9.

39. Helms's spokesman called this a "major victory," "the first time the Republican Congress has succeeded in actually forcing the shutdown of a federal agency." Thomas W. Lippman, "Senate Kills Two Agencies, Reorganizes Foreign Affairs Roles," *Washington Post* (October 22, 1998): A23.

40. "Foreign Aid: GOP Relents on Abortion," 9:37 to 9:43; Robert G. Kaiser, "Foreign Disservice," *Washington Post Outlook* (April 16, 2000): B1–B2.

41. "House Markup Delayed; Senate Panel Avoids Controversy," *1998 Congressional Quarterly Almanac* (Washington, D.C.: Congressional Quarterly, Inc., 1999): 2:48.

42. "House Panel Trims President's IMF Request," *1998 Congressional Quarterly Almanac* (Washington, D.C.: Congressional Quarterly, Inc., 1999): 2:45/46.

43. "House Markup Delayed."

44. "Russia, IMF Lead Debate as Senate Oks Bill," *1998 Congressional Quarterly Almanac* (Washington, D.C.: Congressional Quarterly, Inc., 1999): 2:49/50.

45. "House Panel Approves Its Bill Despite Veto Threat," *1998 Congressional Quarterly Almanac* (Washington, D.C.: Congressional Quarterly, Inc., 1999): 2:52.

46. "Negotiations Continue Over IMF Credit Line," *1998 Congressional Quarterly Almanac* (Washington, D.C.: Congressional Quarterly, Inc., 1999): 2:53.

47. Helen Dewar, "Congress Passes Stopgap Funding to Keep Government Operating," *Washington Post* (September 18, 1998): A4.

48. "Catchall Measure Includes Clinton's IMF Request," *1998 Congressional Quarterly Almanac* (Washington, D.C.: Congressional Quarterly, Inc., 1999): 2:54.

49. Steve Coll and David B. Ottaway, "New Threats Create Doubt in U.S. Policy," *Washington Post* (April 13, 1995): A1, A26–A27.

50. "In many ways Korea poses the greatest security threat to the United

States and the world today," said Defense Secretary William Perry in May 1994. See Coll and Ottaway, "New Threats Create Doubt."

51. "Abortion Fight Halts Foreign Aid Bill," *1995 Congressional Quarterly Almanac* (Washington, D.C.: Congressional Quarterly, Inc., 1996): 11:44.

52. Thomas W. Lippman, "Senate Panel Joins House in Cutting Funds for Nuclear Accord," *Washington Post* (June 20, 1996): A23.

53. Representative Doug Bereuter (R-Nebraska) admitted that "a significant amount of support exists in the Congress, especially in my party and especially in the House," for the idea that China was the new enemy, and aides to several unilateralist legislators formed a so-called Blue Team to publicize and energize an American reaction to the growing threat. Robert G. Kaiser and Steven Mufson, "'Blue Team' Draws a Hard Line on Beijing," *Washington Post* (February 22, 2000): A12.

54. Lippman, "GOP-Controlled Foreign Policy Panels Would Reverse Several Clinton Stands," *Washington Post* (May 21, 1995): A7; Serge F. Kovaleski, "Gingrich Backs Ties with Taiwan," *Washington Post* (July 10, 1995): A1, A12; Michael Dobbs, "House Panel Urges U.S. Force in Taiwan," *Washington Post* (March 15, 1996): A24; "President Vetoes Foreign Policy Bill," *Washington Post* (April 13, 1996): A9.

55. Vote tally from *Congressional Quarterly Weekly* (February 5, 2000): 266–67.

56. "Bosnian War Sparks Conflict at Home," *1995 Congressional Quarterly Almanac,* 10:15.

57. Dov S. Zakheim, "Bosnia," chapter 2 in *Congress and National Security in the Post–Cold War Era* (Washington, D.C.: Nixon Center, October 1998), 17–26.

58. Juliet Eilperin and William Claiborne, "Kosovo Resolution Narrowly Approved," *Washington Post* (March 12, 1999): A28.

59. "Kosovo Vote, Though Won by Clinton, May Signal New Level of Hill Involvement," *Congressional Quarterly Weekly* (March 13, 1999): 621–22; votes at 668–69.

60. S.Con.Res. 21 vote reported in *Congressional Quarterly Weekly* (March 27, 1999): 772. To some extent the split in the Republican party is generational, reflecting the reduced international experience (including military service) of younger members. On this vote, eleven of the sixteen GOP votes in favor of bombing for peace were from senators elected before 1994; and of the twenty-four Republicans elected in 1994 or later, only five voted to put the screws to Milosevic. Carroll J. Doherty, "Two GOP Leaders Personify Party's Rift over Kosovo," *Congressional Quarterly Weekly* (April 10, 1999): 835–36.

61. Juliet Eilperin, "Democrats Blame Kosovo Resolution Failure on Hastert's Silence," *Washington Post* (April 30, 1999): A8–A9; Gebe Martinez, "GOP's Abiding Distrust of Clinton Doesn't Stop at Water's Edge," *Congressional Quarterly Weekly* (May 1, 1999): 1038–39.

62. As Senator McCain put it, "we're in it, now we must win it." Pat Towell, "Congress Set to Provide Money, But No Guidance, for Kosovo Mission," *Congressional Quarterly Weekly* (May 1, 1999): 1036. Miles A. Pomper and Chuck McCutcheon, "As Kosovo Crisis Escalates, Calls Increase to Reconsider Use of Ground Troops," *Congressional Quarterly Weekly* (April 3, 1999): 809–11.

63. Carroll J. Doherty, "New Generation Challenges Established Orthodoxy," *Congressional Quarterly Weekly* (February 3, 1996): 306–8.

64. Doherty, *Congressional Quarterly Weekly*, 307. "Bosnian War Sparks Conflict at Home," 10:10 to 10:15.

65. "Lawmakers Seek to Limit NATO Expansion to Three New Members," *1998 Congressional Quarterly Almanac* (Washington, D.C.: Congressional Quarterly, Inc., 1999), 8:21 to 8:24.

66. Eric Schmitt, "Senate Approves Expansion of NATO by Vote of 80 to 19; Clinton Pleased by Decision," *New York Times* (May 1, 1998): A1, A10.

67. Thomas W. Lippmann, "Chemical Arms Pact in Jeopardy," *Washington Post* (November 13, 1995): A15.

68. SFRC Minutes provided by Taylor Griffin, Senate staff.

69. Thomas W. Lippmann, "Senate Foes Derail Chemical Weapons Treaty," *Washington Post* (September 13, 1996): A1, A24.

70. The other issues on which Helms insisted were UN reform and national ballistic missile defense deployment, plus agreement to submit to the Senate as treaty amendments modifications Clinton was negotiating to the Anti-Ballistic Missile (ABM) and Conventional Forces in Europe (CFE) treaties. Thomas W. Lippmann, "Sen. Helms to Delay Vote on Chemical Arms Pact," *Washington Post* (February 4, 1997): A1, A8.

71. Amendment descriptions and votes from *1997 Congressional Quarterly Almanac*, S:11.

72. "Senate Ratifies [sic] Chemical Arms Pact," *1997 Congressional Quarterly Almanac* (Washington, D.C.: Congressional Quarterly, Inc., 1998), 8:13 to 8:19.

73. Four of these internationalists voted to keep just the fourth killer reservation, on inspectors.

74. In similar fashion to Lott and McConnell, internationalist Warner voted for most of the killers as well as for the treaty—interesting in light of his later vote against the CTBT.

75. "Chemical Weapons Bill Wrapped into Omnibus Spending Package," *1998 Congressional Quarterly Almanac* (Washington, D.C.: Congressional Quarterly, Inc., 1999), 8:20.

76. For the story of the CTBT's defeat, see Terry L. Deibel, "The Death of a Treaty," *Foreign Affairs* 81 (September/October 2002): 142–61. More detail can be found in Deibel, "Inside the Water's Edge: The Senate Votes on the Comprehensive Test Ban Treaty," Case 263, Pew Case Studies in International Affairs (Washington, D.C.: Institute for the Study of Diplomacy, 2003).

77. Robert G. Kaiser and Walter Pincus, "GOP Senators Back Nuclear Test Ban," *Washington Post* (October 15, 1999): A16.

78. Pragmatists, after all, are just idealists restrained by their sense of the possible, but unilateralists have a fundamentally different view of America's role in the world than internationalists. See the first section of this chapter.

79. Here are the rules used to construct the scoring:

> (1) Votes in which a majority of each faction in a party voted against a majority in the other are scored as 1 (these are unquestionably faction-defining votes);

(2) Votes in which at least a third of the faction voted against the majority of the other faction are scored as .5 (in these cases, with the majority of each faction voting the same way, the vote is less faction-defining but the member's decision to vote against the party could be seen as indicating stronger factionalism);
(3) Only the strongest factional vote for each case is scored (in order to avoid consistent votes on one issue overweighting multiple contrary votes on others);
(4) For the CWC vote in the Senate, those who voted yes on the CWC but also voted to keep at least three of the five killer amendments are counted as a no vote;
(5) Members who were in Congress only a short period of time and thus did not participate in enough votes to determine their factional conformity are not scored.

As will be noted from the vote totals (given under "Score" at the top of the column), the conclusions on factional solidarity are much more firmly based for Republicans in the Senate than for Senate Democrats or for either party in the House.

80. I say "apparent" because the events of September 11, 2001, demonstrated that a serious external threat did exist in these years, as indicated by the 1993 World Trade Center bombing, the 1996 bombing of the Khobar Towers complex in Saudi Arabia, the 1998 bombing of the U.S. embassies in Kenya and Tanzania, and the 2000 attack on the USS *Cole* in Aden. It was only the *perception* of threat that was absent, but perceptions are of course all that matters in the politics of foreign policy.

Chapter Five: Explaining Congressional-Executive Rivalry in International Affairs: The Changing Role of Parties, Committees, and the Issue Agenda by Bryan W. Marshall

1. I would like to thank Martin J. Rochester, Brandon Prins, and the participants at the Fulbright Institute's conference on *Divided Power: The Presidency, Congress, and the Formation of American Foreign Policy* for helpful comments. I would also like to thank the University of Missouri for research support. Although I would like to blame someone else for errors and omissions, they are mine.

2. The war resolution, H.J.Res. 114, passed in the House on October 10 by a margin of 296–133 (R215–6; D81–126) and in the Senate the day after by 77–23 (R48–1; D29–21), *Congressional Quarterly Weekly* (October 12, 2002): 2689–92.

3. Helen Fessenden and John Cochran, "Congress Seeks to Find Its Voice as Iraq War Rages," *Congressional Quarterly Weekly* (March 22, 2003): 677.

4. Carolyn Skorneck, "Second Thoughts on Iraq Resolution Not Enough to Prompt a Revote," *Congressional Quarterly Weekly* (March 1, 2003): 518.

5. One salient example came on the Senate floor when John McCain (R-Arizona) brought an amendment to cut a number of earmarks including a lamprey control program for the Great Lakes. Even with Senator McCain's

patriotic pleas, his amendment was soundly rejected, 38–61. Carolyn Skorneck, "White House Battle Hinges on Flexible Spending," *Congressional Quarterly Weekly* (April 5, 2003): 807–11.

6. Gebe Martinez, "Bush Watches as Battles Are Lost in Struggle for His Domestic Agenda," *Congressional Quarterly Weekly* (March 29, 2003): 742.

7. Aaron Wildavsky, "The Two Presidencies," in Aaron Wildavsky, ed., *The Presidency* (Boston: Little, Brown and Company, 1969), 230–43.

8. Stephen Wayne, *The Road to the White House, 2000: The Politics of Presidential Election* (New York: St. Martin's Press, 2001), 50.

9. Louis Fisher, *Constitutional Conflicts between Congress and the President* (Princeton, N.J.: Princeton University Press, 1985).

10. George C. Edwards III and Andrew Barrett, "Presidential Agenda Setting in Congress," in *Polarized Politics: Congress and the President in a Partisan Era*, ed. Jon R. Bond and Richard Fleisher (Washington, D.C.: Congressional Quarterly Press, 2000), 109–33.

11. Pendleton Herring, *Presidential Leadership: The Political Relations of Congress and the Chief Executive* (New York: Farrar and Rinehart, 1940); Clinton Rossiter, *The American Presidency: The Powers and Practices, the Personalities and Problems of the Most Important Office on Earth* (New York: Harvest Book, Harcourt, 1956); Richard E. Neustadt, *Presidential Power: The Politics of Leadership* (New York: John Wiley and Sons, 1962); Aaron Wildavsky, "The Two Presidencies."

12. Some scholars have argued for a more refined distinction that classifies explanations into "presidency-centered" and "president-centered." See, for example, John B. Gilmour, "Institutional and Individual Influences on the President's Veto," *Journal of Politics* 64 (2002): 198–218; and Kenneth R. Mayer, *With the Stroke of a Pen: Executive Orders and Presidential Power* (Princeton, N.J.: Princeton University Press, 2001). The former highlights the constraints imposed by the executive's institutional setting in explaining behavior, while the latter highlights variation in the characteristics of individual presidents in explaining such behavior. See also Richard E. Neustadt, *Presidential Power;* Paul Charles Light, *The President's Agenda: Domestic Policy Choice from Kennedy to Carter* (Baltimore, Md.: Johns Hopkins University Press, 1982); Terry Sullivan, "The Bank Account Presidency: A New Measure and Evidence on the Temporal Path of Presidential Influence," *American Journal of Political Science* 35 (1991): 686–723.

13. Jon R. Bond and Richard Fleisher, *The President in the Legislative Arena* (Chicago: University of Chicago Press, 1990); James Meernik, "Presidential Support in Congress: Conflict and Consensus on Foreign and Defense Policy," *Journal of Politics* 55, 3 (1993): 569–87; David W. Rohde, "Presidential Support in the House of Representatives," in Paul E. Peterson, ed., *The President, the Congress, and the Making of Foreign Policy* (Norman: University of Oklahoma Press, 1994), 101–28. George C. Edwards III, *At the Margins: Presidential Leadership of Congress* (New Haven, Conn.: Yale University Press, 1989); Stephen A. Schull, *Presidential-Congressional Relations: Policy and Time Approaches* (Ann Arbor: University of Michigan Press, 1997); Lance T. Leloup and Steven A. Schull, *The President and Congress: Collaboration and Combat in*

National Policymaking (Needham Heights, Mass.: Allyn and Bacon, 1999); Glen S. Krutz, "Tactical Maneuvering on Omnibus Bills in Congress," *American Journal of Political Science* 45 (2001): 210–23.

14. Wildavsky, "The Two Presidencies," 231.

15. President Kennedy referred to this distinction between foreign and domestic policy. "Domestic policy . . . can only defeat us; foreign policy can kill us." Quoted in Wildavsky, "The Two Presidencies," 242.

16. Edwards, *At the Margins: Presidential Leadership of Congress;* Richard Fleisher, Jon R. Bond, Glen S. Krutz, and Stephen Hanna, "The Demise of the Two Presidencies," *American Politics Quarterly* 28, 1 (2000): 3–25; Scot Schraufnagel and Stephen M. Shellman, "The Two Presidencies, 1994–98," *Presidential Studies Quarterly* 31, 4 (2001): 699–707.

17. James M. McCormick and Eugene Wittkopf, "Bipartisanship, Partisanship, and Ideology in Congressional-Executive Foreign Policy Relations, 1947–1988," *Journal of Politics* 52, 4 (1990): 1077–1100; Meernik, "Presidential Support in Congress: Conflict and Consensus in Foreign and Defense Policy"; I. M. Destler, "Congress and Foreign Policy at Century's End: Requiem or Cooperation?" in Lawrence C. Dodd and Bruce I. Oppenheimer, eds., *Congress Reconsidered* (Washington, D.C.: Congressional Quarterly Press, 2001), 315–33.

18. James M. Lindsay, "Congress and Diplomacy," in Randall B. Ripley and James M. Lindsay, eds., *Congress Resurgent: Foreign and Defense Policy on Capitol Hill* (Ann Arbor: University of Michigan Press, 1993), 261–81; Louis Fisher, *Presidential War Power* (Lawrence: University of Kansas Press, 1995); Barbara Hinckley, *Less than Meets the Eye: Foreign Policy Making and the Myth of an Assertive Congress* (Chicago: University of Chicago Press, 1994); Lee H. Hamilton, "The Making of U.S. Foreign Policy: The Roles of the President and Congress over Four Decades," in James E. Thurber, ed., *Rivals for Power: Presidential-Congressional Relations* (Boulder, Colo.: Rowman and Littlefield, 2002), 207–28.

19. Cecil V. Crabb Jr. and Pat M. Holt, *Invitation to Struggle: Congress, the President, and Foreign Policy* (Washington, D.C.: Congressional Quarterly Press, 1989).

20. Charles W. Kegley Jr. and Eugene Wittkopf, *American Foreign Policy,* 5th ed. (New York: St. Martin's Press, 1998), 434.

21. Kegley and Wittkopf, *American Foreign Policy,* 5th ed.

22. Crabb and Holt, *Invitation to Struggle;* John T. Eliff, "Congress and the Intelligence Community," in Lawrence C. Dodd and Bruce Oppenheimer, eds., *Congress Reconsidered,* 1st ed. (New York: Praeger Publishers, 1977), 193–206. Rohde, "Presidential Support in the House of Representatives." Gerald Felix Warburg, *Conflict and Consensus: The Struggle between Congress and the President over Foreign Policymaking* (New York: Harper and Row Publishers, 1989).

23. Richard F. Fenno Jr., *Congressmen in Committees* (Berkeley, Calif.: Institute of Governmental Studies Press, 1973).

24. David R. Mayhew, *Congress: The Electoral Connection* (New Haven, Conn.: Yale University Press, 1974).

25. Barbara Sinclair, "House Special Rules and the Institutional Design Controversy," in Kenneth A. Shepsle and Barry R. Weingast, eds., *Positive*

Theories of Congressional Institutions (Ann Arbor: University of Michigan Press, 1995), 235–52.

26. Fisher, *Constitutional Conflicts between Congress and the President*. Joseph A. Pika, John Anthony Maltese, and Norman C. Thomas, *The Politics of the Presidency*, 5th ed. (Washington, D.C.: Congressional Quarterly Press, 2002).

27. Joshua Lee Prober, "Congress, the War Powers Resolution, and the Secret Political Life 'a Dead Letter,'" *Journal of Law and Politics* 7 (1990): 173, quoted in Pika, Maltese, and Thomas, *The Politics of the Presidency*, 5th ed., 381.

28. Steven S. Smith, "Congressional Party Leaders," in Paul E. Peterson, ed., *The President, the Congress, and the Making of Foreign Policy* (Norman: University of Oklahoma Press, 1994), 129–60.

29. John E. Cohen, "Historical Reassessment of Wildavsky's 'Two Presidencies' Thesis," in Steven A. Shull, ed., *The Two Presidencies: A Quarter Century Assessment* (Chicago: Nelson-Hall, 1991), 53–60.

30. Sarah A. Binder, "The Dynamics of Legislative Gridlock, 1947–96," *American Political Science Review* 93 (1999): 519–33.

31. V. O. Key Jr., *Southern Politics: In State and Nation* (New York: Alfred A. Knopf, 1949).

32. Bruce A. Ray, "The Responsiveness of the U.S. Congressional Armed Services Committees to Their Parent Bodies," *Legislative Studies Quarterly* 4 (1980): 501–15.

33. Fenno, *Congressmen in Committees*.

34. Steven S. Smith, *Call to Order: Floor Politics in the House and Senate* (Washington, D.C.: Brookings Institute, 1989).

35. David W. Rohde, *Parties and Leaders in the Postreform House* (Chicago: University of Chicago Press, 1991).

36. Bond and Fleisher, *The President in the Legislative Arena*, 126.

37. Rohde, "Presidential Support in the House of Representatives," 92.

38. James M. Scott and Ralph G. Carter, "Acting on the Hill: Congressional Assertiveness in U.S. Foreign Policy," *Congress and the Presidency* 29 (autumn 2002): 151–69; Bryan W. Marshall and Brandon C. Prins, "The Pendulum of Congressional Power: Agenda Change, Partisanship, and the Demise of the Post–World War II Foreign Policy Consensus," *Congress and the Presidency* 29 (autumn 2002): 195–212.

39. Crabb and Holt, *Invitation to Struggle: Congress, the President, and Foreign Policy*.

40. More specifically, the international affairs agenda includes all votes relating to foreign economic, general, military aid, international trade, defense and military issues, veterans' affairs, intelligence, immigration, state department, sanctions, arms control, as well as budget and appropriations measures related to military, defense, and foreign policy.

41. Fleisher, Bond, Krutz, and Hanna, "The Demise of the Two Presidencies."

42. The percentages in each cell are calculated from the total number of international affairs votes the president takes a position on for the given congress.

43. Meernik, "Presidential Support in Congress: Conflict and Consensus on Foreign and Defense Policy"; Edwards, *At the Margins: Presidential Leadership of Congress*.

44. Edwards, *At the Margins: Presidential Leadership of Congress*; Light, *The President's Agenda: Domestic Policy Choice from Kennedy to Carter*.

45. Interestingly, Model 2 shows that with the addition of the two committee opposition variables, the effect of a party-unity vote on international relations is no longer significant. The reason for this appears to be a high level of correlation between the party unity and majority opposition measures for the International Relations Committee. The correlation of these variables for the IR Committee is nearly double that found for the respective variables for the Armed Services Committee (Cramer's V reports .31 and .17, respectively).

46. Rohde argues that the Armed Services and the International Relations Committee tended to insulate presidential priorities from being challenged on the House floor. Rohde, "Presidential Support in the House of Representatives."

47. Fleisher, Bond, Krutz, and Hanna, "The Demise of the Two Presidencies."

Chapter Six: Which Dancer Leads? Foreign Trade Policy Making and Divided Government by Ralph G. Carter

1. Eric Redman, *The Dance of Legislation* (Seattle: University of Washington Press, 2001).

2. Bayless Manning, "The Congress, the Executive, and Intermestic Affairs," *Foreign Affairs* 55 (1977): 306–24.

3. Leroy N. Rieselbach, "It's the Constitution, Stupid! Congress, the President, Divided Government, and Policymaking," in *Divided Government: Change, Uncertainty, and the Constitutional Order*, ed. Peter F. Galderisi, Roberta Q. Herzberg, and Peter McNamara (Lanham, Md.: Rowman and Littlefield, 1996), 109–34.

4. Jon R. Bond and Richard Fleisher, *The President in the Legislative Arena* (Chicago: University of Chicago Press, 1990); George C. Edwards III, *At the Margins: Presidential Leadership of Congress* (New Haven, Conn.: Yale University Press, 1989); Charles O. Jones, *The Presidency in a Separated System* (Washington, D.C.: Brookings Institution Press, 1994); Mark W. Peterson, *Legislating Together* (Cambridge, Mass.: Harvard University Press, 1990).

5. James MacGregor Burns, *The Deadlock of Democracy* (Englewood Cliffs, N.J.: Prentice-Hall, 1963), and *Cobblestone Leadership: Majority Rule, Minority Power* (Norman: University of Oklahoma Press, 1990).

6. Samuel Kernell, "Facing an Opposition Congress: The President's Strategic Circumstance," in *The Politics of Divided Government*, ed. Gary W. Cox and Samuel Kernell (Boulder, Colo.: Westview Press, 1991), 87–112. James L. Sundquist, *Constitutional Reform and Effective Government*, rev. ed. (Washington, D.C.: Brookings Institution Press, 1992).

7. George C. Edwards III, Andrew Barrett, and Jeffrey Peake, "The Legislative Impact of Divided Government," *American Journal of Political Science* 41, 2 (1997): 545–63.

8. Sundquist, *Constitutional Reform and Effective Government*.

9. Gary Cox and Mathew D. McCubbins, "Divided Control of Fiscal Policy," in Cox and Kernell, *The Politics of Divided Government*, 155–75.

10. Mathew D. McCubbins, "Government on Lay-Away: Federal Spending and Deficits under Divided Government Control," in Cox and Kernell, *The Politics of Divided Government*.
11. Bond and Fleisher, *The President in the Legislative Arena*.
12. Rieselbach, "It's the Constitution, Stupid!" 129.
13. Sarah A. Binder, *Stalemate: Causes and Consequences of Legislative Gridlock* (Washington, D.C.: Brookings Institution Press, 2003).
14. Keith Krehbiel, *Pivotal Politics: A Theory of U.S. Lawmaking* (Chicago: University of Chicago Press, 1998); David R. Mayhew, *Divided We Govern* (New Haven, Conn.: Yale University Press, 1991).
15. Jones, *The Presidency in a Separated System*.
16. Peter Trubowitz, *Defining the National Interest: Conflict and Change in American Foreign Policy* (Chicago: University of Chicago Press, 1998).
17. E. E. Schattschneider, *Politics, Pressures and the Tariff* (New York: Prentice-Hall, 1935).
18. John M. Rothgeb, *U.S. Trade Policy: Balancing Economic Dreams and Political Realities* (Washington, D.C.: Congressional Quarterly Press, 2001); John T. Tierney, "Interest Group Involvement in Congressional Foreign and Defense Policy," in *Congress Resurgent*, ed. Randall B. Ripley and James M. Lindsay (Ann Arbor: University of Michigan Press, 1993), 89–111.
19. I. M. Destler, *American Trade Politics*, 3rd ed. (Washington, D.C.: Institute for International Economics/Twentieth-Century Fund, 1995); "Congress and Mexico," in *The Controversial Pivot: The U.S. Congress and North America*, ed. Robert A. Pastor and Rafael Fernandez de Castro (Washington, D.C.: Brookings Institution Press, 1998), 29–49; "Congress, Constituencies, and U.S. Trade Policy," in *Constituent Interests and U.S. Trade Policies*, ed. Alan V. Deardorff and Robert M. Stern (Ann Arbor: University of Michigan Press, 1998), 93–108. Judith Goldstein, "Ideas, Institutions and American Trade Policy," in *The State and American Foreign Economic Policy*, ed. G. John Ikenberry, David A. Lake, and Michael Mastanduno (Ithaca, N.Y.: Cornell University Press, 1988), 179–218. Stephan Haggard, "The Institutional Foundations of Hegemony: Explaining the Reciprocal Trade Agreements Act of 1934," in Ikenberry, Lake, and Mastanduno; Lawrence Margolis, *Executive Agreements and Presidential Power in Foreign Policy* (New York: Praeger, 1986), 91–120. Robert A. Pastor, *Congress and the Politics of U.S. Foreign Economic Policy, 1929–1976* (Berkeley and Los Angeles: University of California Press, 1980); "Cry-and-Sigh Syndrome: Congress and Trade Policy," in *Making Economic Policy in Congress*, ed. Allen Shick (Washington, D.C.: American Enterprise Institute for Public Policy Research, 1983), 158–95.
20. Pastor, *Congress and the Politics of U.S. Foreign Economic Policy, 1929–1976*; Pastor, "Cry-and Sigh Syndrome."
21. I. M. Destler, "Delegating Trade Policy," in *The President, the Congress, and the Making of Foreign Policy*, ed. Paul E. Peterson (Norman: University of Oklahoma Press, 1994), 228–46.
22. Destler, *American Trade Politics*.
23. Rothgeb, *U.S. Trade Policy*; Harold H. Koh, *The National Security Constitution: Sharing Power After the Iran-Contra Affair* (New Haven, Conn.: Yale University Press, 1990).

24. Bruce Stokes, "Organizing to Trade," in *The Domestic Sources of American Foreign Policy: Insights and Evidence,* 2nd ed., ed. Eugene Wittkopf (New York: St. Martin's Press, 1994), 226–35.

25. Stephen D. Cohen, *The Making of United States International Economic Policy: Principles, Problems, and Proposals for Reform,* 5th ed. (Westport, Conn.: Praeger Press, 2000); Martha L. Gibson, *Conflict Amid Consensus in American Trade Policy* (Washington, D.C.: Georgetown University Press, 2000); Jim Kolbe and Robert Matsui, "Forging a New Bipartisan Consensus for Free Trade," in *Trade Strategies for a New Era,* ed. Geza Feketekuty with Bruce Stokes (New York: Council on Foreign Relations Press, 1998), 28–38; C. S. Eliot Kang, "U.S. Politics and Greater Regulation of Inward Foreign Direct Investment," *International Organization* 51 (1997): 301–33; Michael Lusztig, *Risking Free Trade: The Politics of Trade in Britain, Canada, Mexico, and the United States* (Pittsburgh: University of Pittsburgh Press, 1996); James M. Lindsay, "Congress, Foreign Policy, and the New Institutionalism," *International Studies Quarterly* 38 (1994): 281–304.

26. Randall B. Ripley and Grace A. Franklin, *Congress, the Bureaucracy, and Public Policy,* 5th ed. (Pacific Grove, Calif.: Brooks/Cole, 1991).

27. James M. Lindsay and Randall B. Ripley, "How Congress Influences Foreign and Defense Policy," 17–36, in Ripley and Lindsay, *Congress Resurgent.*

28. Lindsay, "Congress, Foreign Policy, and the New Institutionalism"; Mathew D. McCubbins, Roger G. Noll, and Barry R. Weingast, "Administrative Procedures as Instruments of Political Control," *Journal of Law, Economics, and Administration* 3 (1987): 721–48; Terry M. Moe, "The New Economics of Organization," *American Journal of Political Science* 28 (1984): 739–77; Barry R. Weingast, "The Congressional Bureaucratic System: A Principle-Agent Perspective," *Public Choice* 41 (1984): 147–91.

29. Sharyn O'Halloran, "Congress and Foreign Trade Policy," in Ripley and Lindsay, *Congress Resurgent.*

30. Ralph G. Carter, "Congressional Trade Politics, 1985–1995," *Congress and the Presidency* 26, 1 (1999): 61–76.

31. Ralph G. Carter and Lorraine Eden, "Who Makes U.S. Trade Policy?" *International Trade Journal* 13, 1 (1999): 53–100.

32. Stokes, "Organizing to Trade," 227.

33. Ryan J. Barilleaux, "The President, 'Intermestic' Issues, and the Risks of Policy Leadership," in *The Domestic Sources of American Foreign Policy,* ed. Charles W. Kegley Jr. and Eugene R. Wittkopf (New York: St. Martin's Press, 1988); Manning, "The Congress, the Executive, and Intermestic Affairs."

34. Rothgeb, *U.S. Trade Policy*; Richard S. Conley, "Derailing Presidential Fast-Track Authority: The Impact of Constituency Pressures and Political Ideology on Trade Policy in Congress," *Political Research Quarterly* 52 (1999): 785–99; Douglas A. Irwin and Randall S. Kroszner, "Interests, Institutions, and Ideology in Securing Policy Change: The Republican Conversion to Trade Liberalization after Smoot-Hawley," *Journal of Law and Economics* 42 (1999): 643–73; Philip A. Mundo, *National Politics in a Global Economy: The Domestic Sources of U.S. Trade Policy* (Washington, D.C.: Georgetown University Press, 1999); Trubowitz, *Defining the National Interest;* Michael A. Bailey, Judith

Goldstein, and Barry R. Weingast, "The Institutional Roots of American Trade Policy: Politics, Coalitions, and International Trade," *World Politics* 49 (1997): 309–38; Kang, "U.S. Politics and Greater Regulation of Inward Foreign Direct Investment"; John B. Goodman, Debora Spar, and David B. Yoffie, "Foreign Direct Investment and the Demand for Protection in the United States," *International Organization* 50 (1996): 565–91; Wendy L. Hansen and Kee Ok Park, "Nation-State and Pluralistic Decision Making in Trade Policy: The Case of the International Trade Administration," *International Studies Quarterly* 39 (1995): 181–211; Stanley D. Nollen and Dennis P. Quinn, "Free Trade, Fair Trade, Strategic Trade, and Protectionism in the U.S. Congress, 1987–88," *International Organization* 48 (1994): 491–525); Pietro Nivola, "Trade Policy: Refereeing the Playing Field," in *A Question of Balance*, ed. Thomas E. Mann (Washington, D.C.: Brookings Institution Press, 1990), 201–53.

35. Robert E. Baldwin, "U.S. Trade Policies: The Role of the Executive Branch," in Deardorff and Stern, *Constituent Interests and U.S. Trade Policies*, 65–87.

36. Michael Bailey, "Quiet Influence: The Representation of Diffuse Interests on Trade Policy, 1983–94," *Legislative Studies Quarterly* 26, 1 (2001): 45–80; Joseph Quinlan and Marc Chandler, "The U.S. Trade Deficit: A Dangerous Obsession," *Foreign Affairs* 80, 1 (2001): 87–97; Kedron Bardwell, "The Puzzling Decline in House Support for Free Trade: Was Fast Track a Referendum on NAFTA?" *Legislative Studies Quarterly* 25, 4 (2000): 591–610; Bert Rockman, "Presidents, Opinion, and Institutional Leadership," in *The New Politics of American Foreign Policy*, ed. David Deese (New York: St. Martin's Press, 1994), 59–75.

37. Marc Busch and Eric Reinhardt, "Geography, International Trade, and Political Mobilization of U.S. Industries," *American Journal of Political Science* 44, 4 (2000): 703–19.

38. Michael J. Hiscox, "The Magic Bullet: The RTAA, Institutional Reform, and Trade Liberalization," *International Organization* 53 (1999): 669–98; Trubowitz, *Defining the National Interest;* Baldwin, "U.S. Trade Policies: The Role of the Executive Branch"; Bailey, Goldstein, and Weingast, "The Institutional Roots of American Trade Policy: Politics, Coalitions, and International Trade"; Susanne Lohmann and Sharyn O'Halloran, "Divided Government and U.S. Trade Policy: Theory and Evidence," *International Organization* 48 (1994): 595–632; O'Halloran, "Congress and Foreign Trade Policy."

39. O'Halloran, "Congress and Foreign Trade Policy," 284.

40. David Epstein and Sharyn O'Halloran, "The Partisan Paradox and the U.S. Tariff, 1877–1934," *International Organization* 50, 2 (1996): 301–24.

41. Jon R. Bond, Richard Fleisher, and B. Dan Wood, "The Marginal and Time-Varying Effect of Public Approval on Presidential Success in Congress," *Journal of Politics* 65, 1 (2003): 92–110.

42. Ralph G. Carter, "Congress and Post–Cold War U.S. Foreign Policy," in *After the End: Making U.S. Foreign Policy in the Post–Cold War World*, ed. James M. Scott (Durham, N.C.: Duke University Press, 1998), 108–31.

43. Nollen and Quinn, "Free Trade, Fair Trade, Strategic Trade, and Protectionism in the U.S. Congress, 1987–88."

44. David Karol, "Divided Government and U.S. Trade Policy: Much Ado about Nothing?" *International Organization* 54, 4 (2000): 825–44.

45. David Epstein and Sharyn O'Halloran, "Divided Government and the Design of Administrative Procedures: A Formal Model and Empirical Test," *Journal of Politics* 58, 2 (1996): 395.

46. Lohmann and O'Halloran, "Divided Government and U.S. Trade Policy: Theory and Evidence," 628.

47. James M. Scott and Ralph G. Carter, "Acting on the Hill: Congressional Assertiveness in U.S. Foreign Policy," *Congress and the Presidency* 29, 2 (2002): 151–69.

48. Carter, "Congress and Post–Cold War U.S. Foreign Policy."

49. Pastor, "Cry-and-Sigh Syndrome," 161.

50. *Congress and the Nation*, vol. 5, 1977–1980, for the Carter administration; *Congress and the Nation*, vol. 6, 1981–1984, for the first Reagan term; *Congress and the Nation*, vol. 7, 1985–1988, for the second Reagan term; *Congressional Quarterly Almanacs 1989–1992* for the Bush administration; *Congressional Quarterly Almanacs 1993* and *1994* for the first two years of the Clinton administration; *Congressional Quarterly Weekly Report* for the third and fourth years of the Clinton administration (1995–1996); and *Congress and the Nation*, vol. 10, 1997–2000, for the second Clinton term.

51. *Congressional Quarterly Almanac*, 1990, 501.

52. Carter and Eden, "Who Makes U.S. Trade Policy?"

53. John E. Rielly, ed., *American Public Opinion and U.S. Foreign Policy 1991* (Chicago: Chicago Council on Foreign Relations, 1991); *American Public Opinion and U.S. Foreign Policy 1995* (Chicago: Chicago Council on Foreign Relations, 1995); *American Public Opinion and U.S. Foreign Policy 1999* (Chicago: Chicago Council on Foreign Relations, 1999).

54. It is worth noting that the two instances of unified government in the dataset involve governments unified under the Democratic party. Would the results be different if there was an instance of unified government under the Republican party? It does not seem likely, as organizational structure seems to trump party politics in the arena of foreign trade. For example, both Democratic and Republican presidents tend to be free traders, given their national point of view. Centrist viewpoints on trade seem to be more prevalent in the Senate, as senators have diverse constituencies with competing needs. Representatives in the House tend to reflect their more narrow constituents' needs regardless of party affiliation. Thus both Democrats and Republicans from farm states oppose unilateral embargoes that include foodstuffs, and both Democrats and Republicans from manufacturing states tend to support export promotion and oppose embargoes that could cost jobs. Thus it does not appear that the lack of unified government under Republican control skews the findings in any consistent way.

55. Personal communication with the author.

56. See Jon R. Bond and Richard Fleisher, eds., *Polarized Politics: Congress and the President in a Partisan Era* (Washington, D.C.: Congressional Quarterly Press, 2000).

57. Richard Fleisher and Jon R. Bond, "Polarized Politics: Does It Matter?" in *Polarized Politics*, 189.

58. Ibid.

59. See, for example, Barry C. Burden and David C. Kimball, *Why Americans Split Their Tickets: Campaigns, Competition, and Divided Government* (Ann Arbor: University of Michigan Press, 2002).

60. This paper builds on earlier work done with Lorraine Eden. I want to thank both Lorraine and Jim Scott for their past suggestions that have helped to guide this study. I also want to thank Bert Rockman and Marie Henehan for their helpful suggestions on a prior draft of this paper. Unfortunately, I alone am responsible for any mistakes found here.

Chapter Seven: Long-Term Trends in Congressional Foreign Policy Behavior: Explaining Variations in Contention in the U.S. Senate in the Past and in the Future by Marie T. Henehan

1. Randall B. Ripley, "Congress and Foreign Policy: 1945–2005," *Extensions* (spring 2001): 3.

2. Peter Gourevitch, "The Second Image Reversed: The International Sources of Domestic Politics," *International Organization* 32 (autumn 1978): 881–912.

3. It is easy to forget how strong the consensus on containment was because there has been so much attention to the breakdown in the consensus. Of course, Senator Fulbright was a leading critic of the imperial presidency (J. William Fulbright, *The Crippled Giant: American Foreign Policy and Its Domestic Consequences* [New York: Random House, 1972], 227–35). However, in 1961, Fulbright saw our eighteenth-century Constitution not as a protection of separation of powers, but as a hindrance to the exercise of executive power in foreign policy. He called then for the Senate to refrain from attempting to substitute its judgment for that of the president on the grounds that the assumptions guiding the founders' concept of its role no longer applied in the nuclear era. Quoting DeTocqueville approvingly as saying that democracy is unfit to the formulation of an effective foreign policy, he asserted that we could not afford a foreign policy based on public opinion (J. William Fulbright, Doherty Lecture, University of Virginia, Charlottesville, April 21, 1961; *Cornell Law Quarterly* [fall 1961]). He put his faith in the president of that time, JFK, but soon learned that a president whose power is unchecked could act beyond the mandate of even the strongest consensus.

4. See Marie T. Henehan, *Foreign Policy and Congress: An International Relations Perspective* (Ann Arbor: University of Michigan Press, 2000), 52–54, 66–71, 75, for the justification of the temporal domain and the identification of the critical issues.

5. George F. Kennan ("X"), "The Sources of Soviet Conduct," *Foreign Affairs* 25 (1947): 566–82.

6. See, for example, Thomas M. Franck and Edward Weisband, *Foreign Policy by Congress* (New York: Oxford University Press, 1979).

7. Tariff as an issue area is closely related to domestic policy, dominates foreign policy in several years up to 1930, and seems to be unrelated to critical issues. If patterns of behavior are to be explained, it is to be done outside the

framework of this theory. See Henehan, *Foreign Policy and Congress*, 93 and 185n.

8. Joseph M. Jones, *The Fifteen Weeks* (New York: Harcourt, Brace, and World, 1955), 139.

9. Ibid., 139–41.

10. Dean Acheson, *Present at the Creation: My Years in the State Department* (New York: Norton, 1969), 219.

11. Jones, *The Fifteen Weeks*, 142.

12. Philip J. Briggs, *Making American Foreign Policy: President-Congress Relations from the Second World War to Vietnam* (Lanham, Md.: University Press of America, 1991), 51.

13. Briggs, *Making American Foreign Policy*, 54.

14. The peak in 1940 is about the same height as 1898, but the imperialism issue produces high levels of activity and disagreement over that issue from the Spanish-American War until the Panama Canal, so adding 1898, 1900, and 1902 together produces a larger amount of disagreement than that found in 1940. In fact, when the data are smoothed, the period of high disagreement goes from 1898 to 1905, definitely out-stripping 1940. Henehan, *Foreign Policy and Congress*, 114.

15. Talk of isolationism in the post–World War II period has been really more a matter of relative degrees of internationalism or unilateralism vs. multilateralism. The United States has not seriously considered a policy of withdrawing from the world.

16. The upward trend is visible in Figure 1. This is due largely to the growth in foreign aid as an instrument of policy and the necessity for legislation to authorize and appropriate the funds that it requires. This new use of the power of the purse was more consensual than contentious. This inference can be drawn by comparing Figures 1 and 2. Figure 1, activity, clearly has an upward trend, while Figure 2, disagreement (close votes), does not show an upward trend until after Vietnam. The significance of foreign aid, as well as routine diplomatic activity and miscellaneous foreign policy, can be seen when these issues are observed separately. See Henehan, *Foreign Policy and Congress*, 133, 140, and 141.

17. The pre-1968 trend coefficient is .028 and the post-1968 trend coefficient is -.016. The difference between the two is -.044, the trend function, and it is statistically significant.

18. Nixon's downfall, Watergate, might be considered a domestic issue, but it probably would not have happened had it not been for opposition to his Vietnam policy.

19. Cecil V. Crabb Jr. and Pat M. Holt, *Invitation to Struggle: Congress, the President, and Foreign Policy* (Washington, D.C.: Congressional Quarterly Press, 1992), 160–61. Their illustration of the last point is that, since George H. W. Bush would not say that he would wait for congressional authorization before starting the war (Elizabeth Drew, "Letter from Washington," *New Yorker*, February 4, 1991: 87), some members voted for the authorization of the use of force just to avoid a potential constitutional crisis.

20. Ibid., 136.

21. When the same party controls both the presidency and both houses of Congress, the party control variable is coded as 0. When the opposite party from the president controls one or both houses of Congress, the party control variable is coded as 1.

22. Briggs, *Making American Foreign Policy*, 44.

23. Ryan C. Hendrickson, *The Clinton Wars: The Constitution, Congress, and War Powers* (Nashville, Tenn.: Vanderbilt University Press, 2002), 166.

24. Ibid., 90, 96, 164–67.

25. Ibid., 165.

26. Terry L. Deibel, "Intraparty Factionalism on Key Foreign Policy Issues: Congress versus Clinton, 1995–2000," herein.

27. Hrach Gregorian, "Assessing Congressional Involvement in Foreign Policy: Lessons of the Post-Vietnam Period," *Review of Politics* 46 (January 1984): 91–112.

28. Randall B. Ripley and James M. Lindsay, *Congress Resurgent: Foreign and Defense Policy on Capitol Hill* (Ann Arbor: University of Michigan Press, 1993).

29. The six cases are Somalia, Haiti, Bosnia, strikes in Afghanistan and Sudan targeting Osama bin Laden, the NATO war against Serbia, and strikes on Iraq. Hendrickson, *The Clinton Wars*, xiv.

30. "Congress Says 'No, No, No' to War," *Human Events*, Washington, May 7, 1999, 3.

31. Cecil V. Crabb Jr., "Frozen at the Wheel: Congress and the Kosovo Crisis," *Miller Center Report* 15, 3 (fall 1999): 22.

32. Ripley, "Congress and Foreign Policy," 3; Deibel, "Intraparty Factionalism on Key Foreign Policy Issues," herein.

33. Deibel, "Intraparty Factionalism on Key Foreign Policy Issues," herein.

34. Louis Fisher, *Presidential War Power* (Lawrence: University Press of Kansas, 1995), 117.

Index

Acheson, Dean, 48, 49, 154
Afghanistan: American forces in, 17; as "rogue state," 15; military actions in, 14, 175; Soviet invasion of, 22, 36; and Taliban, 27
Africa, 2
Agency on International Development (AID), 79; abolition of, 76; administrative structure of, 78
Albright, Madeleine, 76
al-Qaeda, 15, 179; and terrorist strikes in America, 22
Ambrose, Stephen, 44
American foreign policy, 3–4, 6, 167–68, 170, 173, 178; and the Cold War, 20; conduct of, 21, 32; formulation of, 7, 9, 176
American Implementation Force (IFOR), 83
Amoy, 42
Angola, 162
Anti-Ballistic Missile Treaty, 70
anti-communism, 151–52, 157; critical issue of, 163
Arab American community, 17
Arab nationalism, 48
Archer, William, 74
Armey, Dick, 80–81
Arms Control and Disarmament Agency (ACDA), 70, 78; abolition of, 76
The Arrogance of Power, 20–21
Artic National Wildlife Refuge (ANWR), 112
Ashcroft, John, 90
Asian financial crisis, 81
Aspin, Les, 119
Aziz, Tariq, 58

Baghdad, 12
Baker, James, 35; meeting with Aziz, 58–59; meeting in Geneva, 58; as secretary of state, 58
Ball, George, 52
Berlin Wall, 1, 163
Biden, Joseph, 60, 86, 88, 112; as ranking Foreign Relations Committee Democrat, 76
Binder, Sarah A., 117
Blair, Tony, 26
Blunt, Roy, 85, 90
Boland, Edward, 158, 163
Bond, Jon, 147
Bonior, David E., 90
Bosnia, 68, 161; cutoff of funds for, 89; and Dayton Accords, 68; U.S. involvement in, 70; war in, 83; withdrawal of American troops from, 84
Brazil, 11
Brewster, Daniel, 54
Brezhnev, Leonid, 3
Britain, 46
Buchanan, Pat, 73
Bundy, McGeorge, 52
Burton, Dan, 78, 90
Bush, George H. W., 26; administration of, 66, 71; diary entry of September 13, 57; Gulf War under, 26; implementation of UN resolution, 59; and sanctions against Iraq, 57; student criticism of, 60; and United Nations, 71
Bush, George W., 12, 14, 28; administration of, 31, 39, 41, 61, 112, 150, 164, 177; budget plan of 1992, 112; and confrontation with Iraq, 61;

209

domestic agenda of, 112; as incumbent, 26–27; and supplemental appropriations bill, 112
Byrd, Robert, 26–27, 62, 80, 90

Callahan, Sonny, 80
Camdessus, Michel, 81
Campbell, Thomas, 158, 161
Carter, Jimmy, 32, 140
Carter, Ralph, 18, 131, 133
Central Africa, 68–69
Central Intelligence Agency (CIA), 87
Chafee, John, 79, 84
Chemical Weapons Convention, 70, 89
Chiang Kai-Shek, 45
Chile, 162
China, 2, 26, 177; abusive human rights practices of, 68, 75, 82; and American armies, 54; and Christians, 82; and compulsory abortions, 82; economic growth of, 82; emergence of, 11–12; under Mao, 36; military action of, 43; and Permanent Normal Trade Relations, 75; and political liberalization, 82; and raid on Tachens, 42; and trade, 147
Chou En-Lai, 41
Christopher, Warren, 68
Church, Frank, 115
Churchill, Winston, 45
Civil Rights Bill, 52
Civil War, 135
Clements, Earle C., 43
Cleveland, Grover, 152
Clinton, William Jefferson (Bill), 13, 73–74, 76–79, 80–85, 140, 159, 162, 177; administration of, 12, 30, 67–69, 72–73, 75–76, 79, 81–82, 91, 158, 161, 172; Balkan Policy of, 84; and Comprehensive Test Ban Treaty, 87; and enactment of Mexico City Language, 78–79; and first two years of administration, 68; and foreign affairs agency reorganization, 87; foreign policy of, 66; and IMF and UN funding, 79; impeachment of, 67; and loss of Congress to the Republicans, 68; peacemaking efforts of, 84; and submission of Chemical Weapons Convention to Senate, 86
Coburn, Tom A., 78–79, 90
Cochran, Thad, 88

Cold War, 2, 4, 15, 17, 85, 151, 162, 169, 171; Americans response to, 13; American thinking about, 15; critique of American policy, 20; bipolar quality of, 169; and "defining consensus," 91; and doctrine of containment, 16; early years of, 13, 16; end of, 10, 12, 15, 20, 28–29, 65, 69, 163, 176–77; height of, 117; and perceived threat, 114, 130; post–Cold War, 10–11, 163, 167, 170; realities of, 18
Communism, 154, 171, 177
Communist Manifesto, 14
Comprehensive Test Ban Treaty (CTBT), 89; signed by Clinton, 87
Congress, 24–25, 40, 47–51, 54–55, 57, 59, 61–63, 69, 76, 82–83, 91, 111–20, 128–30, 133–37, 139, 141–43, 145–47, 149–51, 153–54, 156, 158–64, 171, 177–78; 83rd, 121, 128; 86th, 121; 91st, 121, 124; 92nd, 121, 127–28, 131; 93rd, 127–28; 100th, 138; 104th, 76, 78, 121, 124; 105th, 76, 128; 107th, 121; and approval of Vietnam war resolution, 60; authority of, 40, 44; and balance of power in foreign affairs, 115; as challenge to the president, 131–32; China bloc in, 45; and collective action dilemma, 111, 117–19, 130, 132; and constitutional issues, 42, 60, 136; debate in, 26, 34; and declaration of war in Vietnam, 56; delegation of power to the president, 116, 118–19, 135; Democratic party in, 58, 66, 68, 140; and domestic issues, 114; and electoral and institutional changes, 114–17, 132, 135–36; Johnson's message to, 53; and opposition control, 143–45; and presidential influence, 113–14; and Republican party, 66, 71, 76; Republicans in, 66, 76; role of committees in, 130; war-making powers of, 46. *See also* House of Representatives; Senate
Congressional Research Service (CRS), 35
Connally, Thomas, 161
Conrad, Kent, 74
Constitution, 47, 50, 55; ambiguity

inherent in, 7; division of powers and responsibilities mandated by, 17; drafters of, 6; presidential interpretation of, 39
conventional wisdom, 7–9, 11, 74, 168, 176, 179
Cooper, John Sherman, 55
Corwin, Edwin, 4, 8, 40, 179
Cuba, 152, 154, 162
Cuban Missile Crisis, 36
Czech Republic, 85

Daschle, Thomas, 88
Dayton Accords, 68; and end of Bosnian war, 83; signing of in Paris, 83
declarations of war, 43, 59
Delay, Thomas, 78, 80, 83
Democratic Party, 65, 67, 69, 71–79, 82–83, 85–87, 89–91, 147, 158; and baiting of Republicans, 88; basic mission of, 67; and conference in Vienna, 88; and conservative southern voters, 118–19; Democratic Caucus of, 119; and Democratic reforms, 121, 131; factions of, 89; idealists in, 67, 71, 75, 82–83; leadership of, 26, 60, 62; and monopoly hold in the South, 118; and northern voters, 119; pragmatists in, 68–69, 71, 73, 75, 83; unilateralists in, 69
Department of Homeland Security, 16, 175
depression, 135
Desert Storm, 112
DeWine, Michael, 84
Dingell, John D., 90
divided government, 30, 128, 134, 135, 138–40, 142, 144, 145, 147, 149–50, 159–61, 171
Divine, Robert, 45
Dole, Robert, 86, 161
Domenici, Peter, 80
domino effect, 36
Dorgan, Byron, 90
Dulles, John Foster: as defender of Eisenhower Doctrine, 48; as secretary of state, 42–43, 46

Eagleton, Thomas, 158
Eastern Europe, 11

East Timor, 68–69
Eisenhower, Dwight D, 29, 39, 42, 44–47, 49–50; administration of, 159; as commander-in-chief, 50–51; and Eisenhower Doctrine, 46, 48, 50–51; and interpretation of congressional action, 51; leadership of, 51; Middle Eastern policy of, 46; overall strategy of, 45
Estrada, Miquel, A., 112
Europe, 152; U.S. involvement in, 162
European Union, 11
Export–Import Bank, 140–41

Faircloth, Lauch, 74, 90
fast-track trade negotiating authority, 73
Feingold, Russ, 161
Feinstein, Diane, 90
Fleisher, Richard, 147
Foreign Affairs Reform and Restructuring Act of 1998, 79
Formosa, 43–46; attack on, 44; and Formosa resolution, 41, 44, 48, 51; and Formosa Strait, 42; protection of, 43, 45; treaty with, 43
Fowler, Tillie, 84, 89
France, 26, 46
Frank, Barney, 90
Fukuyama, Francis, 12
Fulbright, J. William, 37, 49, 54–57, 115, 167; 1974 and academic exchange program, 1; bid for reelection, 4; as chair of the Senate Foreign Relations Committee, 3, 20–21; as man of many parts, 3; opposition of to Vietnam War, 3; political life of, 2; as public intellectual and practicing politician, 22; as senator, 2; as small-town Arkansas boy, 1; as student of American politics, 1; as supporter of strong presidential initiatives, 3; and support for the bipartisan anti-communist consensus, 2; tenure in office of, 2;
and view of America's place in the world, 2

Gallop Poll, 128
General Accounting Office (GAO), 35
George, Alexander L., 45
Gephardt, Richard, 62, 90
Germany, 26

Gilman, Benjamin, 79
Gingrich, Newt, 161; as champion of free trade, 74; as House Speaker, 74; as internationalist, 85; and support for IMF funds, 80
globalization, 8–9, 28; cultural, 8; debate over, 9–10; economic aspects of, 18; effects of, 69; as threat to American sovereignty, 73
Gorbachev, Mikhail, 161, 163, 177
Gourevitch, Peter, 151
Graham, Lindsey O., 90
Grassley, Charles, 112
Gray, Boyden, 57
Greece, 154
Gregorian, Hrach, 162
Gruenig, Ernest, 55
Gruenther, Alfred, 45
Gulf of Tonkin Resolution, 21, 23, 53–55, 85
Gulf War I, 12–13, 71; debate surrounding, 27; and easy-victory syndrome, 27; rationale for U.S. policy in, 35; and use of military force, 26
Gulf War II, 35, 60–63

Hagel, Chuck, 26–27, 88
Haiti, 161; democracy in, 68
Hamilton, Lee, 159
Harkin, Tom, 90
Hastert, Dennis, 85
Hawaii, 154
Helms, Jesse, 30, 74, 83, 86, 90; as chairman of the Foreign Relations Committee, 30, 32, 76
Hendrickson, Ryan, 161
Hormel, James, 30
House of Representatives, 2, 44, 48, 50, 55, 57, 72, 74–75, 79–80, 89, 120–21, 124, 127, 133, 141, 145, 147, 172; and approval of H.R. 1569, 85; Armed Services Committee of, 118; and Clinton's reorganization plan, 78; Committee of Foreign Affairs of, 48, 141; and debate on H.R. 1757, 77; and delegation of authority, 131, 145; Democratic Party in, 58, 62–63, 73, 140, 159; and Taiwan, 89; and vote on Foreign Affairs Agency Reorganization, 78; and vote on H.Con.Res. 227, 84; and vote on the Taiwan Security Enhancement Act, 82; and vote on UN withdrawal, 77; and votes on Bosnia and the Dayton Accords, 83; and votes on international issues, 113, 121, 124, 128–29; and votes on Kosovo Diplomacy and war, 84. See also Congress
Hungary, 85
Hunter, Duncan, 78
Huntington, Samuel, 9, 11
Hussein, Saddam, 12, 59, 62; character of, 35; and control of Kuwaiti oil resources, 35; overthrow of, 67
Hutchinson, Kay Bailey, 84, 90

Ichiang, 42
imperialism, 152, 154
Inhofe, James, 74, 84, 90
International Atomic Energy Agency (IAEA), 81
internationalism, 151–52, 157
International Monetary Fund (IMF), 70, 79, 80; credits for, 81; funding of, 78, 87; loans of, 80; quota increase for, 80; reform of, 81
Iran, 87
Iran-Contra affair, 163
Iraq, 40, 61, 79; American forces in, 17; and defiance of UN resolutions, 60; military actions in, 14, 164, 175; regime change in, 61, 63; as "rogue state," 15; war in, 31, 112
Iron Curtain, 1
Islam: extremism in, 179; fundamentalism in, 12, 177
isolationism, 7, 152, 157

Japan, 11, 81, 142
Javits, Jacob, 54, 159
Jeffords, James, 79, 84
Johnson, Lyndon B., 39, 41, 50, 52, 55–57, 112, 159; administration of, 20, 36, 56; as commander-in-chief, 57; distortion of, 56; plans of for bringing the Vietnam conflict to an end, 21; as Senate majority leader, 49, 51

Kabul, 22
Karol, David, 138
Kassebaum, Nancy L., 84
Katzenbach, Nicholas, 56

Kefauver, Estes, 49
Kennan, George, 15, 152
Kennedy, Edward, 60, 62
Kennedy, Patrick J., 90
Kennedy, Ted, 26
Kerry, John, 60
Khrushchev, Nikita, 3
Korea: and Korean War armistice, 43; Truman's actions in, 3; war in, 41
Korean Energy Development Organization (KEDO), 81–89; funding related to, 82
Kosovo, 69, 84, 89, 161–62; peacekeeping in, 89; post-settlement peacekeeping force, 84; U.S. involvement in, 70
Kuwait: Iraqi invasion of, 12, 57–58; Iraq's withdrawal from, 112
Kyl, Jon, 80, 86, 88, 90

Lake, Anthony, 68
Largent, Steven, 78
Latin America, 2, 173, 177–78; neocolonialism in, 152
League of Nations, 159
Leahy, Patrick, 60, 62
Lebanon: and Eisenhower Doctrine, 3
legislative branch, 2, 7. *See also* House of Representatives; Senate; Congress
Lenin, Vladimir, 2
Levin, Carl, 62
Lieberman, Joe, 82
Linder, John, 85
Lindsay, James, 112
Lott, Trent, 87–88
Lugar, Richard, 20, 77, 84
Lusitania, 169

Marshall Plan, 154, 159, 164
Marx, Karl, 2, 14
Matsu, 42, 45
Matsui, Robert T., 74; as floor leader, 74; on Ways and Means Trade Subcommittee, 4
McArthur, Douglas, 152
McCain, John, 84, 88
McCarthyism, 17
McConnell, Mitchell, 87; as chair of Senate Appropriations Committee, 80–81
McCormack, John, 47
McKinley, William, 152, 162

McNamara, Robert, 52, 54
Mexico City language, 76–77, 79–80
Mexico, 11, 70
Middle East, 16; anti-Westernism in, 46; crises in, 40; doctrine for stabilizing, 47; and draft Middle East resolution, 42, 51; historical Russian interest in, 46; and Wye River Accords, 79
Milosevic, Slobodan, 84–85
"mission creep," 13
Mitchell, George, 60
Morse, Wayne, 49, 52, 55, 164
Moscow, 70
Most Favored Nation Status (MFN), 141
Moynihan, Daniel Patrick, 60, 88
Mr. X article, 152
Munich analogy, 35–36, 170

Nassar, Gamal Abdal, 48
National Security Council, 53
Nelson, Gaylor, 54–55
nested game, 4–6
Neutrality Acts, 152
New Arrangements to Borrow (NAB): and FY1998 budget, 76, 80
"new world order," 12
Nickles, Don, 90
Nixon, Richard, 57, 158; administration of, 56, 159; bipartisan opposition to, 160; bipartisan support for, 160; as faced with a hostile Senate and Congress, 159
North American Free Trade Association (NAFTA), 73, 75
North Atlantic Treaty, 161
North Atlantic Treaty Organization (NATO), 13, 89, 147, 154, 162; attitudes toward, 85; expansion of, 83, 85; military aid under, 159; prestige of, 85; Russian opposition to, 86
North Korea: and end of nuclear programs, 70; as nuclear threat, 81; as "rogue state," 15
North Vietnam: aggressive designs of, 54; Johnson's protest to, 52; retaliatory air strike on, 53; strong message to, 56
Nuclear Non-Proliferation Treaty (NPT), 81
nuclear weapons, 45

Omnibus Trade Bill, 1988, 140

Panama Canal, 154–55
Passman, Otto, 25, 32
Pastor, Robert, 139
"peace dividend," 12
Pearl Harbor, 150–52, 157, 169
Pelosi, Nancy, 75, 80, 90
Pennsylvania, 14
Pentagon, 14; attack on, 27
Percy, Charles, 115
Perot, Ross, 73
Pescadores, 42; attack on, 44; protecting, 45
peso crisis, 70
Philippines, 154, 154
Phleger, Herman, 44
Platt amendment, 152
Poland, 85
post–September 11 period, 14, 16, 167, 170; analysis of the primary sources of instability in, 15; and "truths" that defined events, 15
post–World War II world, 149, 154
Powell, Colin, 31
presidency, 113, 115–18, 120–21, 124, 127–29, 131–34, 136, 138–43, 145–46, 150–51, 160–61, 164, 167, 171; and behavior of the president, 161; dominant role of, 171
Prober, Joshua Lee, 117

Quemoy, 42; Chinese Communist attack on, 45; defense of, 43–45

Radford, Arthur H., 42
Reagan, Ronald, 8, 158; administration of, 22, 29, 33, 119, 140–41, 163, 177; and M-X missile and aid to contras, 119; repeated veto threats by, 141
Reciprocal Trade Agreements Act, 135
"Red Scares" of the 1930s, 16
Republican Party, 26, 69, 73–75, 77, 79, 85–86, 89, 91, 147, 158–59, 177; anti-China stance of, 83; class of 1994, 83–85; and conservative Southern voters, 118; and Darwinian view, 82; factionalism in, 90; foreign policy priorities of, 86; as internationalists, 70–71, 77, 80, 83, 84–85, 87, 89, 172; leaders of, 60, 74, 80, 88; opposition to Clinton's policy, 161; opposition to the Somalia policy, 161; as pro-defense, 61, 73
Rieselbach, Leroy, 134
Ripley, Randall, 150
Rohrabacher, Dana, 75, 78, 90
Roosevelt, Franklin D. (FDR), 154, 157
Rose, Pete, 145
Rostow, Walt, 15
Roth, William, 84
Rumsfeld, Donald, 31
Rusk, Dean, 52
Russia, 26, 46, 85; aid to, 70; and ratification of CWC, 86

Saltonstall, Leverett, 43
Saxton, James, 80, 90
Scarborough, Joseph, 78, 90
Schuster, Bud, 90
Senate, 43, 49, 55, 57, 63, 72, 79, 84, 87–89, 153–54, 160–61, 168; action of on S.Con.Res., 21, 85; Appropriations Committee of, 80; and approval of S.Con.Res. 44, 84; and Bosnia, 89; Committee on Armed Services of, 48; Committee on Foreign Relations of, 49, 54, 77–78, 86, 141; and control by opposition, 140, 161; and CTBT vote delay, 89; and CWC approval, 89; debate of, 54; Democrats in, 159; disagreement within, 155; and fast-track trade negotiating authority, 74, 89; Finance Committee of, 74, 137; and IMF funding, 89; and invoking of cloture, 74; and KEDO oil money, 89; and Kosovo, 89; and NATO, 90; and passing S.J.Res. 44, 84; rank-and-file membership of, 171; S.903, 77–78; special role in foreign policy of, 25, 34; and vote on Foreign Affairs Agency Reorganization, 78; and vote on funding the Korean Energy Development Organization, 81; and vote on IMF replenishment, 80; and vote on NATO Expansion, 85; and vote on UN arrearages, 77, 90; and votes on Bosnia and the Dayton Accords, 83; and votes on Kosovo Diplomacy and War, 84
Sensenbrenner, Jim, 90

September 11, 2001: terrorist attacks, 13–18
Serbs, 68
Smith, Christopher, 76
Smoke, Richard, 45
Smoot-Hawley tariff bill, 135
Snowe, Olympia, 79
Solomon, Gerald H. B., 78, 90
Somalia, 71, 161; first American casualties in, 68; intervention in, 71
Souder, Mark Edward, 90
South Africa, 141
Southwest Asia, 2, 153; and Collective Defense Treaty, 54; conduct of U.S. policy in, 20; and critique of American policy, 20; and Gulf of Tonkin Resolution, 51; and Resolution to Promote the Maintenance of International Peace and Security, 53
Soviet Union, 46, 66, 152, 177; countries threatened by, 47; "evil empire," 8; invasion of Afghanistan by, 32; and spread of communism, 2; as threatening rival, 2. *See also* Russia
Spain, 152
Spanish-American War, 162
Specter, Arlen, 79
Spence, Floyd, 90
Stalin, Joseph, 3
State Department, 42, 51–52, 70
Suez Crisis, 46

Tachen Islands, 42
Taft, Robert A., 160
Taiwan, 42–42, 70, 82–83; crises within, 40; defense of, 42; invasion of, 42; and Security Enhancement Act, 83
Taliban, 22
terrorism, 164; America's previous experience with, 179; America's war on, 175; as dominating foreign policy, 165
third wave of democratization, 9
Thomas, Craig, 87
Thurmond, Strom, 86
Tibet, 70
Tower, John, 30
trade issues, 72–73
Truman, Harry S., 41, 43, 160; administration of, 154, 159, 161; decision of on Korea, 160; and passage of the Truman Doctrine, 152, 154, 164
Tsebelis, George, 4–5

UN General Assembly, 78
United Nations, 47, 70, 76–77, 79; agreement of to reduce U.S. budget share, 77; arrearage repayment, 78, 89; budget of, 77–78; funding, 77–78; General Assembly of, 61; headquarters of in New York, 87; inspectors in Iraq, 27; and Kosovo action, 162; military or peacekeeping operation of, 78; Resolution 678 of, 58–60; and Security Council reform, 76–77; and Senate involvement in funding, 154; specialized and related agencies of, 70; and U.S. foreign policy, 178; U.S. relationship with, 61
United States General Accounting Office: audit of UN, 77
United States Information Agency (USIA): abolition of, 76–78
U.S. foreign policy, 8, 21
U.S.-Israel Free Trade Area, 141
U.S.-North Korean Agreed Framework, 81

Vandenberg, Arthur H., 154, 161
Versailles Treaty, 152, 156, 159, 162; debate over, 154–56
Vietnam, 8, 14, 32, 41, 51, 53, 54, 57, 112, 118, 159, 60, 162–63, 165; American failure in, 11; commitment of the United States to, 36; end of war in, 175; escalating costs of war in, 29; failure of containment in, 152–53, 157; and post-Vietnam syndrome, 8, 20, 27; protracted political fallout over, 29; U.S. military effort in, 36

Wallace, Henry, 152
War Powers resolutions, 39, 56, 60–61, 63, 68, 117, 153, 159
Warner, John, 86, 88
war resolutions, 41, 53
Washington, George, 113
Ways and Means Committee, 74

Weld, William, 30
The West Wing, 148
White House, 46–47, 51, 53, 62, 66–67, 88, 111, 133–34, 139–41, 147, 171, 175, 178
Wicker, Roger: and amendment proposed, 80
Wildavsky, Aaron, 112, 117, 132; and thesis of two presidencies, 114, 118
Wilson, Woodrow, 152, 154, 159, 162; faced with a hostile Senate/Congress, 159
Wilsonian idealism, 33
World Trade Center, 14; destruction of, 27; earlier attack on, 14
World War I, 10
World War II, 10, 114; end of, 30, 139; U.S. entry into, 29

Yugoslavia, 13, 68, 84